OpenStack Cloud Computing Cookbook

Over 100 recipes to successfully set up and manage your
OpenStack cloud environments with complete coverage
of Nova, Swift, Keystone, Glance, and Horizon

Kevin Jackson

[PACKT] PUBLISHING

open source
community experience distilled

BIRMINGHAM - MUMBAI

OpenStack Cloud Computing Cookbook

First published: September 2012

Production Reference: 1150912

Published by Packt Publishing Ltd.
Livery Place
35 Livery Street
Birmingham B3 2PB, UK.

ISBN 978-1-84951-732-4

www.packtpub.com

Cover Image by Faiz Fattohi (faizfattohi@gmail.com)

Credits

Author

Kevin Jackson

Reviewers

Thierry Carrez

Atul Kumar Jha

Acquisition Editor

Kartikey Pandey

Lead Technical Editor

Azharuddin Sheikh

Technical Editors

Veronica Fernandes

Azharuddin Sheikh

Prasad Dalvi

Joyslita D'Souza

Copy Editor

Brandt D'Mello

Project Coordinator

Yashodhan Dere

Proofreader

Kevin McGowan

Indexer

Tejal R. Soni

Production Coordinator

Nilesh R. Mohite

Cover Work

Nilesh R. Mohite

About the Author

Kevin Jackson is married, with three children. He is an experienced IT professional working with small businesses and online enterprises. He has extensive experience with various flavors of Linux and Unix. He specializes in web and cloud infrastructure technologies for Trader Media Group.

I'd like to thank my wife, Charlene, and the rest of my family for their time, patience, and encouragement throughout the book.

I'd also like to extend my thanks to the OpenStack community, which has helped a great deal during my journey with OpenStack. The talent and support is phenomenal. Without the OpenStack community, there would be no OpenStack.

A specific mention goes to all those who have made this book possible. Your comments, guidance, and motivation have made writing this book an enjoyable experience.

About the Reviewers

Thierry Carrez is an open source project management expert and has been working on OpenStack since 2010, as the project's Release Manager, sponsored by Rackspace.

An Ubuntu Core developer and Debian maintainer, he was previously the Technical Lead for Ubuntu Server edition at Canonical and an Operational Manager for the Gentoo Linux Security Team. He has also worked as an IT Manager for small and large companies.

Atul Kumar Jha has been an ardent Linux enthusiast and free software evangelist for more than eight years. He holds an engineering degree in IT and has been working for over four years on different job roles. He also happens to be one of the co-founders of the free software event series called `mukt.in`.

He currently works as an Evangelist for CSS Corp. Pvt. Ltd., Chennai, India, where most of his work involves free/open software technologies and cloud platforms.

He's been involved with OpenStack since the Bexar release and has been contributing to the project since then. Most of his contributions have been around documentation, bug reporting, and helping folks on IRC.

He can be seen lurking on Freenode, under the `#ubuntu-server` or `#openstack` channels, using the handle `koolhead17`. More information about him can be found at `http://www.atuljha.com`.

www.PacktPub.com

Support files, eBooks, discount offers and more

You might want to visit www.PacktPub.com for support files and downloads related to your book.

Did you know that Packt offers eBook versions of every book published, with PDF and ePub files available? You can upgrade to the eBook version at www.PacktPub.com and as a print book customer, you are entitled to a discount on the eBook copy. Get in touch with us at service@packtpub.com for more details.

At www.PacktPub.com, you can also read a collection of free technical articles, sign up for a range of free newsletters and receive exclusive discounts and offers on Packt books and eBooks.

 PACKTLiB®

http://PacktLib.PacktPub.com

Do you need instant solutions to your IT questions? PacktLib is Packt's online digital book library. Here, you can access, read and search across Packt's entire library of books.

Why Subscribe?

- ▶ Fully searchable across every book published by Packt
- ▶ Copy and paste, print and bookmark content
- ▶ On demand and accessible via web browser

Free Access for Packt account holders

If you have an account with Packt at www.PacktPub.com, you can use this to access PacktLib today and view nine entirely free books. Simply use your login credentials for immediate access.

Table of Contents

Preface

OpenStack is an open source software for building public and private clouds, born from Rackspace and NASA. It is now a global success and is developed and supported by scores of people around the globe and backed by some of the leading players in the cloud space today. This book is specifically designed to quickly help you get up to speed with OpenStack and give you the confidence and understanding to roll it out into your own datacenters. From test installations of OpenStack running under VirtualBox to recipes that help you move out to production environments, this book covers a wide range of topics that help you install and configure a private cloud. This book will show you:

- ▶ How to install and configure all the core components of OpenStack to run an environment that can be managed and operated just like AWS, HP Cloud Services, and Rackspace

- ▶ How to master the complete private cloud stack, from scaling out Compute resources to managing object storage services for highly redundant, highly available storage

- ▶ Practical, real-world examples of each service built upon in each chapter, allowing you to progress with the confidence that they will work in your own environments

OpenStack Cloud Computing Cookbook gives you clear, step-by-step instructions to install and run your own private cloud successfully. It is full of practical and applicable recipes that enable you to use the latest capabilities of OpenStack and implement them.

What this book covers

Chapter 1, Starting OpenStack Compute, teaches you how to set up and use OpenStack Compute running within a VirtualBox environment.

Chapter 2, Administering OpenStack Compute, teaches you how to manage user accounts and security groups as well as how to deal with cloud images to run in an OpenStack environment.

Chapter 3, Keystone OpenStack Identity Service, takes you through installation and configuration of Keystone, which underpins all of the other OpenStack services.

Chapter 4, Installing OpenStack Storage, teaches you how to configure and use OpenStack Storage running within a VirtualBox environment.

Chapter 5, Using OpenStack Storage, teaches you how to use the storage service for storing and retrieving files and objects.

Chapter 6, Administering OpenStack Storage, takes you through how to use tools and techniques that can be used for running OpenStack Storage within datacenters.

Chapter 7, Glance OpenStack Image Service, teaches you how to upload and modify images (templates) for use within an OpenStack environment.

Chapter 8, Nova Volumes, teaches you how to install and configure the persistent storage service for use by instances running in an OpenStack Compute environment.

Chapter 9, Horizon OpenStack Dashboard, teaches you how to install and use the web user interface to perform tasks such as creating users, modifying security groups, and launching instances.

Chapter 10, OpenStack Networking, helps you understand the networking options currently available as well as teaching you how to configure an OpenStack environment so that instances are accessible on the network.

Chapter 11, In the Datacenter, takes you through understanding how to do bare-metal provisioning, scale up OpenStack, and introduces you to adding resilience to our OpenStack installations for high availability.

Chapter 12, Monitoring, shows you how to install and configure various open source tools for monitoring an OpenStack installation.

Chapter 13, Troubleshooting, takes you through an understanding of the logs and where to get help when encountering issues while running an OpenStack environment.

What you need for this book

To use this book, you will need access to computers or servers that have hardware virtualization capabilities. To set up the lab environments you will need Oracle's VirtualBox installed. You will also need access to an Ubuntu 12.04 ISO image, as the methods presented detail steps for Ubuntu environments.

Who this book is for

This book is aimed at system administrators and technical architects moving from a virtualized environment to cloud environments who are familiar with cloud computing platforms. Knowledge of virtualization and managing Linux environments is expected. Prior knowledge or experience of OpenStack is not required, although beneficial.

Conventions

In this book, you will find a number of styles of text that distinguish between different kinds of information. Here are some examples of these styles, and an explanation of their meaning.

Code words in text are shown as follows: "Similar information is presented by the `nova list` and `nova show` commands".

A block of code is set as follows:

```
bind_port = 443
cert_file = /etc/swift/cert.crt
key_file = /etc/swift/cert.key
```

Any command-line input or output is written as follows:

```
sudo apt-get update
sudo apt-get -y install qemu-kvm cloud-utils
```

New terms and **important words** are shown in bold. Words that you see on the screen, in menus or dialog boxes for example, appear in the text like this: "In the **INSTANCE** section, we get details of our running instance".

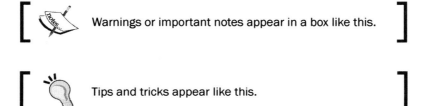

Warnings or important notes appear in a box like this.

Tips and tricks appear like this.

Reader feedback

Feedback from our readers is always welcome. Let us know what you think about this book—what you liked or may have disliked. Reader feedback is important for us to develop titles that you really get the most out of.

To send us general feedback, simply send an e-mail to feedback@packtpub.com, and mention the book title through the subject of your message.

If there is a topic that you have expertise in and you are interested in either writing or contributing to a book, see our author guide on www.packtpub.com/authors.

Customer support

Now that you are the proud owner of a Packt book, we have a number of things to help you to get the most from your purchase.

Errata

Although we have taken every care to ensure the accuracy of our content, mistakes do happen. If you find a mistake in one of our books—maybe a mistake in the text or the code—we would be grateful if you would report this to us. By doing so, you can save other readers from frustration and help us improve subsequent versions of this book. If you find any errata, please report them by visiting http://www.packtpub.com/support, selecting your book, clicking on the **errata submission form** link, and entering the details of your errata. Once your errata are verified, your submission will be accepted and the errata will be uploaded to our website, or added to any list of existing errata, under the Errata section of that title.

Piracy

Piracy of copyright material on the Internet is an ongoing problem across all media. At Packt, we take the protection of our copyright and licenses very seriously. If you come across any illegal copies of our works, in any form, on the Internet, please provide us with the location address or website name immediately so that we can pursue a remedy.

Please contact us at copyright@packtpub.com with a link to the suspected pirated material.

We appreciate your help in protecting our authors, and our ability to bring you valuable content.

Questions

You can contact us at questions@packtpub.com if you are having a problem with any aspect of the book, and we will do our best to address it.

1
Starting OpenStack Compute

In this chapter, we will cover:

- ► Creating a sandbox environment with VirtualBox
- ► Installing OpenStack Compute packages
- ► Configuring database services
- ► Configuring OpenStack Compute
- ► Stopping and starting Nova services
- ► Creating a cloudadmin account and project
- ► Installation of command-line tools
- ► Uploading a sample machine image
- ► Launching your first cloud instance
- ► Terminating your instance

Introduction

OpenStack Compute, also known as Nova, is the **compute** component of the open source cloud operating system, **OpenStack**. It is the component that allows you to run multiple instances of virtual machines on any number of hosts running the OpenStack Compute service, allowing you to create a highly scalable and redundant cloud environment. The open source project strives to be hardware and hypervisor agnostic. Nova compute is analogous to Amazon's **EC2 (Elastic Compute Cloud)** environment and can be managed in a similar way, demonstrating the power and potential of this service.

This chapter gets you up to speed quickly by giving you the information you need to create a cloud environment running entirely from your desktop machine. At the end of this chapter, you will be able to create and access virtual machines using the same command line tools you would use to manage Amazon's own EC2 compute environment.

Creating a sandbox environment with VirtualBox

Creating a sandbox environment using VirtualBox allows us to discover and experiment with the OpenStack Compute service, known as *Nova*. VirtualBox gives us the ability to spin up virtual machines and networks without affecting the rest of our working environment and is freely available from `http://www.virtualbox.org` for Windows, Mac OSX, and Linux. This test environment can then be used for the rest of this chapter.

It is assumed the computer you will be using to run your test environment in has enough processing power and has hardware virtualization support (modern AMDs and Intel iX processors) with at least 4 GB RAM. Remember we're creating a virtual machine that itself will be used to spin up virtual machines, so the more RAM you have, the better.

Getting ready

To begin with, we must download VirtualBox from `http://www.virtualbox.org/` and then follow the installation procedure once this has been downloaded.

We will also need to download the Ubuntu 12.04 LTS Server ISO CD-ROM image from `http://www.ubuntu.com/`.

How to do it...

To create our sandbox environment within VirtualBox, we will create a single virtual machine that allows us to run all of the OpenStack Compute services required to run cloud instances. This virtual machine will be configured with at least 2 GB RAM and 20 GB of hard drive space and have three network interfaces. The first will be a NAT interface that allows our virtual machine to connect to the network outside of VirtualBox to download packages, a second interface which will be the public interface of our OpenStack Compute host, and the third interface will be for our private network that OpenStack Compute uses for internal communication between different OpenStack Compute hosts.

Carry out the following steps to create the virtual machine that will be used to run OpenStack Compute services:

1. In order to use a public and private network in our OpenStack environment, we first create these under VirtualBox. To do this, we can use the VirtualBox GUI by going to **System Preferences** then **Network** or use the `VBoxManage` command from our VirtualBox install and run the following commands in a shell on our computer to create two `HostOnly` interfaces, `vboxnet0` and `vboxnet1`:

```
# Public Network  vboxnet0 (172.16.0.0/16)
VBoxManage hostonlyif create
VBoxManage hostonlyif ipconfig vboxnet0 --ip 172.16.0.254
--netmask 255.255.0.0

# Private Network vboxnet1 (10.0.0.0/8)
VBoxManage hostonlyif create
VBoxManage hostonlyif ipconfig vboxnet1 --ip 10.0.0.254 --netmask
255.0.0.0
```

2. In VirtualBox, create a new virtual machine with the following specifications:

   - 1 CPU
   - 2048 MB
   - 20 GB Hard Disk
   - Three Network Adapters, with the attached Ubuntu 12.04 ISO

This can either be done using the VirtualBox *New Virtual Machine Wizard* or by running the following commands in a shell on our computer:

```
# Create VirtualBox Machine
VboxManage createvm --name openstack1 --ostype Ubuntu_64
--register
VBoxManage modifyvm openstack1 --memory 2048 --nic1 nat
--nic2 hostonly --hostonlyadapter2 vboxnet0 --nic3 hostonly
--hostonlyadapter3 vboxnet1
```

```
# Create CD-Drive and Attach ISO
VBoxManage storagectl openstack1 --name "IDE Controller" --add ide
--controller PIIX4 --hostiocache on --bootable on
VBoxManage storageattach openstack1 --storagectl "IDE Controller"
--type dvddrive --port 0 --device 0 --medium Downloads/ubuntu-
12.04-server-amd64.iso

# Create and attach SATA Interface and Hard Drive
VBoxManage storagectl openstack1 --name "SATA Controller" --add
sata --controller IntelAHCI --hostiocache on --bootable on
VBoxManage createhd --filename openstack1.vdi --size 20480
VBoxManage storageattach openstack1 --storagectl "SATA Controller"
--port 0 --device 0 --type hdd --medium openstack1.vdi
```

3. We are now ready to power on our `OpenStack1` node. Do this by selecting **OpenStack1 Virtual Machine** and then clicking on the **Start** button or by running the following command:

```
VBoxManage startvm openstack1 --type gui
```

4. This will take us through a standard text-based Ubuntu installer, as this is the server edition. Choose appropriate settings for your region and choose **Eth0** as the main interface (this is the first interface in your VirtualBox VM settings—our NATed interface). When prompted for software selection, just choose **SSH Server** and continue. For a user, create a user named `openstack` and the password of `openstack`. This will help with using this book to troubleshoot your own environment.

5. Once installed, log in as the `openstack` user.

6. We can now configure networking on our OpenStack Compute node. To do this we will create a static address on the second interface, `eth1`, which will be the public interface and also configure our host to bring up `eth2` without an address, as this interface will be controlled by OpenStack to provide the private network. To do this, edit the `/etc/network/interfaces` file with the following contents:

```
# The loopback network interface
auto lo
iface lo inet loopback

# The primary network interface
auto eth0
iface eth0 inet dhcp

# Public Interface
auto eth1
iface eth1 inet static
    address 172.16.0.1
    netmask 255.255.0.0
    network 172.16.0.0
    broadcast 172.16.255.255
```

```
# Private Interface
auto eth2
iface eth2 inet manual
  up ifconfig eth2 up
```

 Remember to edit the `/etc/network/interfaces` file with root privileges.

7. Save the file and bring up the interfaces with the following commands:

```
sudo ifup eth1
sudo ifup eth2
```

 Congratulations! We have successfully created the VirtualBox virtual machine running Ubuntu, which is able to run *OpenStack Compute*.

How it works...

What we have done is created a virtual machine that is the basis of our OpenStack Compute host. It has the necessary networking in place to allow us to access this virtual machine from our host personal computer.

There's more...

There are a number of virtualization products available that are suitable for trying OpenStack, for example, *VMware Server* and *VMware Player* are equally suitable. With VirtualBox, you can also script your installations using a tool named *Vagrant*. While outside the scope of this book, the steps provided here allow you to investigate this option at a later date.

Installing OpenStack Compute packages

Now that we have a machine for running OpenStack, we can install the appropriate packages for running OpenStack Compute, which will allow us to spawn its own virtual machine *instances*.

To do this, we will create a machine that runs all the appropriate services for running OpenStack Nova. The services are as follows:

- ► `nova-compute`: The main package for running the virtual machine instances
- ► `nova-scheduler`: The scheduler picks the server for fulfilling the request to run the instance

- ▶ `nova-api`: Service for making requests to OpenStack to operate the services within it; for example, you make a call to this service to start up a new Nova instance
- ▶ `nova-network`: Network service that controls DHCP, DNS, and Routing
- ▶ `nova-objectstore`: File storage service
- ▶ `nova-common`: Common Python libraries that underpin all of the OpenStack environment
- ▶ `nova-cert`: The Nova certificate management service, used for authentication to Nova
- ▶ `glance`: Image Registry and Delivery service
- ▶ `rabbitmq-server`: Message queue service
- ▶ `mysql-server`: Database server that holds the data for all OpenStack services such as Compute nodes available, instances running, state, and so on
- ▶ `ntp`: Network Time Protocol is essential in a multi-node environment and that the nodes have the same time (tolerance is within five seconds and outside of this you get unpredictable results)
- ▶ `dnsmasq`: DNS forwarder and DHCP service that allocates the addresses to your instances in your environment

Getting ready

Ensure that you are logged in to the *openstack1* VirtualBox virtual machine as the `openstack` user.

How to do it...

Installation of OpenStack under Ubuntu 12.04 is simply achieved using the familiar `apt-get` tool due to the OpenStack packages being available from the official *Ubuntu* repositories.

1. We can install the required packages with the following command:

```
sudo apt-get update
sudo apt-get -y install rabbitmq-server nova-api nova-objectstore
nova-scheduler nova-network nova-compute nova-cert glance qemu
unzip
```

2. Once the installation has completed, we need to install and configure NTP as follows:

```
sudo apt-get -y install ntp
```

3. NTP is important in any multi-node environment and in the OpenStack environment it is a requirement that server times are kept in sync. Although we are configuring only one node, not only will accurate time-keeping help with troubleshooting, but also it will allow us to grow our environment as needed in the future. To do this we edit `/etc/ntp.conf` with the following contents:

```
# Replace ntp.ubuntu.com with an NTP server on your network
server ntp.ubuntu.com
server 127.127.1.0
fudge 127.127.1.0 stratum 10
```

4. Once ntp has been configured correctly we restart the service to pick up the change:

```
sudo service ntp restart
```

How it works...

Installation of OpenStack Nova from the main Ubuntu package repository represents a very straightforward and well-understood way of getting OpenStack onto our Ubuntu server. This adds a greater level of certainty around stability and upgrade paths by not deviating away from the main archives.

There's more...

There are various ways to install OpenStack, from source code building to installation from packages, but this represents the easiest and most consistent method available. There are also alternative releases of OpenStack available. The ones available from Ubuntu 12.04 LTS repositories are known as **Essex** and represent the latest *stable* release at the time of writing.

Using an alternative release

Deviating from stable releases is appropriate when you are helping develop or debug OpenStack, or require functionality that is not available in the current release. To enable different releases, add different Personal Package Archives (PPA) to your system. To view the *OpenStack PPAs*, visit `http://wiki.openstack.org/PPAs`. To use them we first install a pre-requisite tool that allows us to easily add PPAs to our system:

```
sudo apt-get update
sudo apt-get -y install python-software-properties
```

To use a particular release PPA we issue the following commands:

- For Milestones (periodic releases leading up to a stable release):

```
sudo add-apt-repository ppa:openstack-ppa/milestone
sudo apt-get update
```

- For Bleeding Edge (Master Development Branch):

```
sudo add-apt-repository ppa:openstack-ppa/bleeding-edge
sudo apt-get update
```

Once you have configured `apt` to look for an alternative place for packages, you can repeat the preceding process for installing packages if you are creating a new machine based on a different package set, or simply type:

```
sudo apt-get upgrade
```

This will make `apt` look in the new package archive areas for later releases of packages (which they will be as they are more recent revisions of code and development).

Configuring database services

OpenStack supports a number of database backends—an internal Sqlite database (the default), MySQL, and Postgres. Sqlite is used only for testing and is not supported or used in a production environment, whereas MySQL or Postgres is down to the experience of the database staff. For the remainder of this book we shall use MySQL.

Setting up MySQL is easy and allows for you to grow this environment as you progress through the chapters of this book.

Getting ready

Ensure that you are logged in to the *openstack1* VirtualBox virtual machine as the `openstack` user.

How to do it...

1. We first set some options to pre-seed our installation of MySQL to streamline the process. This includes the default root password which we'll set as `openstack`. Complete this step as the root user.

```
cat <<MYSQL_PRESEED | debconf-set-selections
mysql-server-5.1 mysql-server/root_password password openstack
mysql-server-5.1 mysql-server/root_password_again password
openstack
mysql-server-5.1 mysql-server/start_on_boot boolean true
MYSQL_PRESEED
```

The steps outlined previously allow for a non-interactive installation of MySQL. You can omit this step, but during installation, it will ask for the root password. If you do opt for an interactive install, set `openstack` as the password for the root user.

2. We can now install and run MySQL by executing the following commands:

```
sudo apt-get update
sudo apt-get -y install mysql-server
sudo sed -i 's/127.0.0.1/0.0.0.0/g' /etc/mysql/my.cnf
sudo service mysql restart
```

3. Once that's done we then configure an appropriate database user, called `nova`, and privileges for use by OpenStack Compute.

```
MYSQL_PASS=openstack
mysql -uroot -p$MYSQL_PASS -e 'CREATE DATABASE nova;'
mysql -uroot -p$MYSQL_PASS -e "GRANT ALL PRIVILEGES ON nova.* TO
'nova'@'%'"
mysql -uroot -p$MYSQL_PASS -e "SET PASSWORD FOR 'nova'@'%' =
PASSWORD('$MYSQL_PASS');"
```

4. We now simply reference our MySQL server in our /etc/nova/nova.conf file to use MySQL by adding in the --sql_connection flag.

```
--sql_connection=mysql://nova:openstack@172.16.0.1/nova
```

How it works...

MySQL is an essential service to OpenStack as a number of services rely on it. Configuring MySQL appropriately ensures your servers operate smoothly. We first configured the Ubuntu `debconf` utility to set some defaults for our installation so that when MySQL gets installed, it finds values for the root user's password and so skips the part where it asks you for this information during installation. We then added in a database called `nova` that will eventually be populated by tables and data from the OpenStack Compute services and granted all privileges to the `nova` database user so that user can use it.

Finally, we configured our OpenStack Compute installation to specify these details so they can use the `nova` database.

See also

▸ The *MySQL clustering using Galera* recipe in *Chapter 11, In the Datacenter*

Configuring OpenStack Compute

The `/etc/nova/nova.conf` file is a very important file and is referred to many times in this book. This file informs each OpenStack Compute service how to run and what to connect to in order to present OpenStack to our end users. This file will be replicated amongst our nodes as our environment grows.

How to do it...

To run our sandbox environment, we will configure OpenStack Compute so that it is accessible from our underlying host computer. We will have the API service (the service our client tools talk to) listen on our public interface and configure the rest of the services to run on the correct ports. The complete `nova.conf` file as used by the sandbox environment is laid out next and an explanation of each line (known as flags) follows.

1. First, we amend the `/etc/nova/nova.conf` file to have the following contents:

    ```
    --dhcpbridge_flagfile=/etc/nova/nova.conf
    --dhcpbridge=/usr/bin/nova-dhcpbridge
    --logdir=/var/log/nova
    --state_path=/var/lib/nova
    --lock_path=/var/lock/nova
    --force_dhcp_release
    --iscsi_helper=tgtadm
    --libvirt_use_virtio_for_bridges
    --connection_type=libvirt
    --root_helper=sudo nova-rootwrap
    --ec2_private_dns_show_ip
    --sql_connection=mysql://nova:openstack@172.16.0.1/nova
    --use_deprecated_auth
    --s3_host=172.16.0.1
    --rabbit_host=172.16.0.1
    --ec2_host=172.16.0.1
    --ec2_dmz_host=172.16.0.1
    --public_interface=eth1
    --image_service=nova.image.glance.GlanceImageService
    --glance_api_servers=172.16.0.1:9292
    --auto_assign_floating_ip=true
    --scheduler_default_filters=AllHostsFilter
    ```

2. For the `openstack-compute` service we specify that we are using software virtualization by specifying the following code in `/etc/nova/nova-compute.conf`:

    ```
    --libvirt_type=qemu
    ```

3. We then issue a command that ensures the database has the correct tables schema installed and initial data populated with the right information:

```
sudo nova-manage db sync
```

4. We can then proceed to create the private network that will be used by our OpenStack Compute instances internally:

```
sudo nova-manage network create vmnet --fixed_range_v4=10.0.0.0/8
--network_size=64 --bridge_interface=eth2
```

5. And finally we can create the public network that will be used to access the instances from our personal computer:

```
sudo nova-manage floating create --ip_range=172.16.1.0/24
```

How it works...

The following are the flags that are present in our `/etc/nova/nova.conf` configuration file--`dhcpbridge_flatfile=` is the location of the configuration (flag) file for the dhcpbridge service.

- ▶ `--dhcpbridge=` is the location of the `dhcpbridge` service.
- ▶ `--force_dhcp_release` releases the DHCP assigned IP address when the instance is terminated.
- ▶ `--logdir=/var/log/nova` writes all service logs to here. This area will be written to as the root user.
- ▶ `--state_path=/var/lib/nova` is an area on your host that Nova will use to maintain various states about the running service.
- ▶ `--lock_path=/var/lock/nova` is where Nova can write its lock files.
- ▶ `--connection_type=libvirt` specifies the connection to use `libvirt`.
- ▶ `--libvirt_use_virtio_for_bridges` uses the virtio driver for bridges.
- ▶ `--root_helper=sudo nova-rootwrap` specifies a helper script to allow the OpenStack Compute services to obtain root privileges.
- ▶ `--use_deprecated_auth` tells Nova to not use the new Keystone authentication service.
- ▶ `--sql_connection=mysql://root:nova@172.16.0.1/nova` is our SQL Connection line created in the previous section. It denotes the `user:password@ Host Address/database` name (in our case `nova`).
- ▶ `--s3_host=172.16.0.1` tells OpenStack services where to look for the `nova-objectstore` service.
- ▶ `--rabbit_host=172.16.0.1` tells OpenStack services where to find the `rabbitmq` message queue service.

- `--ec2_host=172.16.0.1` denotes the external IP address of the `nova-api` service.

- `--ec2_dmz_host=172.16.0.1` denotes the internal IP address of the `nova-api` service.

- `--public_interface=eth1` is the interface on your hosts running `nova` that your clients will use to access your instances.

- `--image_service=nova.image.glance.GlanceImageService` specifies that for this installation we'll be using Glance for managing our images.

- `--glance_api_servers=172.16.0.1:9292` specifies the server that is running the Glance Imaging service.

- `--auto_assign_floating_ip=true` specifies that when an instance is created, it automatically gets an IP address assigned from the range created in step 5 in the previous section.

- `----scheduler_default_filters=AllHostsFilter` specifies the scheduler can send requests to all compute hosts.

- `--libvirt_type=qemu` sets the virtualization mode. Qemu is software virtualization, which is required for running under VirtualBox. Other options include `kvm` and `xen`.

The networking is set up so that internally the guests are given an IP in the range 10.0.0.0/8. We specified that we would use only 64 addresses in this network range. Be mindful of how many you want. It is easy to create a large range of addresses but it will also take a longer time to create these in the database, as each address is a row in the `nova.fixed_ips` table where these ultimately get recorded and updated. Creating a small range now allows you to try OpenStack Compute and later on you can extend this range very easily.

The public range of IP addresses are created in the 172.16.1.0/24 address space. Remember we created our VirtualBox Host-Only adapter with access to 172.16.0.0/16 – this means we will have access to the running instances in that range.

There's more...

There are a wide variety of options that are available for configuring OpenStack Compute. These will be explored in more detail in later chapters as the `nova.conf` file underpins most of OpenStack Compute services.

Information online regarding flags

You can find a description of each flag at the OpenStack website at `http://wiki.openstack.org/NovaConfigOptions`.

Stopping and starting Nova services

Now that we have configured our OpenStack Compute installation, it's time to start our services so that they're running on our OpenStack1 Virtual Machine ready for us to launch our own private cloud instances.

Getting ready

If you haven't done so already, `ssh` to our virtual machine as the *openstack* user—either using a command-line tool or a client, such as *PuTTY* if you're using Windows.

```
ssh openstack@172.16.0.1
```

This ensures that we can access our virtual machine, as we will need access to spin up instances from your personal computer.

The services that run as part of our `openstack1` setup are:

- ► `nova-compute`
- ► `nova-api`
- ► `nova-network`
- ► `nova-objectstore`
- ► `nova-scheduler`
- ► `nova-cert`
- ► `libvirt-bin`
- ► `glance-registry`
- ► `glance-api`

How to do it...

Carry out the following steps to stop the OpenStack Compute services:

1. As part of the package installation, the OpenStack Compute services start up by default so the first thing to do is to stop them by using the following commands:

```
sudo stop nova-compute
sudo stop nova-network
sudo stop nova-api
sudo stop nova-scheduler
sudo stop nova-objectstore
sudo stop nova-cert
```

To stop all of the OpenStack Compute services use the following command:

```
ls /etc/init/nova-* | cut -d '/' -f4 | cut -d
'.' -f1 | while read S; do sudo stop $S; done
```

2. There are also other services that we installed that are stopped in the same way:

```
sudo stop libvirt-bin
sudo stop glance-registry
sudo stop glance-api
```

Carry out the following steps to start the OpenStack Compute services:

1. Starting the OpenStack Compute services is done in a similar way to stopping them:

```
sudo start nova-compute
sudo start nova-network
sudo start nova-api
sudo start nova-scheduler
sudo start nova-objectstore
sudo start nova-cert
```

To start all of the OpenStack Compute services use the following command:

```
ls /etc/init/nova-* | cut -d '/' -f4 | cut -d
'.' -f1 | while read S; do sudo start $S; done
```

2. There are also other services that we installed that are started in the same way:

```
sudo start libvirt-bin
sudo start glance-registry
sudo start glance-api
```

How it works...

Stopping and starting OpenStack Compute services under Ubuntu are controlled using *upstart* scripts. This allows us to simply control the running services by the `start` and `stop` commands followed by the service we wish to control.

Creating a cloudadmin account and project

As part of our installation we specified `--use_deprecated_auth`, which means that we are using a simple way of storing users, roles, and projects within our OpenStack Compute environment. This is an ideal way to start working with OpenStack within a small development environment such as our sandbox. For larger, production ready environments, Keystone is used, which is covered in *Chapter 6, Administering OpenStack Storage*.

The `cloudadmin` account group is the equivalent of the *root* user on a Unix/Linux host. It has access to all aspects of your Nova cloud environment and so the first account we need to create must have this credential.

Each user has a project—a tenancy in the cloud that has access to certain resources and network ranges. In order to spin up instances in your private cloud environment, a user is assigned to a project. This project can then be kept separate from other users' projects, and equally other users can belong to the same project.

Getting ready

The `nova-manage` command must be run with `root` privileges so we execute the `nova-manage` command prefixed with the `sudo` command.

How to do it...

1. We first need to create an admin user which we will call `openstack` as follows:

    ```
    sudo nova-manage user admin openstack
    ```

2. We then assign the `openstack` user to the `cloudadmin` role as follows:

    ```
    sudo nova-manage role add openstack cloudadmin
    ```

3. Once we have that role assigned, which is appropriate for this section to run as the `cloudadmin` role, we can create a project for this user that we will call `cookbook`. We do this as follows:

    ```
    sudo nova-manage project create cookbook openstack
    ```

4. At this point, we have all the required files set up for us to begin to use OpenStack Compute, but we need to ship these over to our underlying host computer (the computer running the VirtualBox software) so that we can access OpenStack Compute from there. OpenStack provides an option to package these credential files up as a ZIP file for this purpose.

    ```
    sudo nova-manage project zipfile cookbook openstack
    ```

5. The result of this is a file called `nova.zip` in your current directory.

How it works...

We first create the initial user, which is an administrator of the cloud project. This admin user is then assigned elevated privileges known as *cloudadmin* by use of the `nova-manage` command. The `nova-manage` command is used throughout this book and is instrumental in administering OpenStack Compute. The `nova-manage` command must be executed with `root` privileges so we always run this with `sudo`.

We then create a project for our user to operate in. This is a tenancy in our OpenStack Compute environment that has access to various resources such as disks and networks. As we are `cloudadmin`, we have access to all resources and this is sufficient for this section.

Once the project has been created, the details of the project are zipped up ready for transporting back to the client that will operate the cloud.

Installation of command line-tools

Management of OpenStack Compute from the command line is achieved by using euca2ools and Nova Client. Euca2ools is a suite of tools that work with the EC2-API presented by OpenStack. This is the same API that allows you to manage your AWS EC2 cloud instances, start them up and terminate them, create security groups, and troubleshoot your instances. The Nova Client tool uses the OpenStack Compute API, OS-API. This API allows greater control of our OpenStack environment. Understanding these tools is invaluable in understanding the flexibility and power of cloud environments, not least allowing you to create powerful scripts to manage your cloud.

Getting ready

The tools will be installed on your host computer and it is assumed that you are running a version of Ubuntu, which is the easiest way to get hold of the Nova Client and euca2ools packages ready to manage your cloud environment.

How to do it...

The *euca2ools* and *Nova Client* packages are conveniently available from the Ubuntu repositories. If the host PC isn't running Ubuntu, creating a Ubuntu virtual machine alongside our OpenStack Compute virtual machine is a convenient way to get access to these tools.

1. As a normal user on our Ubuntu machine, type the following commands:

   ```
   sudo apt-get update
   sudo apt-get install euca2ools python-novaclient unzip
   ```

2. Now the tools have been installed, we need to grab the `nova.zip` file that we created at the end of the previous section and unpack this on your Ubuntu computer. We do this as follows:

   ```
   cd
   mkdir openstack
   cd openstack
   scp openstack@172.16.0.1:nova.zip .
   unzip nova.zip
   ```

3. We can now *source* the credentials file named `novarc` into our shell environment with the following command and set up our environment to allow us to use our command-line tools to communicate with OpenStack:

   ```
   . novarc
   ```

4. We now must create a **keypair** that allows us to access our cloud instance. Keypairs are SSH private and public key combinations that together allow you to access a resource. You keep the private portion safe, but you're able to give the public key to anyone or any computer without fear or compromise to your security, but only your private portion will match enabling you to be authorized. Cloud instances rely on keypairs for access.

   The following commands will create a keypair named `openstack`:

   To create our keypair using euca2ools, use the following commands:

   ```
   euca-add-keypair openstack > openstack.pem
   chmod 0600 *.pem
   ```

5. To create your keypair using Nova Client, use the following commands:

   ```
   nova keypair-add openstack > openstack.pem
   chmod 0600.pem
   ```

How it works...

Using either euca2ools or Nova Client on Ubuntu is a very natural way of managing our OpenStack Cloud environment. We open up a shell and copy the created nova.zip file over from the previous section. When we unpack it, we can source in the contents of the novarc file—the file that contains the details on our *Access Key, Secret Key* (two vital pieces of information required to access our cloud environment using the *EC2-API), Nova API Key* and *Nova Username* (required for accessing the *OS-API*) as well as certificate files, which are used for uploading images to our environment and addresses to use when connecting to our environment.

When you look at your environment now with the env command you will see these details, for example:

```
NOVA_CERT=/home/user/cloud/openstack/cacert.pem
EC2_SECRET_KEY=ea73623f-e18c-4a3c-89f0-92e82f55ebfb
NOVA_PROJECT_ID=cookbook
EC2_USER_ID=42
NOVA_VERSION=1.1
NOVA_USERNAME=openstack
NOVA_API_KEY=a85c6604-8a6e-49da-8957-d0d7746369cc
NOVA_URL=http://172.16.0.1:8774/v1.1/
EC2_URL=http://172.16.0.1:8773/services/Cloud
EC2_ACCESS_KEY=a85c6604-8a6e-49da-8957-d0d7746369cc:cookbook
EC2_PRIVATE_KEY=/home/user/cloud/openstack/pk.pem
EC2_CERT=/home/user/cloud/openstack/cert.pem
```

By also adding a keypair at this point, we can be ready to launch our instance. The euca-add-keypair and nova add-keypair commands create a public and private key combination for you. It stores the public key in the database references by the name you gave it, in our case we matched our username, *openstack*, and output the details of the private key. We must keep the private key safe. If you lose it or delete it, the keypair will be invalid. A requirement to SSH, which we will use to connect to our instance later on, is to have the private key with permissions that are readable/writeable by the owner only, so we set this with the chmod command.

Uploading a sample machine image

Now that we have a running OpenStack Compute environment, it's time to upload an image for us to use. An *image* is a machine template, which is cloned when we spin up new cloud instances. Images used in Amazon, known as AMIs (or Amazon Machine Images) can often be used in OpenStack. For this next section, we will use an Ubuntu Enterprise Cloud image, which can be used in both Amazon and our OpenStack Compute cloud instance.

Getting ready

These steps are to be carried out on your Ubuntu machine under the user that has access to your OpenStack Compute environment credentials (as created in the *Installation of command-line tools* recipe).

Ensure you have sourced your OpenStack Compute environment credentials as follows:

```
cd ~/openstack
. novarc
```

How to do it...

To upload an image into our OpenStack Compute environment, we perform the following steps:

1. We first download the Ubuntu UEC Cloud Image from `ubuntu.com`:

   ```
   wget http://uec-images.ubuntu.com/releases/precise/release/ubuntu-12.04-server-cloudimg-i386.tar.gz
   ```

2. Once downloaded, we need to install the `cloud-utils` package that provides tools to upload images to our OpenStack Compute environment:

   ```
   sudo apt-get update
   sudo apt-get -y install cloud-utils
   ```

3. We can then proceed to upload this to our OpenStack Compute installation using the `cloud-publish-tarball` command provided by the `cloud-utils` package.

   ```
   cloud-publish-tarball ubuntu-12.04-server-cloudimg-i386.tar.gz images i386
   ```

You should see output such as the following:

```
Wed Jun 20 20:40:03 BST 2012: ====== extracting image ======
Warning: no ramdisk found, assuming '--ramdisk none'
kernel : precise-server-cloudimg-i386-vmlinuz-virtual
ramdisk: none
image  : precise-server-cloudimg-i386.img
Wed Jun 20 20:40:16 BST 2012: ====== bundle/upload kernel ======
Wed Jun 20 20:40:18 BST 2012: ====== bundle/upload image ======
```

4. That's it. We now have an image that is ready for use in our OpenStack cloud. This can be checked by issuing the following commands:

   ❑ For euca2ools:

   euca-describe-images

   You should see output like the following:

```
IMAGE aki-00000001     images/precise-server-cloudimg-i386-vmlinuz-virtual.manifest
.xml available private i386 kernel instance-store
IMAGE ami-00000002     images/precise-server-cloudimg-i386.img.manifest.xml availab
le private i386 machine aki-00000001 instance-store
```

   ❑ For Nova Client:

   nova image-list

   You should see output like the following:

```
+--------------------------------------+------------------------------------------------------+--------+--------+
|                  ID                  |                        Name                          | Status | Server |
+--------------------------------------+------------------------------------------------------+--------+--------+
| 0e2f43a8-e614-48ff-92bd-be0c68da19f4 | images/precise-server-cloudimg-i386.img              | ACTIVE |        |
| 8fbe3a28-afe1-4795-8b8f-44c471434392 | images/precise-server-cloudimg-i386-vmlinuz-virtual  | ACTIVE |        |
+--------------------------------------+------------------------------------------------------+--------+--------+
```

The key information from the output are the `aki` and `ami` (and optionally `ari`) IDs from the `euca2ools` output, and the `ID` string generated for the Nova Client output. We use this information to launch our cloud instances.

How it works...

We first downloaded a Ubuntu UEC image that has been created to run in our OpenStack environment. This tarball contained two components that were needed to run our instance: a kernel and a machine image. We used the command-line tool, cloud-publish-tarball from the `cloud-utils` package to upload this to our Glance service, which populated the `Nova-Objectstore` service with the machine images. Note that we specified an option here named images. This references a *bucket* in our *objects tore*, which is a place on the disk(s) where this image can be found by the OpenStack Compute service.

We can interrogate this image store at any point by issuing the `euca-describe-images` or `nova image-list` commands.

When we list the images, the information that gets used when spinning up cloud instances are the `ami-`, `aki-`, and `eri-` values for use with euca2ools and the image IDs for use with the Nova Client tools. Note that a RAM disk doesn't always need to be present for a cloud instance to work (as in the previous example) but sometimes you may come across cloud images that have these.

See also

▸ The *Using public cloud images* recipe in *Chapter 2, Administering OpenStack Compute*

Launching your first cloud instance

Now that we have a running OpenStack Compute environment and a machine image to use, its now time to spin up our first cloud instance! This section explains how to use the information from `euca-describe-images` or the `nova image-list` commands to reference this on the command line to launch the instance that we want.

Getting ready

These steps are to be carried out on our Ubuntu machine under the user that has access to our OpenStack Compute credentials (as created in the *Installation of command-line tools* recipe).

Before we spin up our first instance, we must create the default security settings that define the access rights. We do this only once (or when we need to adjust these) using either the `euca-authorize` command under euca2ools or the `nova secgroup-add-rule` command under Nova Client. The following set of commands gives us SSH access (Port 22) from any IP address and also allows us to ping the instance to help with troubleshooting. Note the *default* group and its rules are always applied if no security group is mentioned on the command line.

- euca2ools;

  ```
  euca-authorize default -P tcp -p 22 -s 0.0.0.0/0
  euca-authorize default -P icmp -t -1:-1
  ```

- Nova Client:

  ```
  nova secgroup-add-rule default tcp 22 22 0.0.0.0/0
  nova secgroup-add-rule default icmp -1 -1 0.0.0.0/0
  ```

How to do it...

1. From our output of `euca-describe-images` or `nova get-images` we were presented with two images. One was the machine image and the other was the kernel image. To launch our instance, we need this information and we specify this on the command line.

   To launch an instance using euca2ools, we issue the following, specifying the machine image ID:

   ```
   euca-run-instances ami-00000002 -t m1.small -k openstack
   ```

   To launch an instance using Nova Client tools, we issue the following, using the ID of our image that is named `precise-server-cloudimg-i386.img`:

   ```
   nova boot myInstance --image 0e2f43a8-e614-48ff-92bd-be0c68da19f4
   --flavor 2 --key_name openstack
   ```

2. You should see output like the following when you launch an instance:

   - `euca-run-instances` output:

   ```
   RESERVATION     r-0vt9ovsl      cookbook        default
   INSTANCE        i-00000001      ami-00000002                    pending     openstack (cookbook
   , None)    0               m1.small        2011-12-02T20:50:53Z    unknown zone    aki-00000001
        ami-00000000
   ```

❏ `nova boot` output:

```
+------------------------------------+-------------------------------------------+
|               Property             |                   Value                   |
+------------------------------------+-------------------------------------------+
| OS-DCF:diskConfig                  | MANUAL                                    |
| OS-EXT-SRV-ATTR:host               | None                                      |
| OS-EXT-SRV-ATTR:hypervisor_hostname| None                                      |
| OS-EXT-SRV-ATTR:instance_name      | instance-00000008                         |
| OS-EXT-STS:power_state             | 0                                         |
| OS-EXT-STS:task_state              | scheduling                                |
| OS-EXT-STS:vm_state                | building                                  |
| accessIPv4                         |                                           |
| accessIPv6                         |                                           |
| adminPass                          | kkrrix8H6ZMq                              |
| config_drive                       |                                           |
| created                            | 2012-06-21T21:08:07Z                      |
| flavor                             | m1.small                                  |
| hostId                             |                                           |
| id                                 | f10fd940-dcaa-4d60-8eda-8ac0c777f69c      |
| image                              | images/precise-server-cloudimg-i386.img  |
| key_name                           | openstack                                 |
| metadata                           | {}                                        |
| name                               | myInstance                                |
| progress                           | 0                                         |
| status                             | BUILD                                     |
| tenant_id                          | cookbook                                  |
| updated                            | 2012-06-21T21:08:07Z                      |
| user_id                            | openstack                                 |
+------------------------------------+-------------------------------------------+
```

3. This will take a few brief moments to spin up. To check the status of your instances, issue the following commands:

    ❏ Listing instances using euca2ools:

    euca-describe-instances

    ❏ Listing instances using Nova Client:

    nova list
    nova show f10fd940-dcaa-4d60-8eda-8ac0c777f69c

4. This brings back output similar to the output of the previous command lines, yet this time it has created the instance and it is now running and has IP addresses assigned to it.

 Note that you can use either command regardless of whether you launched the instance using *euca2ools* or *Nova Client* tools to view the status of instances running in our environment.

5. You can now connect to this instance using SSH and specifying your private key to gain access.

```
ssh -i openstack.pem ubuntu@172.16.1.1
```

 The default user that ships with the Ubuntu cloud images is ubuntu.

Congratulations! We have successfully launched and connected to our first OpenStack cloud instance.

How it works...

After creating the default security settings, we made a note of our machine image identifier, the ami- or ID value, and then called a tool from *euca2ools* or *Nova Client* to launch our instance. Part of that command line refers to the *keypair* to use. We then connect to the instance using the private key as part of that keypair generated.

How does the cloud instance know what key to use? As part of the boot scripts for this image, it makes a call back to the *meta-server* which is a function of the *nova-api* service. The meta-server provides a go-between that bridges our instance and the real world that the cloud init boot process can call and, in this case, it downloaded a script to inject our private key into the Ubuntu user's .ssh/authorized_keys file. We can modify what scripts are called during this boot process, which is covered later on.

When a cloud instance is launched, it produces a number of useful details about that instance—the same details that are output from the commands, euca-describe-instances, and nova list. For euca2ools output there is a **RESERVATION** section and an **INSTANCE** section. In the **INSTANCE** section, we get details of our running instance.

```
INSTANCE
i-00000001                    Instance ID – we refer to this when interrogating it
ami-00000002                  The Machine Image we used to spin this up
172.16.1.1                    The Public IP address assigned to it
10.0.0.3                      The Private IP address assigned to it
running                       The active state of the machine
openstack                     The user who owns the instance
(cookbook, openstack1)        The project and server running the instance
0                             The launch index (greater than 0 if launched multiple instances)
m1.small                      The size of the instance
2011-12-02T20:50:53Z          The time the instance was launched
nova                          The zone the instance is running in
aki-00000001                  The Kernel used in the running instance
ami-00000000                  The Ramdisk used in the running instance (none here)
```

Similar information is presented by the `nova list` and `nova show` commands. The `nova list` command shows a convenient short version listing the ID, name, status, and IP addresses of our instance. The `nova show` command provides more details similar to that of *euca-describe-instances*.

The type of instance we chose, with the `-t` option for `euca-run-instances`, was `m1.small`. This is an Amazon EC2 way of naming instance types. The same type was specified as an ID of 2 when using the `nova boot` command. The instance types supported can be listed by running the following command (there is no euca2ools equivalent):

nova flavor-list

These flavors (specs of instances) are summarized as follows:

Type of instance	Memory	VCPUS	Storage	Version
m1.tiny	512 MB	1	0 GB	32 and 64-bit
m1.small	2048 MB	1	20 GB	32 and 64-bit
m1.medium	4096 MB	2	40 GB	64-bit only
m1.large	8192 MB	4	80 GB	64-bit only
m1.xlarge	16384 MB	8	160 GB	64-bit only

Terminating your instance

Cloud environments are designed to be dynamic and this implies that cloud instances are being spun up and terminated as required. Terminating a cloud instance is easy to do, but equally it is important to understand some basic concepts of cloud instances.

Cloud instances such as the instance we have used are not persistent. This means that the data and work you do on that instance only exists for the time that it is running. A cloud instance can be rebooted, but once it has been terminated, all data is lost.

To ensure no loss of data, an OpenStack Compute service named `nova-volume` provides persistent data store functionality that allows you to attach a volume to it that doesn't get destroyed on termination but allows you to attach it to running instances. A volume is like a USB drive attached to your instance.

How to do it...

From our Ubuntu machine, first list the running instances to identify the instance you want to terminate.

We can terminate instances using either `euca-terminate-instances` or using `nova delete` regardless of whether we launched our instance using euca2ools or Nova Client tools.

- ► Terminating instances using euca2ools:

  `euca-describe-instances`

  - ❏ To terminate an instance:

    `euca-terminate-instances i-00000001`

  - ❏ You can re-run `euca-describe-instances` again to ensure your instance has terminated.

- ► Terminating instances using Nova Client:

  `nova list`

  - ❏ To terminate an instance:

    `nova delete myInstance`

  - ❏ You can re-run `nova list` again to ensure your instance has terminated.

 You can terminate any number of instances with a single command by listing the instance Ids one after the other. For example, `euca-terminate-instances i-00000001 i-00000002 i-00000005`.

How it works...

We simply identify the instance we wish to terminate by its ID, which is in the format `i-00000000` when viewing instances using `euca-describe-instances` or by name (or ID) when using `nova delete`. Once identified, we can specify this as the instance to terminate. Once terminated, that instance no longer exists—it has been destroyed. So if you had any data on there it will have been deleted along with the instance.

2
Administering OpenStack Compute

In this chapter, we will cover:

- ► Creating and modifying user accounts
- ► Managing security groups
- ► Creating and managing keypairs
- ► Using public cloud images
- ► Alternative upload method using euca2ools
- ► Creating custom Windows images
- ► Creating custom CentOS images

Introduction

Administration of OpenStack Compute should be seen as no different from managing a single Linux host. It requires appropriate users, tenants, and security configured, so that any user in a particular tenant doesn't have access to another tenant's environment. Of course, there's added complexity as we're dealing with a very dynamic environment, but the basics should remain.

Dealing with virtualization in a cloud world means we have to create appropriate images that can be used by OpenStack Compute. These should allow the user to run post-boot setup scripts to maintain a high level of flexibility to the end user. After all, our private cloud environment shouldn't limit the functionality required by the end user.

In this chapter, we will be running administrative commands on both our `openstack1` host and our Ubuntu client, to manage our OpenStack Compute environment.

Creating and modifying user accounts

In our sandbox environment, we're running a very basic method of authentication, configured with the `--use_deprecated_auth` flag in our `/etc/nova/nova.conf` file. This method of authentication is appropriate for testing functionality. To add, remove, and modify accounts using this method of authentication, we use the `nova-manage` command directly on our OpenStack Compute host.

Getting ready

To begin with, ensure you're logged in to your OpenStack Compute host.

How to do it...

To add, remove, or modify user accounts, see the following sections.

Adding Users

In our environment, we currently have one user configured, `openstack`. This user had local administration rights to the project that allowed us to configure security groups and upload images as well as site-wide administration rights, courtesy of the `cloudadmin` role assigned.

Normal users are given roles that exist only within their project (tenant). To do this, we perform the following steps:

1. To create a normal account under our cookbook project, we issue the following command:

    ```
    sudo nova-manage user create demoUser
    ```

2. This user isn't assigned to any project yet, though; to do this we issue the following command:

    ```
    sudo nova-manage project add --project=cookbook
        --user=demoUser
    ```

3. Finally, we can create the project `zipfile` bundle that we can then use on our client to utilize the environment, as that user. To do this, we issue the following command:

    ```
    sudo nova-manage project zipfile cookbook demoUser
        demoUser.zip
    ```

 A user can belong to any number of projects. Ensure the credential ZIP files are named separately for each project to allow you to swap between each.

4. This creates the `demoUser.zip` file. We can download this to our client and unpack and source in the `novarc` file within this, ready for use with our OpenStack Compute environment.

Deleting Users

The method for removing users in our environment, when basic authentication is used, is similar to that of creating a user.

To remove a user from our environment when basic authentication is used, we simply issue the following command:

```
sudo nova-manage user delete demoUser
```

Removing a user from a project

A user can belong to any number of projects, so adding and removing users from projects is an essential feature of a cloud environment.

To remove a user from a project we issue the following command:

```
sudo nova-manage project remove --project=cookbook --user=demoUser
```

How it works...

To manage users in OpenStack Compute when using basic authentication, as denoted by the `--use_deprecated_auth` flag in `/etc/nova/nova.conf`, we use the `nova-manage` command on our OpenStack Compute server directly, and we must run this with `root` privileges using `sudo`. We can add a user to a particular role in a particular project. This can be done in three steps:

1. Create the user, as follows:

   ```
   sudo nova-manage user create username
   ```

2. Add the user to the project, as follows:

   ```
   sudo nova-manage project add --project=projectname
       --user=username
   ```

3. Finally, export the credentials to a ZIP file, which can then be transferred to the user's client, as follows:

   ```
   sudo nova-manage project zipfile projectname username
       username.zip
   ```

What this means is that we can now give our users their own appropriate OpenStack credentials, unpack them, and then source in their own details, which allows them to run the commands as their role dictates.

To modify accounts, we issue the following commands:

- To delete a user we issue:

  ```
  sudo nova-manage user delete --name=username
  ```

- To remove a user we issue:

  ```
  sudo nova-manage project remove --project=projectname
  --name=username
  ```

See also

- The *Adding users* recipe in *Chapter 3, Keystone OpenStack Identity Service*
- The *User management by using OpenStack Dashboard* recipe in *Chapter 9, Horizon OpenStack Dashboard*

Managing security groups

Security groups are firewalls for your instances, and they're mandatory in our cloud environment. The firewall actually exists on the nova-compute host that is running the instance and not in the instance itself. They allow us to protect our hosts by restricting and allowing access and also protect our instances from other users' instances running on the same hosts.

Getting ready

To begin with, ensure you're logged in to your Ubuntu client that has access to the euca2ools or Nova Client tools. These packages can be installed using the following commands:

```
sudo apt-get update
sudo apt-get install euca2ools python-novaclient
```

How to do it...

The following sections describe how to create and modify security groups in our OpenStack environment.

Creation of security groups

Recall that we have already created a *default* security group that opened up *TCP port 22* from anywhere and allowed us to ping our instances. We have also added in a new group to allow us to access our Windows environment. To open up another port, we simply run our command again, assigning that port to a particular group.

For example, to open up TCP port 80 and port 443 on our instances using euca2ools, we can do the following:

```
euca-add-group webserver -d "Web Server Access"
euca-authorize webserver -P tcp -p 80 -s 0.0.0.0/0
euca-authorize webserver -P tcp -p 443 -s 0.0.0.0/0
```

And to open up TCP port 80 and port 443 on our instances using Nova Client we can do the following:

```
nova secgroup-create webserver "Web Server Access"
nova secgroup-add-rule webserver tcp 80 80 0.0.0.0/0
nova secgroup-add-rule webserver tcp 443 443 0.0.0.0/0
```

Note that we specified a different group, this time named `webserver`. The reason for this is that we might not want to open up our web server to everyone, *by default*, which would happen every time we spin up a new instance. Putting it into its own security group allows us to open up access to our instance to port 80 by simply specifying this security group when we launch an instance.

For example, when using euca2ools, we use the `-g` option.

```
euca-run-instances ami-00000002 -k openstack -t m1.tiny -g default
   -g webserver
```

Under Nova Client, we specify the `--security_groups` option

```
nova boot myInstance --image 0e2f43a8-e614-48ff-92bd-be0c68da19f4
   --flavor 2 --key_name openstack --security_groups
   default,webserver
```

To remove a rule from a security group

To remove a rule from a security group, we run the `euca-revoke` or `nova secgroup-delete` commands. For example, suppose we want to remove the HTTPS rule from our `webserver` group. To do this using euca2ools, we do the following:

```
euca-revoke webserver -P tcp -p 443 -s 0.0.0.0/0
```

Under Nova Client this would be:

```
nova secgroup-delete-rule webserver tcp 443 443 0.0.0.0/0
```

To delete a security group

To delete a security group, say `webserver`, we run the following under euca2ools:

```
euca-delete-group webserver
```

Under Nova Client this would be:

```
nova secgroup-delete webserver
```

How it works...

Creation of a security group is done in two steps as follows:

1. The first is that we add a group using the `euca-add-group` or `nova secgroup-create` commands.

2. Following that we can define rules in that group using the `euca-authorize` or `nova secgroup-add-rule` tools, and with this we can specify destination ports that we can open up on our instances and the networks that can see these open ports.

Defining groups and rules using euca2ools

The `euca-add-group` command has the following syntax:

```
euca-add-group group_name -d description
```

The `euca-authorize` command has the basic following syntax:

```
euca-authorize -P protocol -p port -s source
```

 To view more advanced syntax, run `euca-authorize -h`.

Removing rules from a security group is done using the `euca-revoke-access` command, which is analogous to the `euca-authorize` command. Removing a security group altogether is done using the `euca-delete-group` command, which is analogous to the `euca-add-group` command.

Defining groups and rules using Nova Client

The `nova secgroup-create` command has the following syntax:

```
nova secgroup-create group_name  "description"
```

The `nova secgroup-add-rule` command has the following basic syntax:

```
nova secgroup-add-rule group_name protocol port_from port_to source
```

Removing rules from a security group is done using the `nova secgroup-delete-rule` command and is analogous to the `nova secgroup-add-rule` command. Removing a security group altogether is done using the `nova secgroup-delete` command and is analogous to the `nova secgroup-create` command.

Creating and managing keypairs

Keypairs refers to SSH keypairs and consists of two elements—a public key and a private key. Only this specific combination of the public and private key will allow us access to our instances.

Getting ready

To begin with, ensure you're logged in to your Ubuntu client that has access to the euca2ools and Nova Client tools. These packages can be installed using the following commands:

```
sudo apt-get update
sudo apt-get install euca2ools python-novaclient
```

How to do it...

To create a keypair, we run the `euca-add-keypair` command when we're using euca2ools, or `nova keypair-add` when using Nova Client. We name the key accordingly, which we will subsequently refer to when launching instances. The output of the command is the SSH private key that we will use to access a shell on our instance.

1. First create the keypair as follows, when using euca2ools:

   ```
   euca-add-keypair myKey > myKey.pem
   ```

   Or for Nova Client, this looks like:

   ```
   nova keypair-add myKey > myKey.pem
   ```

2. We must then protect the private key output:

   ```
   chmod 0600 myKey.pem
   ```

This command has generated a keypair and stored the public portion within our database, at the heart of our OpenStack environment. The private portion has been written to a file on our client, which we then protect by making sure that only our user can access this file.

When we want to launch an instance using our newly created keypair under euca2ools, we specify this with the `-k` option on the `euca-run-instances` command line, as follows:

```
euca-run-instances ami-00000002 -k myKey -t m1.tiny
```

When we want to use this new key under Nova Client, this looks as follows, using the `nova boot` command:

```
nova boot myInstance --image 0e2f43a8-e614-48ff-92bd-be0c68da19f4
    --flavor 2 --key_name myKey
```

And when we want to SSH to this running instance, we specify the private key on the SSH command line with the `-i` option:

```
ssh ubuntu@172.16.1.1 -i myKey.pem
```

 As with most things Unix, the values and files specified are case-sensitive.

Listing and deleting keypairs using euca2ools

To list and delete keypairs using euca2ools, carry out the set of commands in the following sections:

List the keypairs

To list the keypairs in our project, we simply run the `euca-describe-keypairs` command, as follows:

```
euca-describe-keypairs
```

This brings back a list of keypairs in our project, such as the following:

```
KEYPAIR    openstack    bb:af:26:09:8a:c4:72:98:d9:1e:cd
:e5:51:60:50:63
KEYPAIR    myKey  3c:74:65:72:66:19:bd:a5:90:21:45:06:0e:4f:64:29
```

Delete the keypairs

To delete a keypair from our project, we simply specify the name of the key as an option to the `euca-delete-keypair` tool.

▶ To delete the myKey keypair, we do the following:

```
euca-delete-keypair myKey
```

▶ We can verify this by listing the keys available, thus:

```
euca-describe-keypairs
```

Listing and deleting keypairs using Nova Client

To list and delete keypairs using Nova Client, carry out the set of commands in the following sections.

List the keypairs

To list the keypairs in our project using Nova Client, we simply run the `nova keypair-list` command, as follows:

```
nova keypair-list
```

This brings back a list of keypairs in our project, such as the following:

```
+------------+-------------------------------------------------+
|    Name    |                  Fingerprint                    |
+------------+-------------------------------------------------+
| myKey      | 51:3b:4e:f1:02:cc:e5:58:c1:4b:20:0d:a7:f2:48:a1 |
| openstack  | 9b:88:25:8a:d7:73:5e:21:3a:78:c5:53:65:f0:ea:48 |
+------------+-------------------------------------------------+
```

Delete the keypairs

To delete a keypair from our project, we simply specify the name of the key as an option to the `nova keypair-delete` tool.

- To delete the `myKey` keypair, we do the following:

  ```
  nova keypair-delete myKey
  ```

- We can verify this by listing the keys available, thus:

  ```
  nova keypair-list
  ```

 Deleting keypairs is an irreversible action. Deleting a keypair to a running instance will prevent you from accessing that instance.

How it works...

Creation of a keypair allows us SSH access to our instance and is carried out using the `euca-add-keypair` or `nova keypair-add` commands. This stores the public key in our backend database store that will be injected into the `.ssh/authorized_keys` file on our cloud instance, as part of the cloud instance's boot/cloud init script. We can then use the private key that gets generated to access the system by specifying this on the `ssh` command line with the `-i` option.

We can of course also remove keys from our project, and we do this to prevent further access by that particular keypair. The commands `euca-delete-keypair` and `nova keypair-delete` do this for us, and we can verify what keys are available to us in our project, by running the `euca-describe-keypairs` or `nova keypair-list` commands.

Using public cloud images

Images are the templates that get copied and spawned in our OpenStack Compute environment. There are a small handful of places where we can get ready-made images for our use. With these images, we are able to get off the ground very quickly, knowing that the community has tested the images.

> For Ubuntu, download any of the releases at `http://cloud-images.ubuntu.com/releases/`.
>
> For CentOS and Fedora images, download them at `http://open.eucalyptus.com/wiki/EucalyptusUserImageCreatorGuide_v2.0`.

We have already used a public Ubuntu image in *Chapter 1, Starting OpenStack Compute*, where we used the tool `cloud-publish-tarball` to upload this image to our cloud environment. We will recap that and look at an alternative method for images that aren't in the same format.

Getting ready

To begin with, ensure you're logged into your Ubuntu client and have your cloud credentials sourced into your environment.

The `cloud-publish-tarball` tool is provided by the `cloud-utils` package. This can be installed as follows:

```
sudo apt-get update
sudo apt-get -y install cloud-utils
```

How to do it...

There are a few locations from where images can be downloaded for use in our OpenStack environment. These images are usually packaged as tarballs, which allows us to use a convenient tool called `cloud-publish-tarball`, from the `cloud-utils` package, to upload them into our environment.

Ubuntu Cloud Images from ubuntu.com

1. First, we'll download a new Ubuntu image from `http://cloud-images.ubuntu.com/releases/`, as follows:

   ```
   wget http://cloud-images.ubuntu.com/precise/current/
       precise-server-cloudimg-i386.tar.gz
   ```

2. We can now simply upload this to our environment, using the `cloud-publish-tarball` command, as follows:

```
cloud-publish-tarball precise-server-cloudimg-i386.tar.gz images
i386
```

3. Once complete, this is available as an image for use in our OpenStack Compute environment.

   ❑ To display images using euca2ools, use the following command:

   ```
   euca-describe-images
   ```

   ❑ To display images using Nova Client, use the following command:

   ```
   nova image-list
   ```

CentOS/Fedora Images from eucalyptus.com

1. To get a CentOS image from `eucalyptus.com`, we download the tarball, as follows:

```
wget "http://open.eucalyptus.com/sites/all/
    modules/pubdlcnt/pubdlcnt.php?
    file=http://www.eucalyptussoftware.com/downloads/
    eucalyptus-images/euca-centos-5.3-i386.tar.gz&nid=4305"
    -O euca-centos-5.3-i386.tar.gz
```

2. We can now simply upload this to our environment using the same `cloud-publish-tarball` command, as follows:

```
cloud-publish-tarball euca-centos-5.3-i386.tar.gz images i386
```

3. Once complete, this is available as an image for use in our OpenStack Compute environment.

   ❑ To display images using euca2ools, use the following command:

   ```
   euca-describe-images
   ```

   ❑ To display images using Nova Client, use the following command:

   ```
   nova image-list
   ```

How it works...

Cloud images that are publicly available and packaged as tarballs can conveniently be uploaded to our OpenStack Compute environment, with the `cloud-publish-tarball` command, using the following syntax:

```
cloud-publish-tarball tarball.tar.gz bucket architecture
```

`architecture` is optional but recommended, as `cloud-publish-tarball` does its best to work out the architecture from the filename given.

Alternative upload method using euca2ools

Using an alternative method to upload images to our environment offers us greater flexibility in what we can configure. By using the `euca-bundle-image`, `euca-upload-bundle`, and `euca-register` tools, we can upload each part of our machine image independently, allowing us to specify alternative kernel and ramdisk images.

Getting ready

To begin with, ensure you're logged in to your Ubuntu client and have your cloud credentials sourced into your environment.

The `euca-bundle-image`, `euca-upload-bundle`, and `euca-register` tools are provided by the euca2ools package. This can be installed as follows:

```
sudo apt-get update
sudo apt-get -y install euca2ools
```

How to do it...

To have the ability to have more control over how we upload images into our environment, we can use the tools provided by euca2ools. Carry out the following steps to use euca2ools to upload images into your OpenStack environment:

1. Download a cloud image, as described at the beginning of the last section. Once downloaded, we then unpack this as follows:

   ```
   tar zxvf euca-centos-5.3-i386.tar.gz
   cd euca-centos-5.3-i386
   ```

2. Once unpacked, we use a separate set of commands to bundle this up for our OpenStack Compute environment and upload the relevant parts to create our image for use. For this section, we run a command named `euca-bundle-image`, to package up the kernel. There will have been two distinct kernel folders in the tarball: `kvm-kernel` and `xen-kernel`. Our sandbox server is based on `kvm`, so we will bundle up the `kvm-kernel` file. The command is as follows:

   ```
   euca-bundle-image -i kvm-kernel/vmlinuz-2.6.28-11-generic
       --kernel true
   ```

   The previous command will produce the following output:

   ```
   Checking image
   Encrypting image
   Splitting image...
   Part: vmlinuz-2.6.28-11-server.part.00
   Generating manifest /tmp/vmlinuz-2.6.28-11-server.manifest.xml
   ```

3. Note the manifest XML created as we reference this with `euca-upload-bundle` to upload this to our environment. The command is as follows:

```
euca-upload-bundle -b images -m /tmp/vmlinuz-2.6.28-11
    -server.manifest.xml
```

The previous command will produce the following output:

```
Checking bucket: images
Uploading manifest file
Uploading part: vmlinuz-2.6.28-11-server.part.00
Uploaded image as images/vmlinuz-2.6.28-11-server.manifest.xml
```

4. We now proceed to register this using the `euca-register` command (so it is available for use by OpenStack Compute), using the uploaded image manifest XML reference. The command is as follows:

```
euca-register images/vmlinuz-2.6.28-11-server.manifest.xml
```

The previous command will produce the following output:

```
IMAGE    aki-00000003
```

5. Now that we have the kernel uploaded and registered, we can do the same to the ramdisk that accompanies this CentOS image. This is done using the same set of commands, but referencing the ramdisk instead. We do this as follows:

```
euca-bundle-image -i kvm-kernel/initrd.img-2.6.28-11-server
--ramdisk true
```

The previous command will produce the following output:

```
Checking image
Encrypting image
Splitting image...
Part: initrd.img-2.6.28-11-server.part.00
Generating manifest /tmp/initrd.img-2.6.28-11-server.manifest.xml
```

The command to upload is as follows:

```
euca-upload-bundle -b images -m /tmp/initrd.img-2.6.28-11
    -server.manifest.xml
```

The previous command will produce the following output:

```
Checking bucket: images
Uploading manifest file
Uploading part: initrd.img-2.6.28-11-server.part.00
Uploaded image as images/initrd.img-2.6.28-11-server.manifest.xml
```

The command to register is as follows:

```
euca-register images/initrd.img-2.6.28-11-
    server.manifest.xml
```

The previous command will produce the following output:

```
IMAGE    ari-00000004
```

6. We can now bundle all this together along with our machine image in a similar way, so we can reference this for launching instances. The first bundle line only differs slightly in that we reference the uploaded ramdisk and kernel as part of this machine image:

```
euca-bundle-image -i centos.5-3.x86.img --kernel aki-
    00000003 --ramdisk ari-00000004
```

7. This takes a little longer (depending on the size of the image), as it splits it into smaller chunks—10 MB in size—and produces output like the following:

```
Checking image
Encrypting image
Splitting image...
Part: centos.5-3.x86.img.part.00
Part: centos.5-3.x86.img.part.01
Part: centos.5-3.x86.img.part.02
… snip ...
Part: centos.5-3.x86.img.part.21
Part: centos.5-3.x86.img.part.22
Generating manifest /tmp/centos.5-3.x86.img.manifest.xml
```

8. We then continue to upload and register this as before; the only difference is the amount of data to upload. The command is as follows:

```
euca-upload-bundle -b images -m /tmp/centos.5-3.x86.img.manifest.
xml
```

The previous command will produce the following output:

```
Checking bucket: images
Uploading manifest file
Uploading part: centos.5-3.x86.img.part.00
Uploading part: centos.5-3.x86.img.part.01
Uploading part: centos.5-3.x86.img.part.02
… snip …
Uploading part: centos.5-3.x86.img.part.21
Uploading part: centos.5-3.x86.img.part.22
Uploaded image as images/centos.5-3.x86.img.manifest.xml
```

The command to register is as follows:

```
euca-register images/centos.5-3.x86.img.manifest.xml
```

The previous command will produce the following output:

```
IMAGE    ami-00000005
```

9. That's it—we now have a CentOS 5.3 image for use in our Nova environment. To verify this, we can list the available images as follows:

    ```
    euca-describe-images
    ```

10. We can run our newly uploaded image by referencing this output image `ami` and connect to it via `ssh` as the root user for this CentOS image, as follows:

    ```
    euca-run-instances ami-00000005 -k openstack -t m1.tiny
    ssh -i openstack.pem root@172.16.1.1
    ```

How it works...

Uploading images using the tools provided by euca2ools is quite straightforward and is made up of three steps: bundle, upload, and register. You then repeat these steps for each of the kernel, ramdisk, and image files.

```
euca-bundle-image -i kernel   --kernel true
euca-upload-bundle -b bucket -m manifest.xml
euca-register bucket/manifest.xml

euca-bundle-image -i ramdisk   --ramdisk true
euca-upload-bundle -b bucket -m manifest.xml

euca-register bucket/manifest.xml

euca-bundle-image -i image --kernel kernel_id –ramdisk ramdisk_id
euca-upload-bundle -b bucket -m manifest.xml

euca-register bucket/manifest.xml
```

Each command flows to the next: `euca-bundle-image` outputs the manifest XML file path that is used by `euca-upload-bundle` as the value for the parameter `-m`. `euca-upload-bundle` outputs the value to be used by `euca-register`. The last triplet of bundle, upload, and register is for the image itself, as you need to reference the assigned kernel and ramdisk IDs from the preceding steps.

 These procedures can also be used to upload to other Cloud environments such as Amazon EC2.

Creating custom Windows images

If you want to run Windows in your OpenStack environment, you must create the images yourself. This ensures you're not breaching Microsoft's EULA—as you must first agree to this as part of an installation routine—as well as ensuring that your Windows image is suitable for your environment. To do this under OpenStack Compute, we create our image by booting the Windows ISO.

Getting ready

To begin with, ensure you're logged into your Ubuntu client and have your cloud credentials sourced into your environment. We need to install the `qemu-kvm` package to allow us to create the required images and ensure we have euca2ools and cloud-utils available to allow us to upload the resultant Windows image. This is achieved with the following command:

```
sudo apt-get update
sudo apt-get -y install qemu-kvm
```

You also need an ISO of the Windows server you are going to create. For this section, we will be using Windows 2003 SP2 i386.

If you are using Ubuntu as your client through VirtualBox and you don't have enough disk space, simply add in a new disk of at least 20 GB. We will need at least 20 GB to create our new OS cloud installs and temporary files, so that we can upload this to our Nova environment. You also need to use an alternative to `kvm`, named `qemu`.

Your client also needs a VNC client. If you don't have one installed, you can freely download the following:

- For Ubuntu, install `apt-get install gtkvncviewer`
- For Mac OSX, visit `http://sourceforge.net/projects/chicken/`
- For Windows, visit `http://www.tightvnc.com/download.php`

How to do it...

Installation of a Windows image can be achieved by invoking `kvm` commands directly, as described in the following steps:

1. We first need to create the raw image that will essentially be the hard drive for our Windows installation, so it needs to be big enough to install the Windows operating system:

    ```
    kvm-img create -f raw win2k3-i386.img 10G
    ```

2. OpenStack Compute uses VIRTIO to present its disk to the OS, but Windows doesn't ship with these required drivers. We must download these so we can load them during the installation. Browse to `http://alt.fedoraproject.org/pub/alt/virtio-win/latest/images/bin/`. We can download the ISO that is listed, as follows:

3.
```
wget http://alt.fedoraproject.org/pub/alt/virtio-win/latest/images/bin/virtio-win-0.1-22.iso

wget http://www.linuxservices.co.uk/virtio-win-1.1.16.vfd
```

4. We can now launch `kvm`, specifying our Windows 2003 ISO, specifying the disk image we've created, and putting the equivalent of the drivers loaded onto a floppy disk, so Windows can find the required drivers:

```
sudo kvm -m 768 -cdrom
    en_win_srv_2003_r2_standard_with_sp2_cd1.iso -drive
    file=win2k3-i386.img,if=virtio -fda virtio-win-
    1.1.16.vfd -boot d -nographic -vnc :0
```

> If using a guest running under VirtualBox or VMware (or if your client simply doesn't support hardware virtualization) and you encounter a problem running `kvm`, add a `-no-kvm` parameter to the previous command.
>
> You can check for hardware virtualization support by running the command `kvm-ok under Ubuntu`.

5. You can now connect to this using a VNC client. If you're running Ubuntu locally, connect to `localhost`, or else connect to the Ubuntu guest `172.16.0.253`.

6. Go through the installation of Windows. When it completes with the **Rebooting computer** message, press *CTRL + A* and then *X*, to stop `kvm`.

7. You can now boot your Windows image using KVM to complete the installation (note the `-boot c` parameter to boot from the hard drive).

```
sudo kvm -m 768 -cdrom
    en_win_srv_2003_r2_standard_with_sp2_cd1.iso -drive
    file=win2k3-i386.img,if=virtio -fda virtio-win-
    1.1.16.vfd -boot c -nographic -vnc :0 -no-kvm
```

8. This has finished the installation, but we must now configure our Windows image, so that it is suitable for our Nova environment. To do this, we must boot into it again, connect via VNC, configure Remote Desktop Access, and accept the installation of the drivers and any other first-time install steps:

```
sudo kvm -m 768 -drive file=win2k3-i386.img,if=virtio -fda
    virtio-win-1.1.16.vfd -boot c -nographic -vnc :0 -no-
    kvm
```

9. Once completed, power this off by hitting *CTRL + A* and then *X*, to exit kvm. We can then bundle this image up for use in OpenStack Compute.

    ```
    euca-bundle-image -i win2k3-i386.img
    euca-upload-bundle -b images -m /tmp/win2k3-
        i386.img.manifest.xml
    euca-register images/win2k3-i386.img.manifest.xml
    ```

10. Once the image has uploaded (it can take a short while), it will be visible in your image list. To connect to this, we need to open up access to the RDP port (TCP 3389). So, we create an additional security group for this purpose, as follows:

    ```
    euca-describe-images
    euca-add-group windows -d "Windows Group"
    euca-authorize windows -P tcp -p 3389 -s 0.0.0.0/0
    ```

11. We can then launch this instance, for example, under euca2ools do the following:

    ```
    euca-run ami-00000006 -g default -g windows -k openstack -t
        m1.small
    ```

12. Finally, we can connect to this instance once it has launched using RDP.

> Under Mac OSX, you can download an RDP client at http://
> www.microsoft.com/mac/downloads, and for Linux you can
> download rdesktop using your distribution's package manager.
>
> Having trouble accessing your Windows instance? Connect to your
> openstack1 host using VNC. The first instance runs on VNC port
> 5900 (equivalent to :0), the second on 5901 (equivalent to :1).

How it works...

Creating a suitable image running Windows in our Nova environment is simply done by running the installation routine through a kvm session with VNC enabled and then uploading the created disk image to our Nova environment. Creating a guest image in this way is done using the following steps:

1. Create the hard disk image using kvm-img.
2. Create a new kvm session, booting the ISO and specifying the hard drive image as our destination hard drive.
3. Configure it for our use (for example, enabling RDP access).
4. Bundle up the created disk image.

Creating custom CentOS images

For most uses, downloading pre-made Ubuntu or CentOS images will be good enough, as they provide an OS with minimal packages installed and are able to invoke extra commands once booted. Sometimes though, the images need extra work; perhaps they need extra disk space as part of their instance storage, or maybe they need to work with a third party where they expect certain tools or scripts to be present. Creating custom OS images for your cloud allows you to install instances just the way you need to.

Creating custom Linux images is more complex, as we have greater flexibility on how to use these images in our OpenStack Compute environment.

For this next section, we will look at creating the popular CentOS distribution as an OpenStack Compute image. This section is applicable for most Red Hat-based clones in principle.

Getting ready

To begin with, ensure you're logged into your Ubuntu client and have your cloud credentials sourced into your environment. We need to install the `qemu-kvm` package to allow us to create the required images as well as ensure that we have the `cloud-utils` package available, to allow us to upload the image to our OpenStack environment once complete.

```
sudo apt-get update
sudo apt-get -y install qemu-kvm cloud-utils
```

If you are using Ubuntu as your client, through VirtualBox, and you don't have enough disk space, simply add in a new disk of at least 20 GB. We will need at least 20 GB to create our new OS cloud installs and temporary files, so that we can upload this to our OpenStack Compute environment. You also need to use an alternative to `kvm`, named `qemu`.

Your client also needs a VNC client. If you don't have one installed, you can freely download the following:

- For Ubuntu, install `apt-get -y install gtkvncviewer`
- For Mac OSX, visit `http://sourceforge.net/projects/chicken/`
- for Windows, visit `http://www.tightvnc.com/download.php`

How to do it...

Creation of a CentOS image is very similar to that of a Windows image, but since Linux allows for the flexibility of being able to boot alternative kernels and ramdisks, our creation process has to cater to this. For this section, we will describe how to create an appropriate CentOS 6.1 image for use in our OpenStack Compute environment, by calling `kvm` (or `qemu`, where hardware virtualization isn't available) directly.

1. We first need to download CentOS 6.1 from `centos.org`. We do this as follows:

```
wget http://mirrors.manchester.icecolo.com/centos/
     6.2/isos/i386/CentOS-6.2-i386-minimal.iso
```

2. Once downloaded, we can proceed with creating our raw disk image, which will form the basis of the image we'll use to boot our instances:

```
kvm-img create -f raw CentOS-6.2-i386-filesystem.img 5G
```

3. Now that this has been created, we can use it as the hard drive that we will use when we boot the ISO under `kvm`. To have control over partitioning, we must do a graphical installation of CentOS 6.2, and for this we must set at least 1024 MB of RAM. If we install CentOS 6.2 using the text-based installer, we won't be able to produce a valid partition that we can use for our OpenStack Compute instances. To launch the ISO so that we can access it using VNC, execute the following:

```
sudo kvm -m 1024 -cdrom CentOS-6.2-i386-minimal.iso -drive
     file=CentOS-6.2-i386-filesystem.img,if=scsi,index=0
     -boot d -net nic -net user -vnc :0 -usbdevice tablet
```

> Add `-no-kvm`, if running the `kvm` command under your VirtualBox, to enable `qemu`—software virtualization.
>
> If you encounter a failure regarding an MP-BIOS bug launching `kvm`, stop the instance and start it again.

4. Once running, connect to this instance using your VNC viewer, and complete your installation of CentOS ensuring that you choose **Create Custom Layout** when prompted.

 Create Custom Layout
Manually create your own custom layout on the selected device(s) using our partitioning tool.

5. Create a single partition for the / (root) partition and ensure you use all available space.

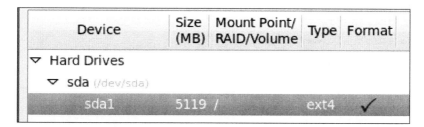

Device	Size (MB)	Mount Point/ RAID/Volume	Type	Format
▽ Hard Drives				
▽ sda (/dev/sda)				
sda1	5119	/	ext4	✓

6. When asked to continue, you will be presented with a warning regarding not specifying a swap partition. It is safe to continue by answering **Yes**.

7. After a while, your installation will complete. When it says **rebooting system**, press *CTRL + C* in the terminal running kvm to power this machine off. We can now relaunch directly into our new image to configure this:

```
sudo kvm -m 1024 -drive file=CentOS-6.2-i386-
    filesystem.img,if=scsi,index=0,boot=on -boot c -net nic
    -net user -nographic -vnc :0 -no-acpi
```

8. When it has booted, log in as root with the password you set during your installation. We first need to get the network interface up and running, followed by a system update.

```
dhclient eth0
yum -y update
```

9. After the update, remove the network persistence udev rules, to ensure that our only required interface remains as eth0, and then power the instance off as follows:

```
rm -rf /etc/udev/rules.d/70-persistent-net.rules
cat > /etc/sysconfig/network-scripts/ifcfg-eth0 << EOF
DEVICE=eth0
BOOTPROTO=dhcp
ONBOOT=yes
EOF
poweroff
```

10. Launch the instance again by repeating the command in step 5 and log in as root again. This reboot is to ensure our image is fully functional after our system update. We're now ready to customize our instance, depending on our requirements. For the purpose of this section, we'll just ensure SSH is running.

```
chkconfig sshd on
poweroff
```

11. We can now extract the EXT4 partition that is the basis of our machine image. We do this by interrogating the image we created and extracting the data partition.

```
sudo losetup -f CentOS-6.2-i386-filesystem.img
sudo losetup -a
sudo fdisk -l /dev/loop0
```

12. This will produce output as shown in the following screenshot:

```
Disk /dev/loop0: 5368 MB, 5368709120 bytes

181 heads, 40 sectors/track, 1448 cylinders, total 10485760 sectors
Units = sectors of 1 * 512 = 512 bytes
Sector size (logical/physical): 512 bytes / 512 bytes
I/O size (minimum/optimal): 512 bytes / 512 bytes
Disk identifier: 0x0007fb12

      Device Boot      Start         End      Blocks   Id  System
/dev/loop0p1   *        2048    10485759     5241856   83  Linux
```

13. The key value to note here is the Start sector, which is specified as 2048. We take this value and multiply it by 512 bytes to give us 1048576. We use this byte value to extract the data for our image.

14. Unmount the loop device and then remount it, using this byte value calculated as the offset.

```
sudo losetup -d /dev/loop0
sudo losetup -f -o 1048576 CentOS-6.2-i386-filesystem.img
sudo losetup -a
```

15. We can then extract the mounted file system, which becomes our machine image.

```
sudo dd if=/dev/loop0 of=CentOS-6.2-i386.img
```

16. We then unmount our offset image, now that we have extracted the data to our image file.

```
sudo losetup -d /dev/loop0
```

17. We're now ready to configure our image for our cloud environment, so we mount this extracted image, so that we can edit the files within it.

```
sudo mount -o loop CentOS-6.2-i386.img /mnt
```

18. We need to edit the `/etc/fstab` file in our image, so that the root file system label remains constant when we spawn different instances:

```
LABEL=uec-rootfs          /              ext4     defaults        0 1
```

19. To ensure we can log in using the keys we specify to run our instances, we add the following to the `rc.local` script:

```
# Download the key from the meta server
mkdir --mode=0700 -p /root/.ssh
echo >> /root/.ssh/authorized_keys
curl -m 10 -s http://169.254.169.254/latest/meta-data/public-
keys/0/openssh-key | grep 'ssh-rsa' >> /root/.ssh/authorized_keys
chmod 0600 /root/.ssh/authorized_keys
echo "AUTHORIZED_KEYS:"
echo "***********************"
cat /root/.ssh/authorized_keys
echo "***********************"
```

20. Once done, we need to copy the kernel and ramdisk for use within Nova.

```
sudo cp /mnt/boot/vmlinuz-2.6.32-220.7.1.el6.i686
    CentOS-6.2-i386-vmlinuz
sudo cp /mnt/boot/initramfs-2.6.32-220.7.1.el6.i686.img
    CentOS-6.2-i386-loader
```

21. We can now unmount our image, ready for upload to our OpenStack Compute environment, thus.

```
sudo umount /mnt
```

22. We now change the label of our image to match what we specified in our `fstab` file.

```
sudo tune2fs -L uec-rootfs CentOS-6.2-i386.img
```

23. We can finally upload this to our OpenStack Compute environment for use, thus.

```
cloud-publish-image -t image -K CentOS-6.2-i386-vmlinuz -R
    CentOS-6.1-i386-loader i386 CentOS-6.1-i386.img images
```

24. After a short while, we can view this in the list of images we can use under OpenStack Compute.

```
euca-describe-images
```

How it works...

Creating custom Linux images is more complex due to the greater flexibility we have to cater to in our OpenStack Compute environment. The steps are outlined as follows:

1. Create the disk image using `kvm-img`.

2. Boot the ISO through `kvm`, specifying the disk image as the destination hard drive.

3. Ensure you only create a single EXT3 or EXT4 partition (/).

4. Extract the data from the disk image (excluding boot sector) by mounting the image and viewing the image drive geometry to find where the data partition begins.

5. Modify any startup scripts and disk configuration to make it flexible in our cloud environment.

6. Extract the kernel and ramdisk from our installation, so we can upload this separately to OpenStack Compute.

7. Upload the disk image, ramdisk, and kernel for use by clients using the `cloud-publish-image` tool.

8. Separating out the kernel, ramdisk, and image allows us to keep the base OS installation separate from kernels and ramdisks. This means we can update our running kernels without affecting the underlying OS installation, just as we would in a traditional Linux installation.

3
Keystone OpenStack Identity Service

In this chapter, we will cover:

- ▶ Installing OpenStack Identity Service
- ▶ Configuring roles
- ▶ Creating tenants
- ▶ Adding users
- ▶ Defining service endpoints
- ▶ Configuring the service tenant and service users
- ▶ Configuring OpenStack Image Service to use OpenStack Identity Service
- ▶ Configuring OpenStack Compute to use OpenStack Identity Service
- ▶ Using OpenStack Compute with OpenStack Identity Service

Introduction

OpenStack Identity Service, known as Keystone, provides services for authenticating and managing user, account, and role information for our OpenStack cloud environment. It is a crucial service that underpins the authentication and verification between all of our OpenStack cloud services. Authentication with OpenStack Identity Service sends back an authorization token that is passed between the services, once validated. This token is subsequently used as your authentication and verification that you can proceed to use that service, such as OpenStack Storage and Compute.

Installing OpenStack Identity Service

Installation and configuration of OpenStack Identity Service is straightforward from Ubuntu packages. Once configured, connecting to our OpenStack cloud environment will be performed through our new OpenStack Identity Service.

The backend datastore for our OpenStack Identity Service is a simple SQLite database.

Getting ready

To begin with, ensure you're logged in to our OpenStack Compute host or an appropriate server on the network where OpenStack Identity Service will be installed, that the rest of the OpenStack hosts have access to.

How to do it...

Carry out the following instructions to install OpenStack Identity Service:

1. Installation of OpenStack Identity Service is done by specifying the keystone package in Ubuntu, and we do this as follows:

   ```
   sudo apt-get update
   sudo apt-get -y install keystone
   ```

2. Once installed, we need to configure the backend database store, so we first create the `keystone` database in MySQL. We do this as follows (where we have a user in MySQL called `root`, with the password `openstack`, that is able to create databases):

   ```
   MYSQL_PASS=openstack
   mysql -uroot -p$MYSQL_PASS -e 'CREATE DATABASE keystone;'
   ```

3. It is good practice to create a user that is specific to our OpenStack Identity Service, so we create this as follows:

   ```
   mysql -uroot -p$MYSQL_PASS -e "GRANT ALL PRIVILEGES ON
       keystone.* TO 'keystone'@'%'"
   mysql -uroot -p$MYSQL_PASS -e "SET PASSWORD FOR
       'keystone'@'%' = PASSWORD('$MYSQL_PASS');"
   ```

4. We then need to configure OpenStack Identity Service to use this database by editing the `/etc/keystone/keystone.conf` file, and then change the `sql_connection` line to match the database credentials. We do this as follows:

   ```
   sudo sed -i "s#^connection.*#connection =
   mysql://keystone:$MYSQL_PASS@172.16.0.1/keystone#"
   /etc/keystone/keystone.conf
   ```

5. We can now restart the `keystone` service:

```
sudo stop keystone
sudo start keystone
```

6. With Keystone started, we can now populate the `keystone` database with the required tables, by issuing the following command:

```
sudo keystone-manage db_sync
```

> Congratulations! We now have OpenStack Identity Service installed for use in our OpenStack environment.

How it works...

A convenient way to install OpenStack Identity Service ready for use in our OpenStack environment is by using the Ubuntu packages. Once installed, we configure our MySQL database server with a `keystone` database and set up the `keystone.conf` configuration file to use this. After starting the Keystone service, running the `keystone-manage db_sync` command populates the `keystone` database with the appropriate tables ready for us to add in the required users, roles, and tenants required in our OpenStack environment.

Configuring roles

Roles are the permissions given to users within a tenant. Here we will configure two roles—an *admin* role that allows for administration of our environment and a *Member* role that is given to ordinary users who will be using the cloud environment.

Getting ready

To begin with, ensure you're logged in to our OpenStack Compute host—where OpenStack Identity Service has been installed—or an appropriate Ubuntu client that has access to where OpenStack Identity Service is installed.

If the `keystone` client tool isn't available, this can be installed on an Ubuntu client to manage our OpenStack Identity Service by issuing the following commands:

```
sudo apt-get update
sudo apt-get -y install python-keystoneclient
```

Ensure that we have our environment set correctly to access our OpenStack environment:

```
export ENDPOINT=172.16.0.1
export SERVICE_TOKEN=ADMIN
export SERVICE_ENDPOINT=http://${ENDPOINT}:35357/v2.0
```

How to do it...

To create the required roles in our OpenStack environment, perform the following steps:

1. Creation of the admin role is done as follows:

```
# admin role
keystone role-create --name admin
```

2. To create the Member role we repeat the step, specifying the Member role:

```
# Member role
keystone role-create --name Member
```

How it works...

Creation of the roles is simply achieved by using the `keystone` client, specifying the `role-create` option with the following syntax:

```
keystone role-create --name role_name
```

The `role_name` attribute can't be arbitrary. The `admin` role has been set in `/etc/keystone/policy.json` as having administrative rights:

```
{
    "admin_required": [["role:admin"], ["is_admin:1"]]
}
```

And when we configure the OpenStack Dashboard, Horizon, it has the *Member* role configured as the default when users are created in that interface.

On creation of the role, this returns an ID associated with it that we use when assigning roles to users. To see a list of roles and the associated IDs in our environment, we can issue the following command:

```
keystone role-list
```

Creating tenants

A tenant in OpenStack is a project. Users can't be created without having a tenant assigned to them so these must be created first. For this section, we will create a tenant for our users, called cookbook.

Getting ready

To begin with, ensure you're logged into our OpenStack Compute host—where OpenStack Identity Service has been installed—or an appropriate Ubuntu client that has access to where OpenStack Identity Service is installed.

If the keystone client tool isn't available, this can be installed on an Ubuntu client—to manage our OpenStack Identity Service—by issuing the following command:

```
sudo apt-get update
sudo apt-get -y install python-keystoneclient
```

Ensure that we have our environment set correctly to access our OpenStack environment:

```
export ENDPOINT=172.16.0.1
export SERVICE_TOKEN=ADMIN
export SERVICE_ENDPOINT=http://${ENDPOINT}:35357/v2.0
```

How to do it...

To create a tenant in our OpenStack environment, perform the following step:

1. Creation of a tenant called cookbook is done as follows:

```
keystone tenant-create --name cookbook --description
    "Default Cookbook Tenant" --enabled true
```

How it works...

Creation of the roles is simply achieved by using the keystone client, specifying the tenant-create option with the following syntax:

```
keystone tenant-create --name tenant_name --description "Default
    Cookbook Tenant" --enabled true
```

The tenant_name is an arbitrary string and must not contain spaces. On creation of the tenant, this returns an ID associated with it that we use when adding users to this tenant. To see a list of tenants and the associated IDs in our environment, we can issue the following command:

```
keystone tenant-list
```

Adding users

Adding users to OpenStack Identity Service requires that the user have a *tenant* they can exist in, and have a *role* defined that can be assigned to them. For this section, we will create two users. The first user will be named admin and will have the *admin* role assigned to them in the cookbook tenant. The second user will be named demo and will have the *Member* role assigned to them in the same cookbook tenant.

Getting ready

To begin with, ensure you're logged into our OpenStack Compute host—where OpenStack Identity Service has been installed—or an appropriate Ubuntu client that has access to where OpenStack Identity Service is installed.

If the keystone client tool isn't available, this can be installed on an Ubuntu client—to manage our OpenStack Identity Service—by issuing the following commands:

```
sudo apt-get update
sudo apt-get -y install python-keystoneclient
```

Ensure that we have our environment set correctly to access our OpenStack environment:

```
export ENDPOINT=172.16.0.1
export SERVICE_TOKEN=ADMIN
export SERVICE_ENDPOINT=http://${ENDPOINT}:35357/v2.0
```

How to do it...

To create the required users in our OpenStack environment, perform the following steps:

1. To create a user in the cookbook tenant, we first need to get the cookbook tenant ID. To do this, issue the following command, which we conveniently store in a variable named TENANT_ID with the tenant-list option:

   ```
   TENANT_ID=$(keystone tenant-list | awk '/\ cookbook\ /
       {print $2}')
   ```

2. Now that we have the tenant ID, creation of the admin user in the cookbook tenant is done as follows, using the user-create option, choosing a password for the user:

   ```
   PASSWORD=openstack
   keystone user-create --name admin --tenant_id $TENANT_ID --
       pass $PASSWORD --email root@localhost --enabled true
   ```

3. As we are creating the `admin` user, to which we are assigning the `admin` role, we need the `admin` role ID. In a similar way to the discovery of the tenant ID in step 1, we pick out the ID of the `admin` role and conveniently store it in a variable to use when assigning the role to the user with the `role-list` option:

```
ROLE_ID=$(keystone role-list | awk '/\ admin\ /
    {print $2}')
```

4. To assign the role to our user, we need to use the user ID that was returned when we created that user. To get this, we can list the users and pick out the ID for that particular user with the following `user-list` option:

```
USER_ID=$(keystone user-list | awk '/\ admin\ /
    {print $2}')
```

5. Finally, with the tenant ID, user ID, and an appropriate role ID available, we can assign that role to the user, with the following `user-role-add` option:

```
keystone user-role-add --user $USER_ID --role $ROLE_ID --
    tenant_id $TENANT_ID
```

6. To create the demo user in the cookbook tenant with the Member role assigned we repeat the process as defined in steps 1 to 5:

```
# Get the cookbook tenant ID
TENANT_ID=$(keystone tenant-list | awk '/\ cookbook\ /
    {print $2}')

# Create the user
PASSWORD=openstack
keystone user-create --name demo --tenant_id $TENANT_ID --
    pass $PASSWORD --email demo@localhost --enabled true

# Get the Member role ID
ROLE_ID=$(keystone role-list | awk '/\ Member\ /
    {print $2}')

# Get the demo user ID
USER_ID=$(keystone user-list | awk '/\ demo\ / {print $2}')

# Assign the Member role to the demo user in cookbook
keystone user-role-add --user $USER_ID --role
    $ROLE_ID --tenant_id $TENANT_ID
```

How it works...

Adding users in OpenStack Identity Service requires that the tenant and roles for that user be created first. Once these are available, in order to use the keystone command-line client, we need the IDs of the tenants and IDs of the roles that are to be assigned to the user in that tenant. Note that a user can be a member of many tenants and can have different roles assigned in each.

To create a user with the `user-create` option, the syntax is as follows:

```
keystone user-create --name user_name --tenant_id TENANT_ID --pass
    password --email email_address --enabled true
```

The `user_name` attribute is an arbitrary name but cannot contain any spaces. A `password` attribute must be present. In the previous examples, these were set to `openstack`. The `email_address` attribute must also be present.

To assign a role to a user with the `user-role-add` option, the syntax is as follows:

```
keystone user-role-add --user USER_ID --role ROLE_ID --tenant_id
    TENANT_ID
```

This means we need to have the ID of the user, the ID of the role, and the ID of the tenant in order to assign roles to users. These IDs can be found using the following commands:

```
keystone tenant-list
```

```
keystone role-list
```

```
keystone user-list
```

Defining service endpoints

Each of the services in our cloud environment runs on a particular URL and port—these are the endpoint addresses for our services. When a client communicates with our OpenStack environment that runs OpenStack Identity Service, it is this service that returns the endpoint URLs, which the user can then use in an OpenStack environment. To enable this feature, we must define these endpoints. In a cloud environment, though, we can define multiple regions. Regions can be thought of as different datacenters, which would imply that they would have different URLs or IP addresses. Under OpenStack Identity Service, we can define these URL endpoints separately for each region. As we only have a single environment, we will reference this as *RegionOne*.

Getting ready

To begin with, ensure you're logged in to our OpenStack Compute host—where OpenStack Identity Service has been installed—or an appropriate Ubuntu client that has access to where OpenStack Identity Service is installed.

If the `keystone` client tool isn't available, it can be installed on an Ubuntu client to manage our OpenStack Identity Service, by issuing the following commands:

```
sudo apt-get update
sudo apt-get -y install python-keystoneclient
```

How to do it...

Defining the services and service endpoints in OpenStack Identity Service involves running the `keystone` client command to specify the different services and the URLs that they run from. Although we might not have all services currently running in our environment, we will be configuring them within OpenStack Identity Service for future use.

 To manage our OpenStack Identity Service, we have to authenticate with the service itself. Without any users configured though, we make use of an *admin token* to send directly back to the *admin port* of OpenStack Identity Service. These are also known as a *service token* and *service port*. These details are configured directly in `/etc/keystone/keystone.conf`, as follows:
```
admin_port = 35357
admin_token = ADMIN
```

To define endpoints for services in our OpenStack environment, carry out the following steps:

1. First, we set the service token and service endpoint, which point to the service port of our OpenStack Identity Service.

   ```
   export ENDPOINT=172.16.0.1
   export SERVICE_TOKEN=ADMIN
   export SERVICE_ENDPOINT=http://${ENDPOINT}:35357/v2.0
   ```

2. We can now define the actual services that OpenStack Identity Service needs to know about in our environment.

   ```
   # OpenStack Compute Nova API Endpoint
   keystone service-create --name nova --type compute
       --description 'OpenStack Compute Service'

   # OpenStack Compute EC2 API Endpoint
   keystone service-create --name ec2 --type ec2
       --description 'EC2 Service'
   ```

```
# Glance Image Service Endpoint
keystone service-create --name glance --type image
    --description 'OpenStack Image Service'


# Keystone Identity Service Endpoint
keystone service-create --name keystone --type identity
    --description 'OpenStack Identity Service'


# Nova Volume Endpoint
keystone service-create --name volume --type volume
    --description 'Volume Service'
```

3. After we have done this, we can add in the service endpoint URLs that these services run on. To do this, we need the ID that was returned for each of the service endpoints created in the previous step. This is then used as a parameter when specifying the endpoint URLS for that service.

> Note that OpenStack Identity Service can be configured to service requests on three URLs: a public facing URL (that the end users use), an administration URL (that users with administrative access can use that might have a different URL), and an internal URL (that is appropriate when presenting the services on either side of a firewall to the public URL).

For the following services, we will configure the public and internal service URLs to be the same, which is appropriate for our environment.

```
# OpenStack Compute Nova API
ID=$(keystone service-list | awk '/\ nova\ / {print $2}')


PUBLIC="http://$ENDPOINT:8774/v2/\$(tenant_id)s"
ADMIN=$PUBLIC
INTERNAL=$PUBLIC


keystone endpoint-create --region RegionOne --service_id $ID
    --publicurl $PUBLIC --adminurl $ADMIN --internalurl $INTERNAL



# OpenStack Compute EC2 API
ID=$(keystone service-list | awk '/\ ec2\ / {print $2}')
```

```
PUBLIC="http://$ENDPOINT:8773/services/Cloud"
ADMIN="http://$ENDPOINT:8773/services/Admin"
INTERNAL=$PUBLIC


keystone endpoint-create --region RegionOne --service_id $ID
    --publicurl $PUBLIC --adminurl $ADMIN --internalurl $INTERNAL



# Glance Image Service
ID=$(keystone service-list | awk '/\ glance\ / {print $2}')

PUBLIC="http://$ENDPOINT:9292/v1"
ADMIN=$PUBLIC
INTERNAL=$PUBLIC


keystone endpoint-create --region RegionOne --service_id $ID
    --publicurl $PUBLIC --adminurl $ADMIN --internalurl $INTERNAL



# Keystone OpenStack Identity Service
ID=$(keystone service-list | awk '/\ keystone\ / {print $2}')

PUBLIC="http://$ENDPOINT:5000/v2.0"
ADMIN="http://$ENDPOINT:35357/v2.0"
INTERNAL=$PUBLIC


keystone endpoint-create --region RegionOne --service_id $ID
    --publicurl $PUBLIC --adminurl $ADMIN --internalurl $INTERNAL



# Nova Volume
ID=$(keystone service-list | awk '/\ volume\ / {print $2}')

PUBLIC="http://$ENDPOINT:8776/v1/%(tenant_id)s"
ADMIN=$PUBLIC
INTERNAL=$PUBLIC


keystone endpoint-create --region RegionOne --service_id $ID
    --publicurl $PUBLIC --adminurl $ADMIN --internalurl $INTERNAL
```

How it works...

Configuring the services and endpoints within OpenStack Identity Service is done with the `keystone` client command.

We first add the service definitions, by using the `keystone` client and the `service-create` option with the following syntax:

```
keystone service-create --name service_name --type service_type
    --description 'description'
```

`service_name` is an arbitrary name or label defining a service of a particular `type`. We refer to the name when defining the endpoint to fetch the ID of the service.

The `type` option can be one of the following: `compute`, `object-store`, `image-service`, and `identity-service`. Note that we haven't configured the OpenStack Storage service (type `object-store`) at this stage.

The `description` field is again an arbitrary field describing the service.

Once we have added in our service definitions, we can tell OpenStack Identity Service where those services run from, by defining the endpoints using the `keystone` client and the `endpoint-create` option, with the following syntax:

```
keystone endpoint-create --region region_name --service_id service_id
    --publicurl public_url --adminurl admin_url --internalurl
    internal_url
```

Where `service_id` is the ID of the service when we created the service definitions in the first step. The list of our services and IDs can be obtained by running the following command:

```
keystone service-list
```

As OpenStack is designed for global deployments, a region defines a physical datacenter or a geographical area that comprises of multiple connected datacenters. For our purpose, we define just a single region—*RegionOne*. This is an arbitrary name that we can reference when specifying what runs in what datacenter/area and we carry this through to when we configure our client for use with these regions. All of our services can be configured to run on three different URLs, as follows, depending on how we want to configure our OpenStack cloud environment:

- ▸ The `public_url` parameter is the URL that end users would connect on. In a public cloud environment, this would be a public URL that resolves to a public IP address.

- ▸ The `admin_url` parameter is a restricted address for conducting administration. In a public deployment, you would keep this separate from the `public_URL` by presenting the service you are configuring on a different, restricted URL. Some services have a different URI for the admin service, so this is configured using this attribute.

- The `internal_url` parameter would be the IP or URL that existed only within the private local area network. The reason for this is that you are able to connect to services from your cloud environment internally without connecting over a public IP address space, which could incur data charges for traversing the Internet. It is also potentially more secure and less complex to do so.

 Once the initial `keystone` database has been set up, after running the initial `keystone-manage db_sync` command on the OpenStack Identity Service server, administration can be done remotely using the `keystone` client.

Configuring the service tenant and service users

With the service endpoints created, we can now configure them so that our OpenStack services can utilize them. To do this, each service is configured with a username and password within a special *service* tenant. For each service that uses OpenStack Identity Service for authentication and authorization, we then specify these details in their relevant configuration file, when setting up that service.

Getting ready

To begin with, ensure you're logged in to our OpenStack Compute host—where OpenStack Identity Service has been installed—or an appropriate Ubuntu client that has access to where OpenStack Identity Service is installed.

If the `keystone` client tool isn't available, this can be installed on an Ubuntu client to manage our OpenStack Identity Service, by issuing the following command:

```
sudo apt-get update
sudo apt-get -y install python-keystoneclient
```

Ensure that we have our environment set correctly to access our OpenStack environment:

```
export ENDPOINT=172.16.0.1
export SERVICE_TOKEN=ADMIN
export SERVICE_ENDPOINT=http://${ENDPOINT}:35357/v2.0
```

How to do it...

To configure an appropriate service tenant, carry out the following steps:

1. Create the *service* tenant as follows:

```
keystone tenant-create --name service --description
    "Service Tenant" --enabled true
```

2. Record the ID of the *service* tenant, so that we can assign service users to this ID, as follows:

```
SERVICE_TENANT_ID=$(keystone tenant-list | awk '/\ service\
    / {print $2}')
```

3. For each of the services in this section, we will create the user accounts to be named the same as the services and set the password to be the same as the service name too. For example, we will add a user called nova, with a password nova in the *service* tenant, using the user-create option, as follows:

```
keystone user-create --name nova --pass nova --tenant_id
    $SERVICE_TENANT_ID --email nova@localhost
    --enabled true
```

4. We then repeat this for each of our other services that will use OpenStack Identity Service:

```
keystone user-create --name glance --pass glance
    --tenant_id $SERVICE_TENANT_ID
    --email glance@localhost --enabled true


keystone user-create --name keystone --pass keystone
    --tenant_id $SERVICE_TENANT_ID --email
    keystone@localhost --enabled true
```

5. We can now assign these users the *admin* role in the *service* tenant. To do this, we use the user-role-add option after retrieving the user ID of the nova user. For example, to add the *admin* role to the nova user in the *service* tenant, we do the following:

```
# Get the nova user id
USER_ID=$(keystone user-list | awk '/\ nova\ / {print $2}')


# Get the admin role id
ROLE_ID=$(keystone role-list | awk '/\ admin\ /
    {print $2}')


# Assign the nova user the admin role in service tenant
keystone user-role-add --user $USER_ID --role $ROLE_ID
    --tenant_id $SERVICE_TENANT_ID
```

6. We then repeat this for our other two service users, *glance* and *keystone*:

```
# Get the glance user id
USER_ID=$(keystone user-list | awk '/\ glance\ /
    {print $2}')

# Assign the glance user the admin role in service tenant
keystone user-role-add --user $USER_ID --role $ROLE_ID
    --tenant_id $SERVICE_TENANT_ID


# Get the keystone user id
USER_ID=$(keystone user-list | awk '/\ keystone\ /
    {print $2}')

# Assign the glance user the admin role in service tenant
keystone user-role-add --user $USER_ID --role $ROLE_ID
    --tenant_id $SERVICE_TENANT_ID
```

How it works...

Creation of the *service* tenant, populated with the services required to run OpenStack, is no different from creating any other users on our system that require the *admin* role. We create the usernames and passwords and ensure they exist in the *service* tenant.

The reason for the *service* tenant is that each service itself has to authenticate with *keystone* in order for it to be available within OpenStack. Configuration of that service is then done using these credentials. For example, for *glance* we specify the following in /etc/glance/glance-registry-api.ini, when used with OpenStack Identity Service, which matches what we created previously:

```
[filter:authtoken]
paste.filter_factory = keystone.middleware.auth_token:filter_factory
service_protocol = http
service_host = 172.16.0.1
service_port = 5000
auth_host = 172.16.0.1
auth_port = 35357
auth_protocol = http
auth_uri = http://172.16.0.1:5000/
admin_tenant_name = service
admin_user = glance
admin_password = glance
```

Configuring OpenStack Image Service to use OpenStack Identity Service

Configuring OpenStack Image Service to use OpenStack Identity Service is required to allow our OpenStack Compute to operate correctly. OpenStack Image Service is covered in more detail in *Chapter 7, Glance OpenStack Image Service*.

Getting ready

To begin with, ensure you're logged in to our OpenStack Compute host or the host that is running OpenStack Image Service.

If the OpenStack Image Service host isn't running on the same server as OpenStack Identity Service, you will need to install the `python-keystone` package, as follows:

```
sudo apt-get update
sudo apt-get -y python-keystone
```

How to do it...

To configure OpenStack Image Service to use OpenStack Identity Service, carry out the following steps:

1. We first edit the `/etc/glance/glance-api-paste.ini` file and configure the `[filter:authtoken]` section found at the bottom of this file, to match our *glance* service user configured previously:

```
[filter:authtoken]
paste.filter_factory = keystone.middleware.auth_token:filter_
factory
service_protocol = http
service_host = 172.16.0.1
service_port = 5000
auth_host = 172.16.0.1
auth_port = 35357
auth_protocol = http
auth_uri = http://172.16.0.1:5000/
admin_tenant_name = service
admin_user = glance
admin_password = glance
```

2. With the file saved, we add in the following at the bottom of the `/etc/glance/glance-api.conf` file, to tell OpenStack Image Service to utilize OpenStack Identity Service and the information in the `glance-api-paste.ini` file:

```
[paste_deploy]
flavor = keystone
```

3. We repeat this process for the `/etc/glance/glance-registry-paste.ini` file, configuring the *glance* service user in the `[filter:authtoken]` section:

```
[filter:authtoken]
paste.filter_factory = keystone.middleware.auth_token:filter_
factory
service_protocol = http
service_host = 172.16.0.1
service_port = 5000
auth_host = 172.16.0.1
auth_port = 35357
auth_protocol = http
auth_uri = http://172.16.0.1:5000/
admin_tenant_name = service
admin_user = glance
admin_password = glance
```

4. Then, we add the following to the corresponding `/etc/glance/glance-registry.conf` file, to use this information and enable it to use OpenStack Identity Service:

```
[paste_deploy]
flavor = keystone
```

5. Finally, we restart the two OpenStack Identity Service processes to pick up the changes:

```
sudo restart glance-api
sudo restart glance-registry
```

How it works...

OpenStack Image Service runs two processes. These are the *glance-api*, which is the service that our clients and services talk to, and the *glance-registry* process that manages the objects on the disk and in the database registry. Both of these services need to have matching credentials that were defined previously in OpenStack Identity Service in their configuration files, in order for these services to allow a user to authenticate with the service successfully.

Refer to the *Managing images with OpenStack Image Service* recipe in *Chapter 7, Glance OpenStack Image Service*, to upload a new image in our OpenStack Identity Service managed environment, as our test images uploaded under `deprecated_auth` will not be accessible.

Configuring OpenStack Compute to use OpenStack Identity Service

In our configuration of OpenStack Compute, we are using `deprecated_auth`, which stores user and project information within the `nova` database, managed by the `nova-manage` command directly on the OpenStack Compute host. This authentication method is limited in its use and will likely be dropped from future versions of OpenStack.

With OpenStack Identity Service installed and configured, we now need to tell our OpenStack Compute service that it can be used instead of the `deprecated_auth` mechanism.

 Note that any existing users and projects created in `deprecated_auth` are not moved over to OpenStack Identity Service automatically and will need recreating again under this new service.

Getting ready

To begin with, ensure you're logged into our OpenStack Compute host.

How to do it...

Replacing the authentication mechanism in our OpenStack Compute sandbox environment is simply achieved with the following steps:

1. We first ensure that our OpenStack Compute host has the required `python-keystone` package installed, if this host is a standalone Compute host, as follows:

```
sudo apt-get update
sudo apt-get -y install python-keystone
```

2. Configuration of the OpenStack Compute service to use the OpenStack Identity Service is first done by filling in the `[filter:authtoken]` section with the details that we created for the `nova` service user in the previous section, as follows:

```
[filter:authtoken]
paste.filter_factory = keystone.middleware.auth_token:
filter_factory
service_protocol = http
service_host = 172.16.0.1
service_port = 5000
auth_host = 172.16.0.1
auth_port = 35357
auth_protocol = http
auth_uri = http://172.16.0.1:5000/
admin_tenant_name = service
admin_user = nova
admin_password = nova
```

3. With the `api-paste.ini` file configured correctly, we edit `/etc/nova/nova.conf` to inform it to use the paste file and set keystone as the authentication mechanism by adding in the following lines:

   ```
   --api-paste_config=/etc/nova/api-paste.ini
   --keystone_ec2_url=http://172.16.0.1:5000/v2.0/ec2tokens
   --auth_strategy=keystone
   ```

4. It is important to remove the following line from `/etc/nova/nova.conf`:

   ```
   --use_deprecated_auth
   ```

5. With our OpenStack Identity Service running, we can restart our OpenStack Compute services to pick up this authentication change, as follows:

   ```
   sudo restart nova-api
   ```

How it works...

Configuration of OpenStack Compute to use OpenStack Identity Service first involves editing the `/etc/nova/api-paste.ini` file and filling in the `[filter:authtoken]` part of the file with details of the `nova` service user we created in the previous section.

We then configure the `/etc/nova/nova.conf` file, which is directed at this paste file, as well as specifying that the `auth_strategy` option is set to `keystone`.

Using OpenStack Compute with OpenStack Identity Service

OpenStack Identity Service underpins all of the OpenStack services. With OpenStack Image Service configured to also use OpenStack Identity Service, the OpenStack Compute environment can now be used.

Getting ready

To begin with, log in to an Ubuntu client and ensure that euca2ools and Nova Client are available. If they aren't, they can be installed as follows:

```
sudo apt-get update
sudo apt-get -y euca2ools python-novaclient
```

How to do it...

To use OpenStack Identity Service as the authentication mechanism in our OpenStack environment, we need to set our environment variables accordingly. This is achieved as follows, for our *demo* user:

1. We first have to configure our environment to use OpenStack Identity Service as our authentication. For Nova Client, we do this by creating an environment resource configuration file with the required variables configured (for example, `/home/user/keystonerc`):

```
NOVA_API_HOST=172.16.0.1
KEYSTONE_API_HOST=172.16.0.1

KEYSTONE_TENANT="cookbook"
KEYSTONE_USERNAME="demo"
KEYSTONE_PASSWORD="openstack"

NOVA_REGION="RegionOne"

export NOVA_USERNAME=$KEYSTONE_USERNAME
export NOVA_PROJECT_ID=$KEYSTONE_TENANT
export NOVA_PASSWORD=$KEYSTONE_PASSWORD
export NOVA_API_KEY=$KEYSTONE_PASSWORD
export NOVA_REGION_NAME=$NOVA_REGION
export NOVA_URL="http://${NOVA_API_HOST}:5000/v2.0/"
export NOVA_VERSION="1.1"

export OS_AUTH_USER=$KEYSTONE_USERNAME
export OS_AUTH_KEY=$KEYSTONE_PASSWORD
export OS_AUTH_TENANT=$KEYSTONE_TENANT
export OS_AUTH_URL="http://${KEYSTONE_API_HOST}:5000/v2.0/"
export OS_AUTH_STRATEGY="keystone"
```

2. We can now simply source this into our environment and use the environment, as before:

```
. keystonerc
```

3. We can test that this is successful by issuing some nova commands, for example:

```
nova list
nova credentials
```

4. To use euca2ools, we create the EC2 credentials in OpenStack Identity Service separately. In order to do this, we use Nova Client to create our *X509* certificates that euca2tools relies on. To do this, we ensure we have sourced in the details, as shown earlier, and then run the following command:

```
nova x509-get-root-cert
nova x509-create-cert
```

5. We can now create our EC2 credentials using the `ec2-credentials-create` option.

 Note that if the environment resource file (for example, `/home/user/keystonerc`) has been sourced into the environment, this will conflict with the `SERVICE_TOKEN` and `SERVICE_ENDPOINT` environment variables as user/password authentication takes precedence.

6. Clear your environment before setting the following environment variables:

```
export ENDPOINT=172.16.0.1
export SERVICE_TOKEN=ADMIN
export SERVICE_ENDPOINT=http://${ENDPOINT}:35357/v2.0

# Get the demo user ID
USER_ID=$(keystone user-list | awk '/\ demo\ / {print $2}')

# Get the cookbook tenant ID
TENANT_ID=$(keystone tenant-list | awk '/\ cookbook\ /
    {print $2}')

# Create the EC2 Credentials
keystone ec2-credentials-create --user $USER_ID
    --tenant_id $TENANT_ID
```

7. We then take the output from the `ec2-credentials-create` option to populate an ec2rc file with the following, replacing the `EC2_ACCESS_KEY` and `EC2_SECRET_KEY` with the corresponding information from the output:

```
NOVA_API_HOST=172.16.01

NOVARC=$(readlink -f "${BASH_SOURCE:-${0}}" 2>/dev/null) ||
    NOVARC=$(python -c 'import os,sys; print
    os.path.abspath(os.path.realpath(sys.argv[1]))'
    "${BASH_SOURCE:-${0}}")
NOVA_KEY_DIR=${NOVARC%/*}
export EC2_ACCESS_KEY=f2aed2792f3a4112bcdf608e6b81ae6f
export EC2_SECRET_KEY=ae3c637e7db94601b98e6729c0c2a0f7
export EC2_URL=http://$NOVA_API_HOST:8773/services/Cloud
```

```
export EC2_USER_ID=42 # nova does not use user id,
    but bundling requires it
export EC2_PRIVATE_KEY=${NOVA_KEY_DIR}/demo.pem
export EC2_CERT=${NOVA_KEY_DIR}/cert.pem
export NOVA_CERT=${NOVA_KEY_DIR}/cacert.pem
export EUCALYPTUS_CERT=${NOVA_CERT} # euca-bundle-image
    requires this set
export S3_URL=http://$NOVA_API_HOST:3333
alias ec2-bundle-image="ec2-bundle-image --cert ${EC2_CERT}
    --privatekey ${EC2_PRIVATE_KEY} --user 42 --ec2cert
    ${NOVA_CERT}"
alias ec2-upload-bundle="ec2-upload-bundle -a
    ${EC2_ACCESS_KEY} -s ${EC2_SECRET_KEY} --url ${S3_URL}
    --ec2cert ${NOVA_CERT}"
```

8. With this created, we can source this in to our environment to use euca2ools:

    ```
    . ec2rc
    ```

9. We then utilize the `euca-` commands as follows, for example:

    ```
    euca-describe-instances
    ```

How it works...

Configuring our environment to use OpenStack Identity Service for authentication for Nova Client and euca2ools so that we can launch our instances involves manually creating an environment resource file with the appropriate environment variables.

To configure our environment to use euca2ools, we run an extra option that creates the appropriate `EC2_ACCESS_KEY` and `EC2_SECRET_KEY` environment variables within OpenStack Identity Service as well as extracting the root cert and creating a cert for our user to allow us to use the `cloud-util` tools to upload images.

Our environment passes on our username, password, and tenant to OpenStack Identity Service for authentication and passes back, behind the scenes, an appropriate token, which validates our user. This then allows us to seamlessly spin up instances within our tenancy (project) of cookbook.

4

Installing OpenStack Storage

In this chapter, we will cover:

- ▶ Creating an OpenStack Storage sandbox environment
- ▶ Installing the OpenStack Storage services
- ▶ Configuring storage
- ▶ Configuring replication
- ▶ Configuring OpenStack Storage Service
- ▶ Configuring the OpenStack Storage proxy server
- ▶ Configuring Account Server
- ▶ Configuring Container Server
- ▶ Configuring Object Server
- ▶ Making the Object, Account, and Container rings
- ▶ Stopping and starting OpenStack Storage
- ▶ Testing OpenStack Storage
- ▶ Setting up SSL access
- ▶ Configuring OpenStack Storage with OpenStack Identity Service

Introduction

OpenStack Object Storage, also known as Swift, is the service that allows for massively scalable and highly redundant storage on commodity hardware. This service is analogous to Amazon's S3 storage service and is managed in a similar way under OpenStack. With OpenStack Storage, we can store many objects of virtually unlimited size—restricted by the available hardware—and grow our environment as needed, to accommodate our storage. The highly redundant nature of OpenStack Storage is ideal for archiving data (such as logs) as well as providing a storage system that OpenStack Compute can use for virtual machine instance templates.

In this chapter, we will set up a single virtual machine that will represent a multi-node test environment for OpenStack Storage. Although we are operating on a single host, the steps involved mimic a four-device setup, so we see a lot of duplication and replication of our configuration files.

Creating an OpenStack Storage sandbox environment

Creating a sandbox environment allows us to discover and experiment with the OpenStack Storage service. This service gives us the ability to store objects such as images or archives of logs.

To do this, we will use an Open Source virtual server program from Oracle, named VirtualBox, which is freely available from `http://www.virtualbox.org` for Windows, Mac OS X, and Linux. The result of this environment will be a virtual machine (with connectivity to any other OpenStack hosts in our sandbox environment) with two disks installed. It will act as the OpenStack Storage host used in the rest of this chapter.

It is assumed the computer you will be using to run your test environment in has enough processing power, with hardware virtualization support (modern AMDs and Intel iX processors) and at least 4 GB of RAM. The virtual machine we will be creating will have all components installed to get you familiar with the OpenStack Storage services.

In this section, we will have created the following specification for a virtual machine:

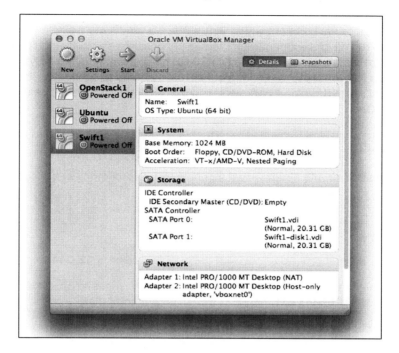

We will install this virtual machine with Ubuntu 12.04 LTS Server 64-bit and assign the name `openstack2`. We will assign `172.16.0.2` as the IP address on `eth1` (the host-only interface that is presented by VirtualBox).

Getting ready

To begin with, we must download VirtualBox from `http://www.virtualbox.org/` and then follow the installation procedure, once it has been downloaded.

We will also need to download the Ubuntu 12.04 LTS Server ISO CD-ROM image from `http://www.ubuntu.com/`.

If a `vboxnet0` host-only adapter doesn't exist in the Virtual Box environment (as created in *Chapter 1, Starting OpenStack Compute*), run the following commands in a shell to create a `172.16.0.0/16` network that our OpenStack Storage virtual machine can use to connect to other virtual machines:

```
# Public Network vboxnet0 (172.16.0.0/16)

VBoxManage hostonlyif create

VBoxManage hostonlyif ipconfig vboxnet0 --ip 172.16.0.254 --netmask
    255.255.0.0
```

How to do it...

To create our sandbox environment within VirtualBox, we will create a single virtual machine that allows us to run all of the OpenStack Storage services. This virtual machine will be configured with at least 2 GB of RAM and two 20 GB hard drives with two network interfaces. The first will be a NAT interface that allows our virtual machine to connect to the network outside of VirtualBox to download packages, and the second interface will be the public interface of our OpenStack Storage host.

Carry out the following steps to create the virtual machine that will be used to run OpenStack Storage services:

1. In VirtualBox, create a new virtual machine with the following specification:

   - One CPU
   - 2048 MB RAM
   - Two 20 GB hard disks
   - Two network adapters, with the attached Ubuntu 12.04 ISO

   This can either be done using the VirtualBox *New Virtual Machine Wizard* or by running the following commands in a shell on our computer:

```
# Create VirtualBox Machine
VBoxManage createvm --name openstack2 --ostype Ubuntu_64
    --register
VBoxManage modifyvm openstack2 --memory 1024 --nic1 nat
    --nic2 hostonly --hostonlyadapter2 vboxnet0


# Create CD-Drive and Attach ISO
VBoxManage storagectl openstack2 --name "IDE Controller"
    --add ide --controller PIIX4 --hostiocache on
    --bootable on
VBoxManage storageattach openstack2 --storagectl "IDE
    Controller" --type dvddrive --port 0 --device 0
    --medium Downloads/ubuntu-12.04-server-amd64.iso


# Create and attach SATA Interface and Hard Drive
VBoxManage storagectl openstack2 --name "SATA Controller"
    --add sata --controller IntelAHCI --hostiocache on
    --bootable on
VBoxManage createhd --filename openstack2.vdi --size 20480
VBoxManage storageattach openstack2 --storagectl
    "SATA Controller" --port 0 --device 0 --type hdd
    --medium openstack2.vdi
```

```
# Create and attach second Hard Drive
VBoxManage createhd --filename openstack2-disk2.vdi
    --size 20480
VBoxManage storageattach openstack2 --storagectl
    "SATA Controller" --port 1 --device 0 --type hdd
    --medium openstack2-disk2.vdi
```

2. Do this by selecting the OpenStack2 virtual machine and then clicking on the **Start** button, or by running the following command:

```
VBoxManage startvm openstack2 --type gui
```

3. This will take us through a standard text-based Ubuntu installer, as this is the server edition. Choose appropriate settings for your region, and choose **Eth0** as the main interface (this is the first interface in your VirtualBox VM settings—our NATed interface). When prompted for software selection, just choose **OpenSSH Server** and continue. For the user, create a user named openstack with the password openstack. This will help in using this book to troubleshoot your own environment.

4. Once installed, log in as the user openstack.

5. We can now configure networking on our OpenStack Storage node. To do this, we will create a static address on the second interface, eth1, which will be the public interface. To do this, edit the /etc/network/interfaces file with the following contents:

```
# The loopback network interface
auto lo
iface lo inet loopback

# The primary network interface
auto eth0
iface eth0 inet dhcp

# Public Interface
auto eth1
iface eth1 inet static
   address 172.16.0.2
   netmask 255.255.0.0
   network 172.16.0.0
   broadcast 172.16.255.255
```

6. Save the file and bring up the interface with the following command:

```
sudo ifup eth1
```

 Congratulations! We have successfully created the VirtualBox virtual machine running Ubuntu, which is able to run OpenStack Storage.

How it works...

What we have done is create a virtual machine that will become the basis of our OpenStack Storage host. It has the necessary disk space and networking in place to allow you to access this virtual machine from your host personal computer and any other virtual machines in our OpenStack sandbox environment.

There's more...

There are a number of virtualization products available that are suitable for trying OpenStack, for example, *VMware Server* and *VMware Player*. With VirtualBox, you can also script your installations by using a tool named *Vagrant*. While Vagrant is outside the scope of this book, the steps provided here allow you to investigate this option at a later date.

See also

▶ The *Creating a sandbox environment with VirtualBox* recipe in *Chapter 1, Starting OpenStack Compute*

Installing the OpenStack Storage services

Now that we have a machine to run our OpenStack Storage service, we can install the packages required to run this service.

To do this, we will create a machine that runs all the appropriate services for running OpenStack Storage:

▶ swift: The underlying common files shared amongst other OpenStack Storage packages, including the swift client

▶ swift-proxy: The proxy service that the clients connect to, that sits in front of the many swift nodes that can be configured

▶ swift-account: The account service for accessing OpenStack Storage

▶ swift-object: The package responsible for object storage and orchestration of rsync

▶ swift-container: The package for the OpenStack Storage Container Server

▶ memcached: A high-performance memory object caching system

▶ ntp: Network Time Protocol is essential in a multi-node environment so that the nodes have the same time (tolerance is up to five seconds, and outside of this you get unpredictable results)

▶ xfsprogs: The underlying filesystem is XFS in our OpenStack Storage installation

▶ curl: Command-line web interface tool

Getting ready

Ensure that you are logged in to your `openstack2` virtual machine.

How to do it...

Installation of OpenStack in Ubuntu 12.04 is simply achieved using the familiar `apt-get` tool as the OpenStack packages are available from the official Ubuntu repositories.

1. We can install the OpenStack Storage packages as follows:

    ```
    sudo apt-get update
    sudo apt-get install -y swift swift-proxy swift-account
        swift-container swift-object memcached xfsprogs curl
    ```

2. Once the installation is complete, we need to install and configure `ntp` as follows:

    ```
    sudo apt-get -y install ntp
    ```

3. NTP is important in any multi-node environment, though in the OpenStack environment it is a requirement for server times to be kept in sync. Although we are configuring only one node, not only will accurate time-keeping help with troubleshooting, but it will also allow us to grow our environment as needed in the future. To do this, we edit `/etc/ntp.conf`, with the following contents:

    ```
    # Replace ntp.ubuntu.com with an NTP server on your network
    server ntp.ubuntu.com
    server 127.127.1.0
    fudge 127.127.1.0 stratum 10
    ```

4. Once `ntp` has been configured correctly, we restart the service to pick up the change:

    ```
    sudo service ntp restart
    ```

How it works...

Installation of OpenStack Storage from the main Ubuntu package repository represents a very straightforward and well-understood way of getting OpenStack onto our Ubuntu server. This adds a greater level of certainty around stability and upgrade paths by not deviating away from the main archives.

There's more...

There are various ways to install OpenStack, from source code building to installation from packages, but this represents the easiest and most consistent method available. There are also alternative releases of OpenStack available. The ones available from Ubuntu 12.04 LTS repositories are known as **Essex** and represent the latest stable release at the time of writing.

Using an alternative release

Deviating from stable releases is appropriate when you are helping develop or debug OpenStack or require functionality that is not available in the current release. To enable different releases, you added different **Personal Package Archives** (**PPAs**) to your system. To view the OpenStack PPAs, visit `http://wiki.openstack.org/PPAs`. To use them, we first install a tool that allows us to easily add PPAs to our system:

```
sudo apt-get update
sudo apt-get -y install python-software-properties
```

To use a particular release PPA, we issue the following commands:

- **Milestones** (periodic releases leading up to a stable release):

  ```
  sudo add-apt-repository ppa:openstack-ppa/milestone
  sudo apt-get update
  ```

- **Bleeding Edge** (Master Development Branch):

  ```
  sudo add-apt-repository ppa:openstack-ppa/bleeding-edge
  sudo apt-get update
  ```

Once you have configured `apt` to look for an alternative place for packages, you can repeat the preceding process for installing packages—if you are creating a new machine based on a different package set—or simply type:

```
sudo apt-get upgrade
```

This will make `apt` look in the new package archive areas for later releases of packages (which they will be as they are more recent revisions of code and development).

Configuring storage

Now that we have our Openstack Storage services installed, we can configure our extra disk, which will form our object storage. As OpenStack Storage is designed to be highly scalable and highly redundant, it is usually installed across multiple nodes. Our test environment will consist of only one node, but OpenStack Storage still expects multiple destinations on our storage to replicate its data to, so we need to configure this appropriately for our test setup.

We will end up with four directories on our OpenStack Storage server specified as /srv/1, /srv/2, /srv/3, and /srv/4, which point to directories on our new disk. The result is an OpenStack Storage setup that looks like it has four other OpenStack Storage nodes to replicate data to.

Getting ready

To begin with, log in to our openstack2 virtual machine.

How to do it...

To configure our OpenStack Storage host, carry out the following steps:

1. We first create a new partition on our extra disk. This extra disk is seen as /dev/sdb, under our Linux installation.

   ```
   sudo fdisk /dev/sdb
   ```

2. Go through fdisk and ensure a single partition has been created.

3. To get Linux to see this new partition without rebooting, run partprobe to reread the disk layout.

   ```
   sudo partprobe
   ```

4. Once completed, we can create our filesystem. For this, we will use the XFS filesystem, as follows:

   ```
   sudo mkfs.xfs -i size=1024 /dev/sdb1
   ```

5. We can now create the required mount point and set up fstab to allow us to mount this new area, as follows:

   ```
   sudo mkdir /mnt/sdb1
   ```

6. Then, edit /etc/fstab to add in the following contents:

   ```
   /dev/sdb1 /mnt/sdb1 xfs
       noatime,nodiratime,nobarrier,logbufs=8 0 0
   ```

7. We can now mount this area, as follows:

   ```
   sudo mount /dev/sdb1
   ```

8. Once done, we can create the required file structure, as follows:

   ```
   sudo mkdir /mnt/sdb1/{1..4}
   sudo chown swift:swift /mnt/sdb1/*
   sudo ln -s /mnt/sdb1/{1..4} /srv
   sudo mkdir -p /etc/swift/{object-server,container-
       server,account-server}
   for S in {1..4}; do sudo mkdir -p /srv/${S}/node/sdb${S};
       done
   sudo mkdir -p /var/run/swift
   sudo chown -R swift:swift /etc/swift /srv/{1..4}/
   ```

9. To ensure OpenStack Storage can always start on boot, add the following commands to /etc/rc.local, before the line exit 0:

   ```
   mkdir -p /var/run/swift
   chown swift:swift /var/run/swift
   ```

Installing OpenStack Storage

How it works...

We first created a new partition on our extra disk and formatted this with the XFS filesystem. XFS is very good at handling large objects and has the necessary extended attributes (`xattr`) required for the objects in this filesystem.

Once created, we mounted this area, and then began to create the directory structure. The commands to create the directories and required symbolic links included a lot of bash shorthand, such as {1..4}. This shorthand essentially prints out 1 2 3 4 when expanded, but repeats the preceding attached text when it does so. Take for example the following piece of code:

mkdir /mnt/sdb1/{1..4}

It is the equivalent of:

mkdir /mnt/sdb1/1 /mnt/sdb1/2 /mnt/sdb1/3 /mnt/sdb1/4

The effect of that short piece of code is the following directory structure:

```
/etc/swift
    /object-server
    /container-server
    /account-server
/mnt/sdb1
    /1 -> /srv/1
    /2 -> /srv/2
    /3 -> /srv/3
    /4 -> /srv/4
/srv/1/node/sdb1
/srv/2/node/sdb2
/srv/3/node/sdb3
/srv/4/node/sdb4
/var/run/swift
```

What we have done is set up a filesystem that will see data replicated into the different device directories to mimic the actions and features OpenStack Storage requires. In production, these device directories would actually be physical servers and physical devices on the servers and won't necessarily have this directory structure.

Configuring replication

As required by a highly redundant and scalable object storage system, replication is a key requirement. The reason we went to great lengths to create multiple directories—named in a particular way so as to mimic actual devices—is that we want to set up replication between these "devices" using rsync.

Rsync is responsible for performing the replication of the objects stored in our OpenStack Storage environment.

Getting ready

To begin with, log in to our `openstack2` server.

How to do it...

Configuring replication in OpenStack Storage means configuring the Rsync service. The following steps set up synchronization modules configured to represent the different ports that we will eventually configure our OpenStack Storage service to run on. As we're configuring a single server, we use different paths and different ports to mimic the multiple servers that would normally be involved.

1. We first create our `/etc/rsyncd.conf` file in its entirety, as follows:

```
uid = swift
gid = swift
log file = /var/log/rsyncd.log
pid file = /var/run/rsyncd.pid
address = 127.0.0.1

[account6012]
max connections = 25
path = /srv/1/node/
read only = false
lock file = /var/lock/account6012.lock

[account6022]
max connections = 25
path = /srv/2/node/
read only = false
lock file = /var/lock/account6022.lock

[account6032]
max connections = 25
path = /srv/3/node/
read only = false
lock file = /var/lock/account6032.lock

[account6042]
max connections = 25
path = /srv/4/node/
read only = false
lock file = /var/lock/account6042.lock
```

```
[container6011]
max connections = 25
path = /srv/1/node/
read only = false
lock file = /var/lock/container6011.lock

[container6021]
max connections = 25
path = /srv/2/node/
read only = false
lock file = /var/lock/container6021.lock

[container6031]
max connections = 25
path = /srv/3/node/
read only = false
lock file = /var/lock/container6031.lock

[container6041]
max connections = 25
path = /srv/4/node/
read only = false
lock file = /var/lock/container6041.lock

[object6010]
max connections = 25
path = /srv/1/node/
read only = false
lock file = /var/lock/object6010.lock

[object6020]
max connections = 25
path = /srv/2/node/
read only = false
lock file = /var/lock/object6020.lock

[object6030]
max connections = 25
path = /srv/3/node/
read only = false
lock file = /var/lock/object6030.lock

[object6040]
max connections = 25
path = /srv/4/node/
read only = false
lock file = /var/lock/object6040.lock
```

2. Once complete, we enable rsync and start the service, as follows:

```
sudo sed -i 's/=false/=true/' /etc/default/rsync
sudo service rsync start
```

How it works...

The vast majority of this section was configuring `rsyncd.conf` appropriately. What we have done is configure various rsync modules that become targets on our rsync server.

For example, the `object6020` module would be accessible using the following command:

```
rsync localhost::object6020
```

It would have the contents of `/srv/node/3/`.

Configuring OpenStack Storage Service

Configuring our OpenStack Storage environment is quick and simple, as it involves just adding in a uniquely generated random alpha numeric string to the `/etc/swift/swift.conf` file. This random string will be included in all nodes as we scale out our environment, so keep it safe.

Getting ready

To begin with, log in to our `openstack2` server.

How to do it...

Configuring the main OpenStack Storage configuration file for our sandbox environment is simply done with the following steps:

1. First, we generate our random string, as follows:

```
< /dev/urandom tr -dc A-Za-z0-9_ | head -c16; echo
```

2. We then create the `/etc/swift/swift.conf`, file adding in the following contents, including our generated random string:

```
[swift-hash]
    # Random unique string used on all nodes
    swift_hash_path_suffix = QAxxUPkzb71P29OJ
```

How it works...

We first generated a random string by outputting characters from the `/dev/urandom` device. We then added this string to our `swift.conf` file, as the `swift_has_path_suffix` parameter. This random string is used as we scale out our OpenStack Storage environment—when creating extra nodes we do not generate a new random string.

Configuring the OpenStack Storage proxy server

Clients connect to OpenStack Storage via a proxy server. This allows us to scale out our OpenStack Storage environment as needed, without affecting the frontend to which the clients connect. Configuration of the proxy service is simply done by editing the `/etc/swift/proxy-server.conf` file.

Getting ready

To begin with, log in to our `openstack2` server.

How to do it...

To configure the OpenStack Storage proxy server, we simply create the file `/etc/swift/proxy-server.conf`, with the following contents:

```
[DEFAULT]
bind_port = 8080
user = swift
log_facility = LOG_LOCAL1

[pipeline:main]
pipeline = healthcheck cache tempauth proxy-server

[app:proxy-server]
use = egg:swift#proxy
allow_account_management = true
account_autocreate = true

[filter:tempauth]
use = egg:swift#tempauth
user_admin_admin = admin .admin .reseller_admin
user_test_tester = testing .admin

[filter:healthcheck]
use = egg:swift#healthcheck

[filter:cache]
use = egg:swift#memcache
```

How it works...

The contents of the `proxy-server.conf` file define how the OpenStack Storage proxy server is configured.

For our purposes, we will run our proxy on port 8080, as the user `swift`, and it will log to `syslog`, using the log level of `LOCAL1` (this allows us to filter against these messages).

We configure our swift proxy server healthcheck behavior to handle caching (by use of `memcached`) and TempAuth (local authentication meaning our proxy server will handle basic authentication).

The `[filter:tempauth]` section defines two users and roles in their own accounts—one called `admin` (with the password `admin`) in the admin account and another called `tester` (with the password `testing`) in the test account. The `admin` user has the `admin` and `reseller_admin` roles. The `tester` user has admin privileges. The `.admin` role is a local administrator role, whereas the `.reseller_admin` role has full access to the whole OpenStack Storage environment. The format of the TempAuth user lines is as follows:

user_account_username = password {.role} {.role …} {endpoint_url}

For example, if we wanted another user in the `tester` account, called `myUser`, as a normal user with the password `myPassword`, we would add the following line:

user_test_myUser = myPassword

The `endpoint_URL` option is useful when there is a requirement for a specific URL to be returned that differs from the default. This is used in scenarios where the endpoint URL comes back on an address that is inaccessible on the network or you want to present this differently to the end user, to fit your network.

See also

- ▸ There are more complex options and features described in `/usr/share/doc/swift-proxy/proxy-server.conf-sample.gz`
- ▸ A good overview of TempAuth can be found at `http://swiftstack.com/blog/2012/01/04/swift-tempauth/`

Configuring Account Server

Account Server lists the available containers on our node. As we are creating a setup where we have four virtual devices available under the one hood, they each have their own list of available containers, but they run on different ports. These represent the rsync account numbers seen previously, for example, port 6012 is represented by `[account6012]` within rsync.

Getting ready

To begin with, log in to our `openstack2` server.

How to do it...

For this section, we're creating four different Account Server configuration files that differ only in the port that the service will run on and the path on our single disk that corresponds to that service on that particular port.

1. We begin by creating an initial Account Server configuration file for our first node. Edit `/etc/swift/account-server/1.conf` with the following contents:

```
[DEFAULT]
devices = /srv/1/node
mount_check = false
bind_port = 6012
user = swift
log_facility = LOG_LOCAL2

[pipeline:main]
pipeline = account-server

[app:account-server]
use = egg:swift#account

[account-replicator]
vm_test_mode = yes

[account-auditor]

[account-reaper]
```

2. We then use this to create the remaining three virtual nodes, each with their appropriate unique values as follows:

```
cd /etc/swift/account-server
sed -e "s/srv\/1/srv\/2/" -e "s/601/602/" -e
    "s/LOG_LOCAL2/LOG_LOCAL3/" 1.conf | sudo tee -a 2.conf

sed -e "s/srv\/1/srv\/3/" -e "s/601/603/" -e
    "s/LOG_LOCAL2/LOG_LOCAL4/" 1.conf | sudo tee -a 3.conf

sed -e "s/srv\/1/srv\/4/" -e "s/601/604/" -e
    "s/LOG_LOCAL2/LOG_LOCAL5/" 1.conf | sudo tee -a 4.conf
```

How it works...

What we have accomplished is to create the first Account Server device node, which we named 1.conf, under the /etc/swift/swift-account directory. This defined our Account Server for node 1, which will run on port 6012.

We then took this file and made the subsequent Account Servers run on their respective ports, with a search and replace, using sed.

We ended up with four files, under our swift-account configuration directory, which defined the following services:

```
account-server 1: Port 6012, device /srv/1/node, Log Level LOCAL2
account-server 2: Port 6022, device /srv/2/node, Log Level LOCAL3
account-server 3: Port 6032, device /srv/3/node, Log Level LOCAL4
account-server 4: Port 6042, device /srv/4/node, Log Level LOCAL5
```

Configuring Container Server

Container Servers contains Object Servers seen in our OpenStack Storage environment. The configuration of this is similar to configuring Account Server.

Getting ready

To begin with, log in to our openstack2 server.

How to do it...

As with configuring the Account Server, we follow a similar procedure for Container Server, creating the four different configuration files that correspond to a particular port and area on our disk.

1. We begin by creating an initial Container Server configuration file for our first node. Edit /etc/swift/container-server/1.conf with the following contents:

```
[DEFAULT]
devices = /srv/1/node
mount_check = false
bind_port = 6011
user = swift
log_facility = LOG_LOCAL2

[pipeline:main]
pipeline = container-server
```

```
[app:container-server]
use = egg:swift#container

[account-replicator]
vm_test_mode = yes

[account-updater]

[account-auditor]

[account-sync]
```

2. We then use this to create the remaining three virtual nodes, each with their appropriate unique values, as follows:

```
cd /etc/swift/container-server
sed -e "s/srv\/1/srv\/2/" -e "s/601/602/" -e
    "s/LOG_LOCAL2/LOG_LOCAL3/" 1.conf | sudo tee -a 2.conf

sed -e "s/srv\/1/srv\/3/" -e "s/601/603/" -e
    "s/LOG_LOCAL2/LOG_LOCAL4/" 1.conf | sudo tee -a 3.conf

sed -e "s/srv\/1/srv\/4/" -e "s/601/604/" -e
    "s/LOG_LOCAL2/LOG_LOCAL5/" 1.conf | sudo tee -a 4.conf
```

How it works...

What we have accomplished is to create the first Container Server node configuration file, which we named 1.conf, under the /etc/swift/swift-container directory. This defined our Container Server for node 1, which will run on port 6011.

We then took this file and made subsequent Container Servers run on their respective ports, with a search and replace, using sed.

We ended up with four files, under our swift-container configuration directory, which defined the following:

```
container-server 1: Port 6011, device /srv/1/node, Log Level LOCAL2
container-server 2: Port 6021, device /srv/2/node, Log Level LOCAL3
container-server 3: Port 6031, device /srv/3/node, Log Level LOCAL4
container-server 4: Port 6041, device /srv/4/node, Log Level LOCAL5
```

Configuring Object Server

Object Server contains the actual objects seen in our OpenStack Storage environment and the configuration of this is similar to configuring the Account Server and Container Server.

Getting ready

To begin with, log in to our `openstack2` server.

How to do it...

As with configuring the Container Server, we follow a similar procedure for Object Server, creating the four different configuration files that correspond to a particular port and area on our disk.

1. We begin by creating an initial Object Server configuration file for our first node. Edit `/etc/swift/object-server/1.conf` with the following contents:

```
[DEFAULT]
devices = /srv/1/node
mount_check = false
bind_port = 6010
user = swift
log_facility = LOG_LOCAL2

[pipeline:main]
pipeline = object-server

[app:object-server]
use = egg:swift#object

[object-replicator]
vm_test_mode = yes

[object-updater]

[object-auditor]
```

2. We then use this to create the remaining three virtual nodes, each with their appropriate unique values, as follows:

```
cd /etc/swift/object-server
sed -e "s/srv\/1/srv\/2/" -e "s/601/602/" -e
    "s/LOG_LOCAL2/LOG_LOCAL3/" 1.conf | sudo tee -a 2.conf

sed -e "s/srv\/1/srv\/3/" -e "s/601/603/" -e
    "s/LOG_LOCAL2/LOG_LOCAL4/" 1.conf | sudo tee -a 3.conf

sed -e "s/srv\/1/srv\/4/" -e "s/601/604/" -e
    "s/LOG_LOCAL2/LOG_LOCAL5/" 1.conf | sudo tee -a 4.conf
```

How it works...

What we have accomplished is to create the first Object Server node configuration file, which we named `1.conf`, under the `/etc/swift/swift-container` directory. This defined our Object Server for `node 1`, which will run on port 6010.

We then took this file and made subsequent Object Servers run on their respective ports, with a search and replace, using `sed`.

We end up with four files, under our `swift-object` configuration directory, which defined the following:

```
object-server 1: Port 6010, device /srv/1/node, Log Level LOCAL2
object-server 2: Port 6020, device /srv/2/node, Log Level LOCAL3
object-server 3: Port 6030, device /srv/3/node, Log Level LOCAL4
object-server 4: Port 6040, device /srv/4/node, Log Level LOCAL5
```

 The three preceding sections have seen us configure Account Servers, Object Servers, and Container Servers, each running on their respective ports. These sections all tie up to the modules configured in our `rsyncd.conf` file.

Making the Object, Account, and Container rings

The final step is to create the Object ring, Account ring, and Container ring that each of our virtual nodes exist in.

Getting ready

To begin with, log in to our `openstack2` server.

How to do it...

The OpenStack Storage ring keeps track of where our data exists in our cluster. There are three rings that OpenStack Storage understands, and they are the Account, Container, and Object rings. To facilitate quick rebuilding of the rings in our cluster, we will create a script that performs the necessary steps.

1. The most convenient way to create the rings for our OpenStack Storage environment is to create a script. Create `/usr/local/bin/remakerings`:

    ```
    #!/bin/bash
    cd /etc/swift
    ```

```
rm -f *.builder *.ring.gz backups/*.builder backups/*.ring.gz
# Object Ring
swift-ring-builder object.builder create 18 3 1
swift-ring-builder object.builder add z1-127.0.0.1:6010/sdb1 1
swift-ring-builder object.builder add z2-127.0.0.1:6020/sdb2 1
swift-ring-builder object.builder add z3-127.0.0.1:6030/sdb3 1
swift-ring-builder object.builder add z4-127.0.0.1:6040/sdb4 1
swift-ring-builder object.builder rebalance

# Container Ring
swift-ring-builder container.builder create 18 3 1
swift-ring-builder container.builder add z1-127.0.0.1:6011/sdb1 1
swift-ring-builder container.builder add z2-127.0.0.1:6021/sdb2 1
swift-ring-builder container.builder add z3-127.0.0.1:6031/sdb3 1
swift-ring-builder container.builder add z4-127.0.0.1:6041/sdb4 1
swift-ring-builder container.builder rebalance

# Account Ring
swift-ring-builder account.builder create 18 3 1
swift-ring-builder account.builder add z1-127.0.0.1:6012/sdb1 1
swift-ring-builder account.builder add z2-127.0.0.1:6022/sdb2 1
swift-ring-builder account.builder add z3-127.0.0.1:6032/sdb3 1
swift-ring-builder account.builder add z4-127.0.0.1:6042/sdb4 1
swift-ring-builder account.builder rebalance
```

2. Now we can run the script as follows:

    sudo chmod +x /usr/local/bin/remakerings
    sudo /usr/local/bin/remakerings

3. You will see output similar to the following:

```
Device z1-127.0.0.1:6010/sdb1_"" with 1.0 weight got id 0
Device z2-127.0.0.1:6020/sdb2_"" with 1.0 weight got id 1
Device z3-127.0.0.1:6030/sdb3_"" with 1.0 weight got id 2
Device z4-127.0.0.1:6040/sdb4_"" with 1.0 weight got id 3
Reassigned 262144 (100.00%) partitions. Balance is now
    0.00.
Device z1-127.0.0.1:6011/sdb1_"" with 1.0 weight got id 0
Device z2-127.0.0.1:6021/sdb2_"" with 1.0 weight got id 1
Device z3-127.0.0.1:6031/sdb3_"" with 1.0 weight got id 2
Device z4-127.0.0.1:6041/sdb4_"" with 1.0 weight got id 3
Reassigned 262144 (100.00%) partitions. Balance is now
    0.00.
Device z1-127.0.0.1:6012/sdb1_"" with 1.0 weight got id 0
Device z2-127.0.0.1:6022/sdb2_"" with 1.0 weight got id 1
Device z3-127.0.0.1:6032/sdb3_"" with 1.0 weight got id 2
Device z4-127.0.0.1:6042/sdb4_"" with 1.0 weight got id 3
Reassigned 262144 (100.00%) partitions. Balance is now
    0.00.
```

How it works...

Creation of the rings is done using the `swift-ring-builder` command and involves the following steps, repeated for each ring type (Object, Container, and Account):

1. Creating the ring (of type Object, Container, or Account).
2. Assigning a device to the ring.
3. Rebalancing the ring.

Creating the ring

To create the ring, we use the following syntax:

```
swift-ring-builder builder_file create part_power replicas
    min_part_hours
```

Creation of the ring specifies a builder file to create three parameters: `part_power`, `replicas`, and `min_part_hours`. This means `2^part_power` (18 is used in this instance) is the number of partitions to create, `replicas` are the number of replicas (3 is used in this case) of the data within the ring, and `min_part_hours` (1 is specified in this case) is the time in hours before a specific partition can be moved in succession.

Assigning a device to the ring

To assign a device to a ring, we use the following syntax:

```
swift-ring-builder builder_file add zzone-ip:port/device_name weight
```

Adding a node to the ring specifies the same `builder_file` created in the first step. We then specify a zone (for example, `1`, prefixed with `z`) that the device will be in, `ip` (`127.0.0.1`) is the IP address of the server that the device is in, `port` (for example, `6010`) is the port number that the server is running on, and `device_name` is the name of the device on the server (for example, `sdb1`). The weight is a float weight that determines how many partitions are put on the device, relative to the rest of the devices in the cluster.

Rebalancing the ring

To rebalance the ring, we use the following syntax within the `/etc/swift` directory:

```
swift-ring-builder builder_file rebalance
```

This command will distribute the partitions across the drives in the ring.

The previous process is run for each of the rings: object, container, and account.

Stopping and starting OpenStack Storage

Now that we have configured our OpenStack Storage installation, it's time to start our services, so that they're running on our `openstack2` virtual machine, ready for us to use for storing objects and images in our OpenStack environment.

Getting ready

To begin with, log in to our `openstack2` server.

How to do it...

Controlling OpenStack Storage services is achieved using SysV Init scripts, utilizing the `service` command.

Since the OpenStack Storage services may have started following installation of the packages, we will restart the needed services to ensure the services have the correct configuration and are running as expected.

```
sudo service swift-account restart
sudo service swift-object restart
sudo service swift-container restart
sudo service swift-proxy restart
```

How it works...

The OpenStack Storage services are simply started, stopped, and restarted, using the following syntax:

```
service swift-account { start | stop | restart }
service swift-object { start | stop | restart }
service swift-container { start | stop | restart }
service swift-proxy { start | stop | restart }
```

Testing OpenStack Storage

We are now ready to test our installation of OpenStack Storage, and we can achieve this in a couple of ways—by using `curl` and using the `swift` command-line utility.

Getting ready

For this section, we will log in to our `swift1` host.

How to do it...

As OpenStack Storage is a web service, we will use `curl` to do some basic tests to ensure our services are running as they should. We will perform some basic authentication and connect to our web service using these details.

Using curl to test OpenStack Storage

1. We first authenticate to our swift proxy server running on port 8080, on our host.

    ```
    curl -v -H 'X-Storage-User: test:tester' -H 'X-Storage-
        Pass: testing' http://127.0.0.1:8080/auth/v1.0
    ```

2. We should see output similar to the following, where we should get a **HTTP 200 OK** message back when successful:

    ```
    * About to connect() to 127.0.0.1 port 8080 (#0)
    *    Trying 127.0.0.1... connected
    * Connected to 127.0.0.1 (127.0.0.1) port 8080 (#0)
    > GET /auth/v1.0 HTTP/1.1
    > User-Agent: curl/7.21.6 (x86_64-pc-linux-gnu) libcurl/7.21.6
    OpenSSL/1.0.0e
          zlib/1.2.3.4 libidn/1.22 librtmp/2.3
    > Host: 127.0.0.1:8080
    > Accept: */*
    > X-Storage-User: test:tester
    > X-Storage-Pass: testing
    >
    < HTTP/1.1 200 OK
    < X-Storage-Url: http://127.0.0.1:8080/v1/AUTH_test
    < X-Storage-Token: AUTH_tkea3bbcb73a524cca8b244d0f0b10b824
    < X-Auth-Token: AUTH_tkea3bbcb73a524cca8b244d0f0b10b824
    < Content-Length: 0
    < Date: Mon, 02 Jan 2012 20:28:57 GMT
    <
    * Connection #0 to host 127.0.0.1 left intact
    * Closing connection #0
    ```

3. We take the `X-Storage-Url` and `X-Auth-Token` reply headers and send this back, using `curl` again:

    ```
    curl -v -H 'X-Auth-Token:
        AUTH_tkea3bbcb73a524cca8b244d0f0b10b824'
        http://127.0.0.1:8080/v1/AUTH_test
    ```

4. We should now get output similar to the following, on acceptance (where we get a **HTTP 204 No Content**, which says we have successfully connected but returned no content as we have nothing stored there yet):

```
* About to connect() to 127.0.0.1 port 8080 (#0)
*    Trying 127.0.0.1... connected
* Connected to 127.0.0.1 (127.0.0.1) port 8080 (#0)
> GET /v1/AUTH_test HTTP/1.1
> User-Agent: curl/7.21.6 (x86_64-pc-linux-gnu) libcurl/7.21.6
OpenSSL/1.0.0e
      zlib/1.2.3.4 libidn/1.22 librtmp/2.3
> Host: 127.0.0.1:8080
> Accept: */*
> X-Auth-Token: AUTH_tkea3bbcb73a524cca8b244d0f0b10b824
>
< HTTP/1.1 204 No Content
< X-Account-Object-Count: 0
< X-Account-Bytes-Used: 0
< X-Account-Container-Count: 0
< Accept-Ranges: bytes
< Content-Length: 0
< Date: Mon, 02 Jan 2012 20:30:04 GMT
<
* Connection #0 to host 127.0.0.1 left intact
* Closing connection #0
```

Using a swift command to test OpenStack Storage

Rather than seeing the web service output, we can use the command-line tool `swift` (previously known as `st`) to ensure we have a working setup. Note the output matches the reply headers seen when queried using `curl`.

```
swift -A http://127.0.0.1:8080/auth/v1.0 -U test:tester -K testing
    stat
```

You should see the following output:

```
Account: AUTH_test
Containers: 0
Objects: 0
Bytes: 0
Accept-Ranges: bytes
```

How it works...

OpenStack Storage is a web service so we can use traditional command-line web clients to troubleshoot and verify our OpenStack Storage installation. This becomes very useful for debugging OpenStack Storage at this low level, just as you would debug any web service.

Using `curl` allows us to get a glimpse of how authentication and service discovery works. We first send through our authentication details (that we specified in our /etc/swift/ proxy-server.conf file, as we're using the proxy server to provide our authentication) and in return, we're presented with some reply headers that we can then use to find the objects we have access to via the URL returned to us.

The `swift` command wraps this process into a single line, but the result is the same. Behind the scenes, the authentication returns a URL after successful authentication, and then lists the statistics of that container.

Setting up SSL access

Setting up SSL access provides secure access between the client and our OpenStack Storage environment in exactly the same way SSL provides secure access to any other web service. To do this, we configure our proxy server with *SSL certificates*.

Getting ready

To begin with, log in to our openstack2 server.

How to do it...

Configuration of OpenStack Storage to secure communication between the client and the proxy server is done as follows:

1. In order to provide SSL access to our proxy server, we first create the certificates, as follows:

```
cd /etc/swift
sudo openssl req -new -x509 -nodes -out cert.crt -keyout
    cert.key
```

2. We need to answer the following questions that the certificate process asks us:

```
Generating a 1024 bit RSA private key
...............++++++
.++++++
writing new private key to 'cert.key'
-----
You are about to be asked to enter information that will be incorporated
into your certificate request.
What you are about to enter is what is called a Distinguished Name or a DN.
There are quite a few fields but you can leave some blank
For some fields there will be a default value,
If you enter '.', the field will be left blank.
-----
Country Name (2 letter code) [AU]:GB
State or Province Name (full name) [Some-State]:.
Locality Name (eg, city) []:
Organization Name (eg, company) [Internet Widgits Pty Ltd]:Cookbook
Organizational Unit Name (eg, section) []:
Common Name (e.g. server FQDN or YOUR name) []:172.16.0.2
Email Address []:
```

3. Once created, we configure our proxy server to use the certificate and key by editing the `/etc/swift/proxy-server.conf` file:

   ```
   bind_port = 443
   cert_file = /etc/swift/cert.crt
   key_file = /etc/swift/cert.key
   ```

4. With this in place, we can restart the proxy server, using the `swift-init` command, to pick up the change:

   ```
   sudo swift-init proxy-server restart
   ```

How it works...

Configuring OpenStack Storage to use SSL involves configuring the proxy server to use SSL. We first configure a self-signed certificate using the `openssl` command, which asks for various fields to be filled in. An important field is the **Common Name** field. Put in the fully qualified domain name (FQDN) hostname or IP address that you would use to connect to the Swift server.

Once that has been done, we specify the port that we want our proxy server to listen on. As we are configuring an SSL HTTPS connection, we will use the standard TCP port 443 that HTTPS defaults to. We also specify the certificate and key that we created in the first step, so when a request is made, this information is presented to the end user to allow secure data transfer.

With this in place, we then restart our proxy server to listen on port 443.

Configuring OpenStack Storage with OpenStack Identity Service

The OpenStack Storage service configured in the previous sections uses the inbuilt TempAuth mechanism to manage accounts. This is analogous to the `deprecated_auth` mechanism we can configure with the OpenStack Compute service. This section shows you how to move from TempAuth to OpenStack Identity Service to manage accounts.

Getting ready

For this section, we will log in to our `openstack2` host for configuration of OpenStack Storage Service as well as to a client that has access to the `keystone` client, to manage OpenStack Identity Service.

How to do it...

Configuring OpenStack Storage to use OpenStack Identity Service is carried out as follows:

1. We first use the `keystone` client to configure the required endpoints and accounts under OpenStack Identity Service, as follows:

```
# Set up environment
export ENDPOINT=172.16.0.1
export SERVICE_TOKEN=ADMIN
export SERVICE_ENDPOINT=http://${ENDPOINT}:35357/v2.0

# Swift Proxy Address
export SWIFT_PROXY_SERVER=172.16.0.2

# Configure the OpenStack Storage Endpoint
keystone --token $SERVICE_TOKEN --endpoint $SERVICE_ENDPOINT
service-create --name swift --type object-store --description
'OpenStack Storage Service'

# Service Endpoint URLs
ID=$(keystone service-list | awk '/\ swift\ / {print $2}')

# Note we're using SSL
PUBLIC_URL="https://$SWIFT_PROXY_SERVER:443/v1/AUTH_\$(tenant_id)
s"
ADMIN_URL="https://$SWIFT_PROXY_SERVER:443/v1"
INTERNAL_URL=$PUBLIC_URL

keystone endpoint-create --region RegionOne --service_id
    $ID --publicurl $PUBLIC_URL --adminurl $ADMIN_URL
    --internalurl $INTERNAL_URL
```

2. With the endpoints configured to point to our OpenStack Storage server, we can now set up the `swift` user, so our proxy server can authenticate with the OpenStack Identity server.

```
# Get the service tenant ID
SERVICE_TENANT_ID=$(keystone tenant-list | awk '/\ service\
    / {print $2}')

# Create the swift user
keystone user-create --name swift --pass swift --tenant_id
    $SERVICE_TENANT_ID --email swift@localhost
    --enabled true

# Get the swift user id
USER_ID=$(keystone user-list | awk '/\ swift\ /
    {print $2}')

# Get the admin role id
ROLE_ID=$(keystone role-list | awk '/\ admin\ /
    {print $2}')

# Assign the swift user admin role in service tenant
keystone user-role-add --user $USER_ID --role $ROLE_ID
    --tenant_id $SERVICE_TENANT_ID
```

3. On the OpenStack Storage server (`openstack2`), we now install the Keystone Python libraries, so that OpenStack Identity Service can be used. This is done as follows:

```
sudo apt-get update
sudo apt-get install python-keystone
```

4. We can now edit the proxy server configuration, `/etc/swift/proxy-server.conf`, to utilize OpenStack Identity Server, as follows:

```
[DEFAULT]
bind_port = 443
cert_file = /etc/swift/cert.crt
key_file = /etc/swift/cert.key
user = swift
log_facility = LOG_LOCAL1

[pipeline:main]
pipeline = catch_errors healthcheck cache authtoken keystone
proxy-server

[app:proxy-server]
use = egg:swift#proxy
account_autocreate = true
```

```
[filter:healthcheck]
use = egg:swift#healthcheck

[filter:cache]
use = egg:swift#memcache

[filter:keystone]
paste.filter_factory = keystone.middleware.swift_auth:
filter_factory
operator_roles = Member,admin

[filter:authtoken]
paste.filter_factory = keystone.middleware.auth_token:
filter_factory
service_port = 5000
service_host = 172.16.0.1
auth_port = 35357
auth_host = 172.16.0.1
auth_protocol = http
auth_token = ADMIN
admin_token = ADMIN
admin_tenant_name = service
admin_user = swift
admin_password = swift
cache = swift.cache

[filter:catch_errors]
use = egg:swift#catch_errors

[filter:swift3]
use = egg:swift#swift3
```

5. We pick up these changes by restarting the proxy server service, as follows:

    `sudo swift-init proxy-server restart`

How it works...

Configuring OpenStack Storage to use OpenStack Identity Service involves altering the pipeline so that `keystone` is used as the authentication.

After setting the relevant endpoint within the OpenStack Identity Service to be an SSL endpoint, we can configure our OpenStack Storage proxy server.

To do this, we first define the pipeline to include `keystone` and `authtoken`, and then configure these further down the file in the `[filter:keystone]` and `[filter:authtoken]` sections. In the `[filter:keystone]` section, we set someone with `admin` and `Member` roles assigned to be an operator of our OpenStack Storage. This allows those of our users who have one of those roles to have write permissions in our OpenStack Storage environment.

In the `[filter:authtoken]` section, we tell our proxy server where to find the OpenStack Identity Service. Here, we also set the service username and password for this service that we have configured within OpenStack Identity Service.

5
Using OpenStack Storage

In this chapter, we will cover:

- ▶ Installing the swift client tool
- ▶ Creating containers
- ▶ Uploading objects
- ▶ Uploading large objects
- ▶ Listing containers and objects
- ▶ Downloading objects
- ▶ Deleting containers and objects
- ▶ Using OpenStack Storage ACLs

Introduction

Now that we have an OpenStack Storage environment running, we can use it to store our files. To do this, we can use a tool provided, named `swift`. This allows us to operate our OpenStack Storage environment by allowing us to create containers, upload files, retrieve them, and set required permissions on them, as appropriate.

Installing the swift client tool

In order to operate our OpenStack Storage environment, we need to install an appropriate tool on our client. Swift ships with the `swift` tool, which allows us to upload, download, and modify files in our OpenStack Storage environment.

Getting ready

To begin with, ensure you are logged into your Ubuntu client, where we can install the `swift` client.

We will be using OpenStack Storage, authenticating against the OpenStack Identity Service, Keystone.

How to do it...

Installation of the `swift` client can be done on any appropriate machine on the network; it can conveniently be downloaded from the Ubuntu repositories using the familiar `apt-get` utility.

1. Installation of the `swift` client is done by installing the `swift` package as well as the python libraries for the OpenStack Identity Service, Keystone. We do this as follows:

   ```
   sudo apt-get update

   sudo apt-get -y swift python-keystone
   ```

2. The preceding command will download the required package and a number of supporting python libraries. No further configuration is required. To test that you have successfully installed `swift` and can connect to your OpenStack Storage server, issue the following command:

   ```
   swift -V 2.0 -A http://172.16.0.1:5000/v2.0/ -U cookbook:demo -K
   openstack stat
   ```

3. This will bring back statistics about our OpenStack Storage environment to which our `demo` user has access.

How it works...

The `swift` client package is easily installed under Ubuntu and requires no further configuration after downloading, as all parameters needed to communicate with OpenStack Storage using the command line are installed.

 When confirming that OpenStack Storage uses the OpenStack Identity Service authentication, you configure your client to communicate to OpenStack Identity Server, not OpenStack Storage Proxy Server.

Creating containers

A **container** can be thought of as a `root` folder under OpenStack Storage. They allow for objects to be stored within them. Under S3, they are known as **buckets**. Creating objects and containers can be achieved in a number of ways. A simple way is by using the `swift` client tool. We run this client tool against OpenStack Identity Service, which in turn has been configured to communicate to our OpenStack Storage proxy server and allows us to create, delete, and modify containers and objects in our OpenStack Storage environment.

Getting ready

Log in to a computer or a server that has the `swift` client package installed.

How to do it...

Carry out the following steps to create a container under OpenStack Storage:

1. To create a container named `test`, under our OpenStack Storage server, using the `swift` tool, we do the following:

    ```
    swift -V 2.0 -A http://172.16.0.1:5000/v2.0/ -U cookbook:demo -K
    openstack post test
    ```

2. To verify the creation of our container, we can list the containers in our OpenStack Storage environment, as follows:

    ```
    swift -V 2.0 -A http://172.16.0.1:5000/v2.0/ -U demo:cookbook -K
    openstack list
    ```

This will simply list the containers in our OpenStack Storage environment.

How it works...

Creation of containers using the supplied `swift` tool is very simple. The syntax is as follows:

```
swift -V 2.0 -A http://keystone_server:5000/v2.0 -U tenant:user -K
password post container
```

This authenticates our user through OpenStack Identity Service using Version 2.0 authentication, which in turn connects to the OpenStack Storage endpoint configured for this tenant and executes the required command to create the container.

Uploading objects

Objects are the files or directories that are stored within a container. Uploading objects can be achieved in a number of ways. A simple way is by using the `swift` client tool. We run this client tool against our OpenStack Identity Service, which in turn has been configured to communicate to our OpenStack Storage proxy server and allow us to create, delete, and modify containers and objects in our OpenStack Storage environment.

Getting ready

Log in to a computer or server that has the `swift` client package installed.

How to do it...

Carry out the following steps to upload objects into our OpenStack Storage environment:

Uploading objects

1. Create a 500 MB file under `/tmp` as an example file to upload, as follows:

   ```
   dd if=/dev/zero of=/tmp/example-500Mb bs=1M count=500
   ```

2. We can upload this file to our OpenStack Storage account using the following command:

   ```
   swift -V 2.0 -A http://172.16.0.1:5000/v2.0/ -U cookbook:demo -K
   openstack upload test /tmp/example-500Mb
   ```

 When using OpenStack Storage, objects uploaded will be stored with the full path of that object under our container. Although the objects appear to be a regular file system, with a notion of a path structure, OpenStack Storage is not a regular filesystem.

Uploading directories

Create a directory and two files to upload to our OpenStack Storage environment, as follows:

```
mkdir /tmp/test
dd if=/dev/zero of=/tmp/test/test1 bs=1M count=20
dd if=/dev/zero of=/tmp/test/test2 bs=1M count=20
```

To upload directories and their contents, we issue the same command, but just specify the directory. The files within the directory are recursively uploaded. We do this as follows:

```
swift -V 2.0 -A http://172.16.0.1:5000/v2.0/ -U cookbook:demo -K
openstack upload test /tmp/test
```

Uploading multiple objects

We are able to upload a number of objects at once. To do this, we simply specify each of them on our command line. To upload our `test1` and `test2` files, we issue the following command:

```
swift -V 2.0 -A http://172.16.0.1:5000/v2.0/ -U cookbook:demo -K
openstack upload test /tmp/test/test1 /tmp/test/test2
```

How it works...

Uploading files to our OpenStack Storage environment is simple to achieve with the `swift` client tool. We can upload individual files or complete directories. The syntax is as follows:

```
swift -V 2.0 -A http://keystone_server:5000/v2.0 -U tenant:user -K
password upload container file|directory {file|directory … }
```

Note that when uploading files, the objects that are created are of the form that we specify to the `swift` client, including the full paths. For example, uploading `/tmp/example-500Mb` uploads that object as `tmp/example-500Mb`. This is because OpenStack Storage is not a traditional tree-based hierarchical file system that our computers and desktops usually employ, where paths are delimited by a single slash (/ or \). OpenStack Storage consists of a flat set of objects that exist in containers where that slash forms the object name itself.

Uploading large objects

Individual objects up to 5 GB in size can be uploaded to OpenStack Storage. However, by splitting the objects into segments, the download size of a single object is virtually unlimited. Segments of the larger object are uploaded and a special manifest file is created that, when downloaded, sends all the segments concatenated as a single object. By splitting objects into smaller chunks, you also gain efficiency by allowing parallel uploads.

Getting ready

Log in to a computer or server that has the `swift` client package installed.

How to do it...

Carry out the following steps to upload large objects, split into smaller segments:

Uploading objects

1. We will first start by creating a 1 GB file under /tmp as an example file to upload. We do this as follows:

   ```
   dd if=/dev/zero of=/tmp/example-1Gb bs=1M count=1024
   ```

2. Rather than upload this file as a single object, we will utilize segmenting to split this into smaller chunks, in this case, 100 MB segments. To do this, we specify the size of the segments with the -s option, as follows:

   ```
   swift -V 2.0 -A http://172.16.0.1:5000/v2.0/ -U cookbook:demo -K
   openstack upload test  -S 102400000 /tmp/example-1Gb
   ```

You will see output similar to the following, showing the status of each upload:

```
tmp/example-1Gb segment 7
tmp/example-1Gb segment 5
tmp/example-1Gb segment 2
tmp/example-1Gb segment 0
tmp/example-1Gb segment 3
tmp/example-1Gb segment 6
tmp/example-1Gb segment 4
tmp/example-1Gb segment 10
tmp/example-1Gb segment 1
tmp/example-1Gb segment 8
tmp/example-1Gb segment 9
tmp/example-1Gb
```

How it works...

OpenStack Storage is very good at storing and retrieving large objects. To efficiently do this in our OpenStack Storage environment, we have the ability to split large objects into smaller objects with OpenStack Storage, maintaining this relationship between the segments and the objects that appear as a single file. This allows us to upload large objects in parallel, rather than stream a single large file. To achieve this, we use the following syntax:

```
swift -V 2.0 -A http://keystone_server:5000/v2.0 -U tenant:user -K
password upload container -S bytes large_file
```

Now, when we list our containers under our account, we have an extra container, named `test_segments` created, holding the actual segmented data fragments for our file. Our test container holds the view that our large object is a single object. Behind the scenes, the metadata within this single object will pull back the individual objects from the `test_segments` container, to reconstruct the large object.

```
swift -V 2.0 -A http://172.16.0.1:5000/v2.0/ -U cookbook:demo -K
openstack list
```

When the preceding command is executed, we get the following output:

```
test
test_segments
```

Now, execute the following command:

```
swift -V 2.0 -A http://172.16.0.1:5000/v2.0/ -U cookbook:demo -K
openstack list test
```

The following output is generated:

```
tmp/example-1Gb
```

Execute:

```
swift -V 2.0 -A http://172.16.0.1:5000/v2.0/ -U cookbook:demo -K
openstack list test_segments
```

The following output is generated:

```
tmp/example-1Gb/1332326501.5/1073741824/00000000
tmp/example-1Gb/1332326501.5/1073741824/00000001
tmp/example-1Gb/1332326501.5/1073741824/00000002
tmp/example-1Gb/1332326501.5/1073741824/00000003
tmp/example-1Gb/1332326501.5/1073741824/00000004
tmp/example-1Gb/1332326501.5/1073741824/00000005
tmp/example-1Gb/1332326501.5/1073741824/00000006
tmp/example-1Gb/1332326501.5/1073741824/00000007
tmp/example-1Gb/1332326501.5/1073741824/00000008
tmp/example-1Gb/1332326501.5/1073741824/00000009
tmp/example-1Gb/1332326501.5/1073741824/00000010
```

Listing containers and objects

The `swift` client tool allows you to easily list containers and objects within your OpenStack Storage account.

Getting ready

Log in to a computer or server that has the `swift` client package installed.

How to do it...

Carry out the following to list objects within the OpenStack Storage environment:

Listing all objects in a container

In the preceding recipes, we uploaded a small number of files. To simply list the objects within our `test` container, we issue the following command:

```
swift -V 2.0 -A http://172.16.0.1:5000/v2.0/ -U cookbook:demo -K
openstack list test
```

This will show output similar to the following:

```
tmp/example-500Mb
tmp/test/test1
tmp/test/test2
```

Listing specific object paths within a container

To list just the files within the `tmp/test` path, we specify this with the `-p` parameter, as follows:

```
swift -V 2.0 -A http://172.16.0.1:5000/v2.0/ -U cookbook:demo -K
openstack list -p tmp/test test
```

This will list our two files, as follows:

```
tmp/test/test1
tmp/test/test2
```

We can put partial matches in the `-p` parameter too. For example, to list all files starting with `tmp/ex` we issue the following command:

```
swift -V 2.0 -A http://172.16.0.1:5000/v2.0/ -U cookbook:demo -K
openstack list -p tmp/ex test
```

This will list files that match that string:

```
tmp/example-500Mb
```

How it works...

The tool `swift` is a basic but versatile utility that allows us to do many of the things we want to do with files. Listing them in a way that suits the user is also possible. To simply list the contents of our container, the syntax is as follows:

```
swift -V 2.0 -A http://keystone_server:5000/v2.0 -U tenant:user -K
password list container
```

To list a file in a particular path within the container, we add in the `-p` parameter to the syntax:

```
swift -V 2.0 -A http://keystone_server:5000/v2.0 -U tenant:user -K
password list -p path container
```

Downloading objects

Now that we have a usable OpenStack Storage environment with containers and objects, there comes a time when we want to retrieve the objects. The `swift` client tool allows us to do this.

Getting ready

Log in to a computer or server that has the `swift` client package installed.

How to do it...

Carry out the following to download objects from our OpenStack Storage environment:

Downloading objects

To download the object `tmp/test/test1`, we issue the following command:

```
swift -V 2.0 -A http://172.16.0.1:5000/v2.0/ -U cookbook:demo -K
openstack download test tmp/test/test1
```

This downloads the object to our file system. As we downloaded a file with the full path, *this directory structure is preserved*, so we end up with a new directory structure of `tmp/test` with a file in it called `test1`.

Downloading objects with the -o parameter

To download the file without preserving the file structure, or to simply rename it to something else, we specify the `-o` parameter, as follows:

```
swift -V 2.0 -A http://172.16.0.1:5000/v2.0/ -U cookbook:demo -K
openstack download test tmp/test/test1 -o test1
```

Downloading all objects from a container

We are also able to download complete containers to our local filesystem. To do this, we simply specify the container we want to download, as follows:

```
swift -V 2.0 -A http://172.16.0.1:5000/v2.0/ -U cookbook:demo -K
openstack download test
```

This will download all objects found under the `test` container.

Downloading all objects from our OpenStack Storage account

We can download all objects that reside under our OpenStack Storage account. If we have multiple containers, all objects from all containers will be downloaded. We do this with the `--all` parameter, as follows:

```
swift -V 2.0 -A http://172.16.0.1:5000/v2.0/ -U cookbook:demo -K
openstack download --all
```

This will download all objects with full paths preceded by the container name, for example:

```
test/tmp/test/test1
test/tmp/test/test2
test/tmp/example-500Mb
```

How it works...

The `swift` client is a basic but versatile tool that allows us to do many of the things we want to do with files. Downloading *objects* and *containers* is achieved using the following syntax:

```
swift -V 2.0 -A http://keystone_server:5000/v2.0 -U tenant:user -K
password download container {object … }
```

To download all *objects* from our account (for example, from all containers), we specify the following syntax:

```
swift -V 2.0 -A http://keystone_server:5000/v2.0 -U tenant:user -K
password download --all
```

Deleting containers and objects

The `swift` client tool allows us to directly delete containers and objects within our OpenStack Storage environment.

Getting ready

Log in to a computer or server that has the `swift` client package installed.

How to do it...

Carry out the following to delete objects in our OpenStack Storage environment:

Deleting objects

To delete the object `tmp/test/test1`, we issue the following:

```
swift -V 2.0 -A http://172.16.0.1:5000/v2.0/ -U cookbook:demo -K
openstack delete test tmp/test/test1
```

This deletes the object `tmp/test/test1` from the container `test`.

Deleting multiple objects

To delete the objects `tmp/test/test2` and `tmp/example-500Mb`, we issue the following command:

```
swift -V 2.0 -A http://172.16.0.1:5000/v2.0/ -U cookbook:demo -K
openstack delete test tmp/test/test2 tmp/example-500Mb
```

This deletes the objects `tmp/test/test2` and `tmp/example-500Mb` from the container `test`.

Deleting containers

To delete our `test` container we issue the following command:

```
swift -V 2.0 -A http://172.16.0.1:5000/v2.0/ -U cookbook:demo -K
openstack delete test
```

This will delete the *container* and any *objects* under this container.

Deleting everything from our account

To delete all *containers* and *objects* in our account, we issue the following command:

```
swift -V 2.0 -A http://172.16.0.1:5000/v2.0/ -U cookbook:demo -K
openstack delete --all
```

This will delete *all* containers and any objects under these containers.

How it works...

The `swift` client is a basic but versatile tool that allows us to do many of the things we want to do with files. Deleting objects and containers is achieved using the following syntax:

```
swift -V 2.0 -A http://keystone_server:5000/v2.0 -U tenant:user -K
password delete container {object … }
```

To download all objects from our account (for example, from all containers), we specify the following syntax:

```
swift -V 2.0 -A http://keystone_server:5000/v2.0 -U tenant:user -K
password delete -all
```

Using OpenStack Storage ACLs

ACLs allow us to have greater control over individual objects and containers without requiring full read/write access to a particular container.

Getting ready

Log in to a computer that has the `keystone` and `swift` clients available.

How to do it...

Carry out the following steps:

We will first create an account in our OpenStack Identity Server that is only a `Member` in the `cookbook` tenant. We will call this user, `user`.

```
export ENDPOINT=172.16.0.1

export SERVICE_TOKEN=ADMIN

export SERVICE_ENDPOINT=http://${ENDPOINT}:35357/v2.0


# First get TENANT_ID related to our 'cookbook' tenant

TENANT_ID=$(tenant-list | awk ' / cookbook / {print $2}')


# We then create the user specifying the TENANT_ID

keystone user-create --name user --tenant_id $TENANT_ID --pass openstack
--email user@localhost --enabled true
```

```
# We get this new user's ID
USER_ID=$(keystone user-list | awk ' / user / {print $2}')


# We get the ID of the 'Member' role
ROLE_ID=$(keystone role-list | awk ' / Member / {print $2}')


# Finally add the user to the 'Member' role in cookbook
keystone --token 999888777666 --endpoint http://172.16.0.1:35357/v2.0/
user-role-add --user $USER_ID --role $ROLE_ID --tenant_id $TENANT_ID
```

1. With our new user created, we will now create a container using a user that has admin privileges (and therefore a container that our new user initially doesn't have access to), as follows:

    ```
    swift -V 2.0 -A http://172.16.0.1:5000/v2.0/ -U cookbook:demo -K
    openstack post testACL
    ```

2. We will try to upload a file to this container using our new user, as follows:

    ```
    swift -V 2.0 -A http://172.16.0.1:5000/v2.0/ -U cookbook:user -K
    openstack upload testACL /tmp/test/test1
    ```

    This brings back an *HTTP 403 Forbidden* message similar to the following:

    ```
    Object HEAD failed: https://172.16.0.2:443/v1/AUTH_53d87d9b6679490
    4aa2c84c17274392b/testACL/tmp/test/test1 403 Forbidden
    ```

3. We will now give write access to the testACL container for our user by allowing them access to the Member role.

    ```
    swift -V 2.0 -A http://172.16.0.1:5000/v2.0/ -U cookbook:demo -K
    openstack post testACL -w Member -r Member
    ```

4. When we repeat the upload of the file, it now succeeds:

    ```
    swift -V 2.0 -A http://172.16.0.1:5000/v2.0/ -U cookbook:user -K
    openstack upload testACL /tmp/test/test1
    ```

How it works...

Granting access control is done on a *container* basis and is achieved at the *role* level. When a user creates a container by using the role they are in, other users can be granted that access by adding other roles to the container. The users in the new role will then be granted read and write access to containers, for example:

```
swift -V 2.0 -A http://keystone_server:5000/v2.0 -U tenant:user -K
password post container -w role -r role
```

Note that the roles that are allowed to use our OpenStack Storage environment are defined in the proxy server, as follows:

```
[filter:keystone]
paste.filter_factory = keystone.middleware.swift_auth:filter_factory
operator_roles = Member,admin
```

6
Administering
OpenStack Storage

In this chapter, we will cover:

- ▶ Preparing drives for OpenStack Storage
- ▶ Managing the OpenStack Storage cluster with swift-init
- ▶ Checking cluster health
- ▶ OpenStack Storage benchmarking
- ▶ Managing capacity
- ▶ Removing nodes from a cluster
- ▶ Detecting and replacing failed hard drives
- ▶ Collecting usage statistics

Introduction

Day to day administration of our OpenStack Storage cluster involves ensuring the files within the cluster are replicated to the right number of nodes, reporting on usage within the cluster, and dealing with failure of the cluster. This section introduces the tools and processes required to administer OpenStack Storage.

Preparing drives for OpenStack Storage

OpenStack Storage doesn't have any dependencies on any particular filesystem, as long as that filesystem supports extended attributes (xattr). But, it has been generally acknowledged that the XFS filesystem yields the best all-round performance and resilience.

Getting ready

Log in to a swift node that has a disk ready to be formatted for use with OpenStack Storage.

How to do it...

Carry out the following steps to prepare a hard drive for use within an OpenStack Storage node:

1. For this, we will assume our new drive is ready for use, has been set up with an appropriate partition, and is ready for formatting. Take for example the partition /dev/sdb1. To format it for use, using XFS, we run the following command:

   sudo mkfs.xfs -i size=1024 /dev/sdb1

2. This produces a summary screen of the new drive and partition, as follows:

   ```
   meta-data=/dev/sdb1              isize=1024   agcount=4, agsize=1310656 blks
            =                       sectsz=512   attr=2, projid32bit=0
   data     =                       bsize=4096   blocks=5242624, imaxpct=25
            =                       sunit=0      swidth=0 blks
   naming   =version 2              bsize=4096   ascii-ci=0
   log      =internal log           bsize=4096   blocks=2560, version=2
            =                       sectsz=512   sunit=0 blks, lazy-count=1
   realtime =none                   extsz=4096   blocks=0, rtextents=0
   ```

3. Once formatted, we set the mount options in our /etc/fstab file, as follows:

   /dev/sdb1 /srv/node/sdb1 xfs noatime,nodiratime,nobarrier,logbu fs=8 0 0

4. If the directory mount point doesn't exist, create it, and then mount the filesystem as follows:

   mkdir -p /srv/node/sdb1
   mount /srv/node/sdb1

How it works...

While it is recommended you do thorough testing of OpenStack Storage for your own environments, it is generally recommended that you use the XFS filesystem. OpenStack Storage requires a filesystem that supports extended attributes (xattr) and it has been shown that XFS offers good all-round performance in all areas.

In order to accommodate the metadata used by OpenStack Storage, we increase the inode size to 1024. This is set at the time of the format with the -i size=1024 parameter.

Further performance considerations are set at mount time. We don't need to record file access times (`noatime`) and directory access times (`nodiratime`). Barrier support flushes the write-back cache to disk at an appropriate time. Disabling this yields a performance boost, as the highly available nature of OpenStack Storage allows for failure of a drive (and therefore, write of data), so this safety net in our filesystem can be disabled (with the `nobarrier` option), to increase speed.

Managing the OpenStack Storage cluster with swift-init

Services in our OpenStack Storage environment can be managed using the `swift-init` tool. This tool allows us to control all the daemons in OpenStack Storage in a convenient way.

Getting ready

Log in to any OpenStack Storage node.

How to do it...

The `swift-init` tool can be used to control any of the running daemons in our OpenStack Storage cluster, which makes it a convenient tool, rather than calling individual init scripts.

Each command can be succeeded with the following:

Controlling OpenStack Storage proxy

```
swift-init proxy-server { command }
```

Controlling OpenStack Storage object daemons

```
swift-init object { command }
swift-init object-replicator {command }
swift-init object-auditor { command }
swift-init object-updater { command }
```

Controlling OpenStack Storage container daemons

```
swift-init container { command }
swift-init container-update { command }
swift-init container-replicator { command }
swift-init container-auditor { command }
```

Controlling OpenStack Storage account daemons

```
swift-init account { command }
swift-init account-auditor { command }
swift-init account-reaper { command }
swift-init account-replicator { command }
```

Controlling all daemons

```
swift-init all { command }
```

{ command } can be one of the following:

Command	Description
stop, start, and restart	As stated
force-reload and reload	These mean the same thing—graceful shutdown and restart
shutdown	Shutdown after waiting for current processes to finish
no-daemon	Start a server within the current shell
no-wait	Spawn server and return immediately
once	Start server and run one pass
status	Display the status of the processes for the server

How it works...

The swift-init tool is a single tool that can be used to manage any of the running OpenStack Storage daemons. This allows for consistency in managing our cluster.

Checking cluster health

We are able to measure the health of our cluster by using the swift-dispersion-report tool. This is done by checking the set of our distributed containers, to ensure that the objects are in their proper places within the cluster.

Getting ready

Log in to the OpenStack Storage Proxy Server.

How to do it...

Carry out the following steps to set up the `swift-dispersion` tools to report on cluster health:

1. We first create the configuration file (`/etc/swift/dispersion.conf`) required by the `swift-dispersion` tools, as follows:

```
[dispersion]
auth_url = http://172.16.0.1:5000/auth/v2.0
auth_user = cookbook:admin
auth_key = openstack
```

2. Once this is in place, we need to create containers and objects throughout our cluster, so that they are in distinct places, by using the `swift-dispersion-populate` tool. We do this as follows:

```
sudo swift-dispersion-populate
```

3. Once these containers and objects have been set up, we can then run `swift-dispersion-report`, as follows:

```
sudo swift-dispersion-report
```

This produces the following result:

```
Queried 2621 containers for dispersion reporting, 19s, 0 retries
100.00% of container copies found (7863 of 7863)
Sample represents 1.00% of the container partition space

Queried 2621 objects for dispersion reporting, 7s, 0 retries
100.00% of object copies found (7857 of 7857)
Sample represents 1.00% of the object partition space
```

4. We can then set up a cron job that repeatedly checks the health of these containers and objects. We do this as follows:

```
echo "/usr/bin/swift-dispersion-report" | sudo tee -a /etc/cron.hourly/swift-dispersion-report
```

How it works...

The health of objects can be measured by checking whether the replicas are correct. If our OpenStack Storage cluster replicates an object 3 times and 2 of the 3 are in the correct place, the object would be 66.66% healthy.

To ensure we have enough replicated objects in our cluster, we populate it with the `swift-dispersion-populate` tool, which creates 2,621 containers and objects, thereby increasing our cluster size. Once in place, we can then set up a cron job that will run hourly to ensure our cluster is consistent and therefore giving a good indication that our cluster is healthy.

By setting up a cron job on our proxy node (which has access to all our nodes), we can constantly measure the health of our entire cluster. The cron job runs hourly, executing the `swift-dispersion-report` tool.

OpenStack Storage benchmarking

Understanding the capabilities of your OpenStack Storage environment is crucial to determining limits for capacity planning and areas for performance tuning. OpenStack Storage provides a tool named `swift-bench` that helps you understand these capabilities.

Getting ready

Log in to the swift-proxy node as the root user.

How to do it...

Carry out the following to benchmark an OpenStack Storage cluster:

1. First, create a configuration file named `/etc/swift/swift-bench.conf`, with the following contents:

    ```
    [bench]
    auth = http://172.16.0.1:5000/v2.0
    user = cookbook:admin
    key = openstack
    concurrency = 10
    object_size = 1
    num_objects = 1000
    num_gets = 10000
    delete = yes
    ```

2. With this in place, we can simply execute `swift-bench`, specifying our configuration file:

    ```
    swift-bench /etc/swift/swift-bench.conf
    ```

3. This produces the following output:

```
swift-bench 2012-04-06 19:56:10,417 INFO 76 PUTS [0 failures], 37.9/s
swift-bench 2012-04-06 19:56:25,429 INFO 531 PUTS [0 failures], 31.2/s
swift-bench 2012-04-06 19:56:38,665 INFO 1000 PUTS **FINAL** [0 failures], 33.1/s
swift-bench 2012-04-06 19:56:40,673 INFO 348 GETS [0 failures], 173.6/s
swift-bench 2012-04-06 19:56:55,676 INFO 3405 GETS [0 failures], 200.2/s
swift-bench 2012-04-06 19:57:10,677 INFO 4218 GETS [0 failures], 131.8/s
swift-bench 2012-04-06 19:57:25,693 INFO 6026 GETS [0 failures], 128.1/s
swift-bench 2012-04-06 19:57:40,701 INFO 9125 GETS [0 failures], 147.1/s
swift-bench 2012-04-06 19:57:44,830 INFO 10000 GETS **FINAL** [0 failures], 151.1/s
swift-bench 2012-04-06 19:57:46,852 INFO 84 DEL [0 failures], 41.6/s
swift-bench 2012-04-06 19:58:01,873 INFO 578 DEL [0 failures], 33.9/s
swift-bench 2012-04-06 19:58:14,467 INFO 1000 DEL **FINAL** [0 failures], 33.7/
```

How it works...

OpenStack Storage comes with a benchmarking tool named `swift-bench`. This runs through a series of puts, gets, and deletions, calculating the throughput and reporting of any failures in our OpenStack Storage environment. The configuration file is as follows:

```
[bench]
auth = Keystone authentication URL or OpenStack Storage Proxy
Tempauth Address
user = tenant:username
key = key/password
concurrency = number of concurrent operations
object_size = the size of the object in Bytes
num_objects = number of objects to upload
num_gets = number of objects to download
delete = whether to perform deletions
```

The user specified must be capable of performing the required operations in our environment, including the creation of containers.

Managing capacity

A **zone** is a group of nodes that is as isolated as possible from other nodes (separate servers, network, power, even geography). The ring guarantees that every replica is stored in a separate zone. To increase capacity in our environment, we can add an extra zone, to which data will then replicate. In this example, we will add an extra storage node, with its second disk, `/dev/sdb`, used for our OpenStack Storage. *This node makes up the only node in this zone.*

To add additional capacity to existing zones, we repeat the instructions for each existing zone in our cluster. For example, the following steps assume zone 5 (`z5`) doesn't exist, so this gets created when we build the rings. To simply add additional capacity to existing zones, we specify the new servers in the existing zones (zones 1-4). The instructions remain the same throughout.

Getting ready

Log in to the OpenStack Storage proxy server node as well as a new storage node (that will form the basis of our new zone).

How to do it...

To add an extra zone to our OpenStack Storage cluster, carry out the following:

Proxy Server

1. We first need to add the following entries to the ring where STORAGE_LOCAL_NET_ IP is the IP address of our new node and ZONE is our new zone:

    ```
    cd /etc/swift

    ZONE=5
    STORAGE_LOCAL_NET_IP=172.16.0.4
    WEIGHT=100
    DEVICE=sdb1

    swift-ring-builder account.builder add z$ZONE-$STORAGE_LOCAL_NET_
    IP:6002/$DEVICE $WEIGHT
    swift-ring-builder container.builder add z$ZONE-$STORAGE_LOCAL_
    NET_IP:6001/$DEVICE $WEIGHT
    swift-ring-builder object.builder add z$ZONE-$STORAGE_LOCAL_NET_
    IP:6000/$DEVICE $WEIGHT
    ```

2. We need to verify the contents of the rings by issuing the following commands:

    ```
    swift-ring-builder account.builder
    swift-ring-builder container.builder
    swift-ring-builder object.builder
    ```

     Ensure you run these commands while in the /etc/swift directory.

3. Finally, we rebalance the rings, which could take some time to run:

    ```
    swift-ring-builder account.builder rebalance
    swift-ring-builder container.builder rebalance
    swift-ring-builder object.builder rebalance
    ```

4. Once this has finished, we need to copy `account.ring.gz`, `container.ring.gz`, and `object.ring.gz` over to our *new* storage node *and all other storage nodes*:

```
scp *.ring.gz $STORAGE_LOCAL_NET_IP:/tmp
# And scp to other storage nodes
```

Storage Node

1. We first move the copied `account.ring.gz`, `container.ring.gz`, and `object.ring.gz` files to the `/etc/swift` directory and ensure they're owned by `swift`:

```
sudo mv /tmp/*.ring.gz /etc/swift
sudo chown swift:swift /etc/swift/*.ring.gz
```

2. We can now prepare the storage on this node, as described in the first recipe of this chapter, *Preparing drives for OpenStack Storage*.

3. Edit the `/etc/swift/swift.conf` file, so that the `[swift-hash]` section matches that of all other nodes, as follows:

```
[swift-hash]
# Random unique string used on all nodes
swift_hash_path_suffix = QAxxUPkzb7lP29OJ
```

4. We now need to create the appropriate `/etc/rsyncd.conf` file with the following contents:

```
uid = swift
gid = swift
log file = /var/log/rsyncd.log
pid file = /var/run/rsyncd.pid
address = 172.16.0.4

[account]
max connections = 2
path = /srv/node/
read only = false
lock file = /var/lock/account.lock

[container]
max connections = 2
path = /srv/node/
read only = false
lock file = /var/lock/container.lock

[object]
max connections = 2
path = /srv/node/
read only = false
lock file = /var/lock/object.lock
```

5. Enable and start `rsync`, as follows:

```
sudo sed -i 's/=false/=true/' /etc/default/rsync
sudo service rsync start
```

6. We need to create the `/etc/swift/account-server.conf` file with the following contents:

```
[DEFAULT]
bind_ip = 172.16.0.4
workers = 2

[pipeline:main]
pipeline = account-server

[app:account-server]
use = egg:swift#account

[account-replicator]

[account-auditor]

[account-reaper]
```

7. Also create the `/etc/swift/container-server.conf` file with the following contents:

```
[DEFAULT]
bind_ip = 172.16.0.4
workers = 2

[pipeline:main]
pipeline = container-server

[app:container-server]
use = egg:swift#container

[container-replicator]

[container-updater]

[container-auditor]
```

8. Finally, create the `/etc/swift/object-server.conf` file with the following contents:

```
[DEFAULT]
bind_ip = 172.16.0.4
workers = 2
```

```
[pipeline:main]
pipeline = object-server

[app:object-server]
use = egg:swift#object

[object-replicator]

[object-updater]

[object-auditor]
```

9. We can now simply start this storage node, which we have configured to be in our fifth zone, as follows:

    ```
    sudo swift-init all start
    ```

How it works...

Adding extra capacity by adding additional nodes or zones is done with the following two steps:

1. Configuring the zones and nodes on the proxy server
2. Configuring the storage node(s)

For each storage node, and the devices on those storage nodes, we run the following command, which adds the storage node and device to our new zone:

```
swift-ring-builder account.builder add zzone-storage_ip:6002/device
weight
```

```
swift-ring-builder container.builder add zzone-storage_ip:6001/device
weight
```

```
swift-ring-builder object.builder add zzone-storage_ip:6000/device weight
```

Once this has been configured on our proxy node, we rebalance the rings. This updates the object, account, and container rings. We copy the updated gzipped files as well as the swift hash key used within our environment, to all our storage node(s).

On the storage node, we simply run through the following steps:

1. Configure the disk (partition and format with XFS).
2. Configure and start `rsyncd`.
3. Configure the account, container, and object services.
4. Start the OpenStack Storage services on the storage node(s).

Data is then redistributed within our OpenStack Storage environment onto this new zone's node.

Removing nodes from a cluster

Converse to adding capacity to our OpenStack Storage cluster, there may be times where we need to scale back. We can do this by removing nodes from the zones in our cluster. In the following example, we will remove the node 172.16.0.4 in z5, which only has one storage device attached, /dev/sdb1.

Getting ready

Log in to the OpenStack Storage proxy server node.

How to do it...

Carry out the following to remove a storage node from a zone:

Proxy Server

1. To remove a node from OpenStack Storage, we first set its weight to be 0, so that when the rings get rebalanced, data is drained away from this node:

    ```
    cd /etc/swift

    swift-ring-builder account.builder set_weight z5-172.16.0.4:6002/
    sdb1 0
    swift-ring-builder container.builder set_weight z5-
    172.16.0.4:6001/sdb1 0
    swift-ring-builder object.builder set_weight z5-172.16.0.4:6000/
    sdb1 0
    ```

2. We then rebalance the rings as follows:

    ```
    swift-ring-builder account.builder rebalance
    swift-ring-builder container.builder rebalance
    swift-ring-builder object.builder rebalance
    ```

3. Once this is done, we can remove the node in this zone from the ring, as follows:

    ```
    swift-ring-builder account.builder remove z5-172.16.0.4:6002/sdb1
    swift-ring-builder container.builder remove z5-172.16.0.4:6001/
    sdb1
    swift-ring-builder object.builder remove z5-172.16.0.4:6000/sdb1
    ```

4. We then copy the resultant account.ring.gz, container.ring.gz, and object.ring.gz files over to the rest of the nodes in our cluster. We are now free to decommission this storage node by physically removing this device.

How it works...

Manually removing a node from our OpenStack Storage cluster is done in three steps:

1. Setting the node's `weight` to be `0`, so data isn't being replicated to it, by using the `swift-ring-builder <ring> set_weight` command.
2. Rebalancing the rings to update the data replication.
3. Removing the node from the OpenStack Storage cluster, using the `swift-ring-builder <ring> remove` command.

Once done, we are then free to decommission that node. We repeat this for each node (or device) in the zone.

Detecting and replacing failed hard drives

OpenStack Storage won't be of much use if it can't access the hard drives where our data is stored; so being able to detect and replace failed hard drives is essential.

Getting ready

Log in to an OpenStack Storage node as well as the proxy server.

How to do it...

To detect a failing hard drive, carry out the following:

Storage node

1. We first need to configure a cron job that monitors `/var/log/kern.log` for failed disk errors on our storage nodes. To do this, we create a configuration file named `/etc/swift/swift-drive-audit.conf`, as follows:

```
[drive-audit]
log_facility=LOG_LOCAL0
log_level=INFO
device_dir=/srv/node
minutes=60
error_limit=1
```

2. We then add a cron job that executes `swift-drive-audit` hourly, as follows:

```
echo '/usr/bin/swift-drive-audit /etc/swift/swift-drive-audit.
conf' | sudo tee -a /etc/cron.hourly/swift-drive-audit
```

3. With this in place, when a drive has been detected as faulty, the script will unmount it, so that OpenStack Storage can work around the issue. Therefore, when a disk has been marked as faulty and taken offline, you can now replace it.

> Without `swift-drive-audit` taking care of this automatically, should you need to act manually, ensure the disk has been unmounted and removed from the ring.

4. Once the disk has been physically replaced, we can follow the instructions as described in the *Managing capacity* recipe to add our node or device back into our cluster.

How it works...

Detection of failed hard drives can be picked up automatically by the `swift-drive-audit` tool, which we set up as a cron job to run hourly. With this in place, it detects failures, unmounts the drive so it can't be used, and updates the ring, so that data isn't being stored or replicated to it.

Once the drive has been removed from the rings, we can run maintenance on that device and replace the drive.

With a new drive in place, we can then put the device back in service on the storage node by adding it back into the rings. We can then rebalance the rings by running the `swift-ring-builder` commands.

Collecting usage statistics

OpenStack Storage can report on usage metrics by using the `swift-recon` middleware added to our `object-server` configuration. By using a tool, also named `swift-recon`, we can then query these collected metrics.

Getting ready

Log in to an OpenStack Storage node as well as the proxy server.

How to do it...

To collect usage statistics from our OpenStack Storage cluster, carry out the following:

1. We first need to modify our /etc/swift/object-server.conf configuration file to include the swift-recon middleware, so that it looks similar to the following:

```
[DEFAULT]
bind_ip = 0.0.0.0
workers = 2

[pipeline:main]
pipeline = recon object-server

[app:object-server]
use = egg:swift#object

[object-replicator]

[object-updater]

[object-auditor]

[filter:recon]
use = egg:swift#recon
recon_cache_path = /var/cache/swift
```

2. Once this is in place, we simply restart our object-server service, using swift-init, as follows:

```
swift-init object-server restart
```

Now that the command is running, we can use the swift-recon tool on the proxy server to get usage statistics, as follows:

Disk usage

```
swift-recon -d
```

This will report on disk usage in our cluster.

```
swift-recon -d -z5
```

This will report on disk usage in zone 5.

Load average

```
swift-recon -l
```

This will report on the load average in our cluster.

```
swift-recon -l -z5
```

This will report on the load average of the nodes in zone 5.

Quarantined statistics

```
swift-recon -q
```

This will report on any quarantined containers, objects, and accounts in the cluster.

```
swift-recon -q -z5
```

This will report on this information just for zone 5.

Check for unmounted devices

```
swift-recon -u
```

This will check for any unmounted drives in our cluster.

```
swift-recon -z5 -u
```

This will do the same just for zone 5.

Check replication metrics

```
swift-recon -r
```

This will report on the replication status within our cluster.

```
swift-recon -r -z5
```

This will just perform this for nodes in zone 5.

We can perform all these actions with a single command to get all telemetry data back about our cluster, as follows:

```
swift-recon --all
```

We can just get this information for nodes within zone 5 by adding -z5 at the end, as follows:

```
swift-recon --all -z5
```

22

How it works...

To enable usage statistics within OpenStack Storage, we add in the `swift-recon` middleware, so metrics are collected. We add this to the *object server* by adding the following lines to `/etc/swift/object-server.conf`, on each of our storage nodes:

```
[pipeline:main]
pipeline = recon object-server

[filter:recon]
use = egg:swift#recon
recon_cache_path = /var/cache/swift
```

With this in place and our object servers restarted, we can query this telemetry data by using the `swift-recon` tool. We can collect the statistics from the cluster as a whole, or from specific zones, with the `-z` parameter.

Note that we can also collect all or multiple statistics by specifying the `--all` flag or appending multiple flags to the command line. For example, to collect load average and replication statistics from our nodes in zone 5, we would execute the following command:

swift-recon -r -l -z5

7
Glance OpenStack Image Service

In this chapter, we will cover:

- ▶ Installing OpenStack Image Service
- ▶ Configuring OpenStack Image Service with MySQL
- ▶ Configuring OpenStack Image Service with OpenStack Storage
- ▶ Configuring OpenStack Compute with OpenStack Image Service
- ▶ Managing images with OpenStack
- ▶ Image Service
- ▶ Registering a remotely stored image

Introduction

OpenStack Image Service, known as **Glance**, is the service that allows you to register, discover, and retrieve virtual machine images for use in our OpenStack environment. Images made available through OpenStack Image Service can be stored in a variety of backend locations, from local filesystem storage to distributed filesystems such as OpenStack Storage.

Installing OpenStack Image Service

Installation of OpenStack Image Service is simply achieved by using the packages provided from the Ubuntu repositories. If you followed the guide in *Chapter 1, Starting OpenStack Compute*, we already installed and configured OpenStack Image Service appropriately for our test setup, but as OpenStack has been designed so that the components and services can be deployed across multiple machines, we will go through the steps here to specifically set up the service.

Getting ready

To begin with, ensure you are logged in to the server on which you want to install OpenStack Image Service.

How to do it...

Installation of OpenStack Image Service is very simple, using `apt`. We do this as follows:

```
sudo apt-get update
sudo apt-get -y install glance
```

To install just the client that allows us to administer and use OpenStack Image Service without needing to log onto our server, we do the following:

```
sudo apt-get update
sudo apt-get -y install glance-client
```

How it works...

The Ubuntu stable repositories have an appropriate version of OpenStack Image Service for our environment.

There's more...

There are various ways to install OpenStack, from source code building to installation from packages, but this represents the easiest and most consistent method available. There are also alternative releases of OpenStack available. The ones available from Ubuntu 12.04 LTS repositories are known as **Essex** and represent the latest *stable* release, at the time of writing.

Using an alternative release

Deviating from stable releases is appropriate when you are helping develop or debug OpenStack, or require functionality that is not available in the current release. To enable different releases, add different **Personal Package Archives** (**PPA**) to your system. To view the OpenStack PPAs, visit `http://wiki.openstack.org/PPAs`. To use them, we first install a tool that allows us to easily add PPAs to our system, as follows:

```
sudo apt-get update
sudo apt-get -y install python-software-properties
```

To use a particular release PPA we issue the following command:

- ▶ **Milestones** (periodic releases leading up to a stable release)

  ```
  sudo add-apt-repository ppa:openstack-ppa/milestone
  sudo apt-get update
  ```

- ▶ **Bleeding Edge** (Master Development Branch)

  ```
  sudo add-apt-repository ppa:openstack-ppa/bleeding-edge
  sudo apt-get update
  ```

Once you have configured apt to look for an alternative place for packages, you can repeat the preceding process for installing packages, if you are creating a new machine based on a different package set. Or, you can simply type:

```
sudo apt-get upgrade
```

This will make apt look in the new package archive areas for later releases of packages.

Configuring OpenStack Image Service with MySQL

In order to scale OpenStack effectively, we must move our local database store for OpenStack Image Service to a central, scalable, and more resilient database tier. For this, we will use our MySQL database.

Getting ready

To begin with, ensure you are logged into the server where OpenStack Image Service is installed, and become the root user.

How to do it...

Carry out the following steps:

1. Once OpenStack Image Service is installed, we can now create the glance database in our MySQL database server. We do this as follows:

   ```
   PASSWORD=openstack
   mysql -uroot -p$PASSWORD -e 'CREATE DATABASE glance;'
   ```

2. We now create a glance user, with the password openstack and with privileges to use this database, as follows:

   ```
   mysql -uroot -p$PASSWORD -e "GRANT ALL PRIVILEGES ON glance.* TO
   'glance'@'%';"
   mysql -u root -p$PASSWORD -e "SET PASSWORD FOR 'glance'@'%' =
   PASSWORD('openstack');"
   ```

3. Then, we need to configure OpenStack Image Service to use this database by editing the `/etc/glance/glance-registry.conf` file and change the `sql_connection` line to match the database credentials. We do this as follows:

```
sudo sed -i 's#^sql_connection.*#sql_connection = mysql://
glance:openstack@172.16.0.1/glance#' /etc/glance/glance-registry.
conf
```

4. We can now restart the keystone service, as follows:

```
sudo stop glance-registry
sudo start glance-registry
```

5. On start-up, the OpenStack Image Service Registry database is automatically populated with the correct tables.

How it works...

OpenStack Image Service is split into two running services—glance-api and glance-registry—and it is the glance-registry service that connects to the database backend. The first step is to create our glance database and glance user, so it can perform operations on the glance database that we have created.

Once this is done, we modify the `/etc/glance/glance-registry.conf` file so that glance knows where to find and connect to our MySQL database. This is provided by the standard SQLAlchemy connection string that has the following syntax:

```
sql_connection = mysql://USER:PASSWORD@HOST/DBNAME
```

Configuring OpenStack Compute with OpenStack Image Service

Once we have OpenStack Image Service configured and running, in order for our OpenStack Compute environment to connect to this service for our images, we modify the `--image_service` and `--glance_api_servers` flags in our `/etc/nova/nova.conf` file.

Getting ready

To begin with, ensure you are logged in to the server where OpenStack Image Service is installed.

How to do it...

Carry out the following steps to configure OpenStack Compute to use OpenStack Image Service:

1. To get our OpenStack Compute service to communicate with OpenStack Image Service instead of the default image service, we edit `/etc/nova/nova.conf` to include the following lines:

   ```
   --image_service=nova.image.glance.GlanceImageService
   --glance_api_servers=172.16.0.1:9292
   ```

2. We then restart the `nova-api` and `nova-objectstore` services to pick up this change.

   ```
   sudo restart nova-api
   sudo restart nova-objectstore
   ```

How it works...

As we configure OpenStack Compute to use OpenStack Image Service, we modify the file `/etc/nova/nova.conf`, with the following flags:

- The `--image_service` flag specifies the libraries to load for managing images. We point this to the `GlanceImageService` libraries.

- The `--glance_api_servers` flag is used to direct OpenStack Compute to where we have installed OpenStack Image Service and the port we have configured the `glance-api` service to run on. By default, the `glance-api` service runs on TCP port `9292`.

Configuring OpenStack Image Service with OpenStack Storage

Configuring OpenStack Image Service to use OpenStack Storage allows us to keep our images on easily accessible storage.

Getting ready

To begin with, ensure you are logged in to the server where OpenStack Image Service is installed.

How to do it...

Carry out the following steps to configure OpenStack Image Service to use OpenStack Storage:

1. We first need to install a package on our OpenStack Image Service host, that allows it to communicate to our OpenStack Storage service. We do this as follows:

   ```
   sudo apt-get update
   sudo apt-get -y install python-swift
   ```

2. We now ensure that we are able to authenticate to our OpenStack proxy server using the swift user Identity Service credentials created in *Chapter 4, Installing OpenStack Storage*. We can do this as follows, using the `swift` command:

   ```
   swift -V 2.0 -A http://172.16.0.1:5000/v2.0/ -U service:swift -K
   swift stat
   ```

3. We will get stats on our environment, such as the number of containers and objects, and so on, when successful.

4. We can now configure the `/etc/glance/glance-api.conf` file as required, in order to use OpenStack Storage as our file store, as follows:

   ```
   sudo sed -i 's/^default_store.*/default_store = swift/' /etc/
   glance/glance-api.conf
   ```

5. Once done, we can configure the same `/etc/glance/glance-api.conf` file to put values that are appropriate for connecting to OpenStack Storage:

   ```
   swift_store_auth_address = http://172.16.0.1:5000/v2.0/

   swift_store_user = service:swift

   swift_store_key = swift

   swift_store_container = glance
   ```

6. We must also ensure there is a container in our OpenStack Storage datastore called `glance`, as this is specified in `/etc/glance/glance-api.conf`, too. To create this container using the `swift` tool, we can do the following:

   ```
   swift -V 2.0 -A http://172.16.0.1:5000/v2.0/ -U
   service:swift -K swift post glance
   ```

7. Once done, we can restart our `glance-api` service to pick up these changes, as follows:

   ```
   sudo restart glance-api
   ```

8. Once restarted, when we upload images, they will now be stored in OpenStack Storage.

> Warning: If you have previously uploaded images to OpenStack Image Service prior to changing over to OpenStack Storage, you will need to re-upload your images so that they exist in OpenStack Storage.

How it works...

Setting up OpenStack Image Service to use OpenStack Storage as its backing store is straightforward. Once you have created an appropriate account that OpenStack Image Service can use to store images in OpenStack Storage, you configure the `glance-api.conf` file appropriately to point to your OpenStack Storage proxy server with these account details. The key configuration lines are:

```
swift_store_auth_address = http://KEYSTONE_HOST:5000/v2.0/

swift_store_user = service:USER

swift_store_key = PASSWORD
swift_store_container = glance
```

You also must ensure that the target `swift_store_container` exists within the OpenStack Storage datastore, before you can use OpenStack Image Service.

See also

▸ The *Configuring OpenStack Storage with OpenStack Identity Service* recipe in *Chapter 4, Installing OpenStack Storage*

Managing images with OpenStack Image Service

Uploading and managing images within OpenStack Storage is achieved using the `glance` command-line tool. This tool allows us to upload, remove, and change information about the stored images for use within our OpenStack environment.

Getting ready

To begin with, ensure you are logged in to our Ubuntu client, where we can run the `glance` tool. This can be installed using:

```
sudo apt-get update
sudo apt-get -y install glance-client
```

How to do it...

We can upload and view images in OpenStack Image Service in a number of ways. Carry out the following steps to upload and show details of our uploaded images:

Uploading Ubuntu images

To upload tarball cloud bundles using `glance` through the `cloud-publish-tarball` command, we can do the following, using the `glance` client:

1. First, we download an Ubuntu cloud image from `ubuntu.com`, as follows:

```
wget http://cloud-images.ubuntu.com/releases/precise/release/
ubuntu-12.04-server-cloudimg-i386.tar.gz
```

2. We then unpack this using the following command:

```
tar zvxf ubuntu-12.04-server-cloudimg-i386.tar.gz
```

3. We can now upload the kernel from the tarball into `glance`, specifying a name for this kernel, as follows:

```
# Source in our OpenStack Credentials
. keystonerc

# Upload the kernel (and store ID)
KERNEL=$(glance add name='Ubuntu 12.04 i386 Kernel'
disk_format=aki container_format=aki distro='Ubuntu' is_
public=true < precise-server-cloudimg-i386-vmlinuz-virtual |
awk '/ ID/ { print $6 }')
```

4. We then use the kernel ID that we have stored in `KERNEL`, to upload our machine image, as follows:

```
# Upload Machine Image
glance add name='Ubuntu 12.04 i386 Server' disk_format=ami
container_format=ami distro='Ubuntu' kernel_id=$KERNEL is_
public=true < precise-server-cloudimg-i386.img
```

You will see output similar to the following:

```
Uploading image 'Ubuntu 12.04 i386 Server'
=========================[100%] 6.68M/s, ETA  0h  0m  0s
Added new image with ID: 469460b0-464d-43f8-810d-ce1c919b25e9
```

Listing images

To list the images in our OpenStack Image Service repository, we can use the familiar `euca-describe-images` or `nova image-list` commands from our client, as using OpenStack Image Service doesn't change how we access our cloud environment. However, to get detailed information, we use the `glance` tool.

To list the private images for our demo user and public contents of our `glance` registry, we need to send a valid user authorization token, as follows:

```
glance index
```

This produces the following result:

```
ID    Name                    Disk Format      Container Format        Size
16    oneiric-server-i386         ami               ami             1476395008
```

Viewing image details

We can view further details about our images in the repository. To show all the details for our images, we issue the following command:

```
glance details
```

This returns a detailed list of all our images, for example:

```
URI: http://172.16.0.1:9292/v1/images/f4b75e07-38fa-482b-a9c5-e5dfcc977b02
Id: f4b75e07-38fa-482b-a9c5-e5dfcc977b02
Public: Yes
Protected: No
Name: ubuntu-12.04-i386
Status: active
Size: 200542828
Disk format: raw
Container format: ovf
Minimum Ram Required (MB): 0
Minimum Disk Required (GB): 0
Owner: 950534b6b9d740ad887cce62011de77a
Property 'distro': Ubuntu
```

To see a specific image detail, we issue the following command:

```
glance show f4b75e07-38fa-482b-a9c5-e5dfcc977b02
```

Deleting images

There will be times when you will need to remove images from being able to be called within your OpenStack cloud environment. You can delete public and private images from the `glance` server.

1. To delete an image, issue the following command:

    ```
    glance delete f4b75e07-38fa-482b-a9c5-e5dfcc977b02
    ```

2. You will then be asked to confirm. Press *Y* to confirm.

3. Once confirmation is complete, OpenStack Image Service will respond that the image has been removed. You can verify this with the `glance` index command.

To remove all public images from OpenStack Image Service, we can issue the following command:

1. Removing all our images from `glance` is achieved with:

    `glance clear --verbose`

2. You will then be asked to confirm where it will print out the images it is deleting.

Making private images public

When you upload an image using `cloud/euca2ools` commands, such as `euca-upload-bundle` and `cloud-publish-tarball`, they get entered into OpenStack Image Service and are only accessible by the user who uploaded them. This marks them as private. If an image is uploaded this way but you want to make it public, you do the following in OpenStack Image Service:

1. First, list and view the image(s) that you want to make public. In this case, we will choose our first uploaded image.

    `glance show f4b75e07-38fa-482b-a9c5-e5dfcc977b02`

    This produces results somewhat similar to the following:

    ```
    URI: http://172.16.0.1:9292/v1/images/f4b75e07-38fa-482b-a9c5-e5dfcc977b02
    Id: f4b75e07-38fa-482b-a9c5-e5dfcc977b02
    Public: Yes
    Protected: No
    Name: ubuntu-12.04-i386
    Status: active
    Size: 200542828
    Disk format: raw
    Container format: ovf
    Minimum Ram Required (MB): 0
    Minimum Disk Required (GB): 0
    Owner: 950534b6b9d740ad887cce62011de77a
    Property 'distro': Ubuntu
    ```

2. We can now convert this to a public image, available to all users of our cloud environment, with the following command:

    `glance update f4b75e07-38fa-482b-a9c5-e5dfcc977b02 is_public=True`

3. Issue a public `glance` listing as follows:

glance details

We will now see this:

```
URI: http://172.16.0.1:9292/v1/images/f4b75e07-38fa-482b-a9c5-e5dfcc977b02
Id: f4b75e07-38fa-482b-a9c5-e5dfcc977b02
Public: Yes
Protected: No
Name: ubuntu-12.04-i386
Status: active
Size: 200542828
Disk format: raw
Container format: ovf
Minimum Ram Required (MB): 0
Minimum Disk Required (GB): 0
Owner: 950534b6b9d740ad887cce62011de77a
Property 'distro': Ubuntu
```

How it works...

OpenStack Image Service is a very flexible system for managing images in our private cloud environment. It allows us to modify many aspects of our OpenStack Image Service registry—from adding new images, deleting them, and updating information, such as the name that is used so end users can easily identify them, to making private images public and vice-versa.

To do all this, we use the `glance` tool from any connected client. To use the `glance` tool, we source in our OpenStack Identity Service credentials.

Registering a remotely stored image

OpenStack Image Service provides a mechanism to remotely add an image that is stored at an externally accessible location. This allows for a convenient method of adding images we might want to use for our private cloud that has been uploaded to an external third-party server.

Getting ready

To begin with, ensure you are logged in to our Ubuntu client, where we can run the `glance` tool. This can be installed using the following command:

```
sudo apt-get update
sudo apt-get -y install glance-client
```

How to do it...

Carry out the following steps to remotely store an image into OpenStack Image Service:

1. To register a remote virtual image into our environment, we add a location parameter instead of streaming the image through a pipe on our `glance` command line:

```
glance  add name="CentOS 5.3" is_public=true distro="CentOS"
container_format=ovf disk_format=vhd location="http://a.webserver.
com/images/centos-5.3.vhd"
```

2. This returns information similar to the following that is then stored in OpenStack Image Service:

```
Added new image with ID: 44576f07-a8da-2d2b-b0c5-e4dfff977ba2
Returned the following metadata for the new image:
container_format => ovf
created_at => 2012-01-19T16:42:04.765890
deleted => False
deleted_at => None
disk_format => vhd
id => 44576f07-a8da-2d2b-b0c5-e4dfff977ba2
is_public => True
location => http://a.webserver.com/images/centos-5.3vhd
name => CentOS 5.3
properties => {}
size => 0
status => active
updated_at => None
```

How it works...

Using the `glance` tool to specify remote images directly provides a quick and convenient way to add images to our OpenStack Image Service repository. The way this happens is with the `location` parameter. We add in our usual meta information to accompany this, as we would with a locally specified image.

8
Nova Volumes

In this chapter, we will cover:

- ▸ Configuring nova-volume services
- ▸ Configuring OpenStack Compute for nova-volume
- ▸ Creating volumes
- ▸ Attaching volumes to instances
- ▸ Detaching volumes from an instance
- ▸ Deleting volumes

Introduction

Data written to currently running instances on disks is not persistent—meaning that when you terminate such instances, any disk writes will be lost. Volumes are persistent storage that you can attach to your running OpenStack Compute instances; the best analogy is that of a USB drive that you can attach to an instance. Like USB drives, you can only attach instances to one computer at a time. Nova Volumes are very similar to Amazon EC2's Elastic Block Storage—the difference is how these are presented to the running instances. Under OpenStack Compute, these can easily be managed using an iSCSI exposed LVM volume group named `nova-volumes`, so this must be present on any host running the service `nova-volume`.

nova-volume is the running service.

nova-volumes is the name of the *LVM Volume Group* that is exposed by the nova-volume service.

Configuring nova-volume services

In this section, we will add a new disk to our VirtualBox VM, OpenStack1, and add the prerequisites that `nova-volume` requires to attach volumes to our instances.

Getting ready

To use Nova Volumes, we will make some changes to our OpenStack1 Virtual Machine. This is because we need to power it off and add a new volume to this VM, so that we have an LVM-managed volume named `nova-volumes`. We will then configure this drive under Ubuntu and make the volume available to `nova-volume`.

How to do it...

We first need to configure our storage for use by `nova-volume`. We can then set up LVM appropriately, by creating a volume group named `nova-volumes`, on that new storage. Following this, we install and configure prerequisites such as `open-iscsi`. Once complete, we simply set up `nova-volume`.

Adding a new disk to a VirtualBox Virtual Machine

1. Ensure your host is powered off. Add new storage by clicking on your OpenStack1 VirtualBox Virtual Machine and clicking on **Settings**.

2. Under **Storage Tree**, click on the second **+** sign at the end of the section that says **SATA Controller**, as shown in the following screenshot (note that there are two—the first is a CD-ROM drive and the second is the option to add in a new disk):

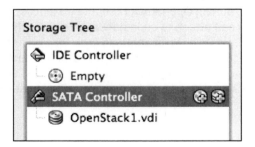

3. When presented with a dialog box, select **Create new disk** of type VDI and size 20 GB. For a name, for ease of administration in VirtualBox, call this **Nova-Volumes-OpenStack1**, as shown in the following screenshot:

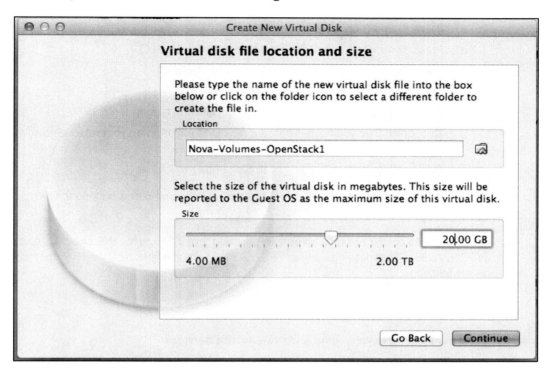

4. Once done, power the OpenStack1 VM back on.

Alternatively, using the command line:

We can use the VBoxManage command from our VirtualBox install and run the following in a shell on our computer, to add in a new disk:

```
VBoxManage createhd --filename Nova-Volumes-OpenStack1.vdi --size 20480
VBoxManage storageattach openstack1 --storagectl "SATA Controller" --port 1 --device 0 --type hdd --medium Nova-Volumes-OpenStack1.vdi
```

Configuring your new storage for use by nova-volume

1. Now we must use fdisk to configure the new volume:

```
sudo fdisk /dev/sdb
```

2. Under the `fdisk` menu, we do the following:

   - ❏ Press *n*, and then hit *Enter*
   - ❏ Press *p*, and then hit *Enter*
   - ❏ Press *1*, and then hit *Enter*
   - ❏ Press *Enter* when asked for start sector (default `2048`)
   - ❏ Press *Enter* when asked for the last sector (default)
   - ❏ Back at the main fdisk menu press *t*, then *Enter*
   - ❏ Type in `8e`, and then press *Enter* (to set partition type to Linux LVM)
   - ❏ To confirm that you have created a new LVM partition on your new volume, at the main menu press *p* and then *Enter*
   - ❏ Press *w* to write these changes to disk and to exit fdisk.

3. To force Linux to see these changes, we run the `partprobe` command, as follows:

   ```
   sudo partprobe
   ```

4. As we chose to create our LVM volume in partition 1 of `/dev/sdb`, this should display as `/dev/sdb1`. To create our `nova-volumes` LVM volume group on `/dev/sdb1`, we do the following:

   ```
   sudo pvcreate /dev/sdb1
   sudo vgcreate nova-volumes /dev/sdb1
   ```

Installing and configuring nova-volume and prerequisite services

1. `nova-volume` relies on the Open iSCSI service, so we install both `nova-volume` and the required `iscsi` services on our `openstack1` server, as follows:

   ```
   sudo apt-get -y install nova-volume tgt
   ```

2. Once complete, we need to start the required `tgt` service on our `nova-volume` host. We do this as follows:

   ```
   sudo start tgt
   ```

3. Now, restart the `nova-volume` service to pick up the change, via the following command:

   ```
   sudo service nova-volume restart
   ```

How it works...

In order for us to use `nova-volume`, we need to prepare a suitable disk or partition that has been configured as an LVM volume and that is specifically named `nova-volumes`. For our virtual environment, we simply add a new disk that we can then set up to be part of this LVM volume group. In a physical installation, the steps are no different. We simply configure a partition to be of type `8e` (Linux LVM) in fdisk and then add this partition to a volume group named `nova-volumes`.

Once done, we then install the required `nova-volume` packages and supporting services. As `nova-volume` uses iSCSI as the mechanism for attaching a volume to an instance, we install the appropriate packages that are required to run iSCSI targets.

Configuring OpenStack Compute for nova-volume

We now need to tell our OpenStack Compute service about our new `nova-volume` service.

Getting ready

Ensure you are logged in to your compute nodes, so we can install and configure the appropriate packages in order to use the `nova-volume` attached storage.

How to do it...

Configuring OpenStack Compute nodes to use `nova-volume` involves installing the appropriate package (that can communicate back to the iSCSI target) on our node.

1. First, install the `open-iscsi` package on our OpenStack Compute host. The OpenStack Compute host is known as an *iSCSI Initiator*.

    ```
    sudo apt-get -y install open-iscsi
    ```

2. Start the iSCSI service through the following command:

    ```
    sudo service open-iscsi start
    ```

3. Finally, we instruct OpenStack Compute to use this iSCSI service for `nova-volume`, by adding the following lines to our `/etc/nova/nova.conf` file:

    ```
    iscsi_ip_address=172.16.0.1
    --iscsi_helper=tgtadm
    ```

4. We can now restart the `nova-compute` service as follows:

    ```
    sudo service nova-compute restart
    ```

5. We can verify that we have all services running correctly, by running the following:

    ```
    sudo nova-manage service list
    ```

This should present us with an extra service line, now saying that `nova-volume` is happily running on `openstack1`.

How it works...

The host running `nova-volume` is known as an **iSCSI Target**. The host running our compute service is known as the **iSCSI Initiator**. The iSCSI Initiator package is started, which our OpenStack Compute service then controls.

To make our OpenStack Compute host aware of our new `nova-volume` service, we add the following to `/etc/nova/nova.conf`:

```
--iscsi_ip_address=NOVA-VOLUME-ADDRESS
```

```
--iscsi_helper=tgtadm
```

These lines tell the OpenStack Compute where the iSCSI Target is (which is the address of our `nova-volume` server), and the service to use to locate the iSCSI services.

Creating volumes

Now that we have a usable `nova-volume` service, we can create volumes for use by our instances. We do this under our Ubuntu client using one of the euca2ools, `euca-create-volumes`, or the Nova Client tool, so we are creating volumes specific to our tenancy (project).

Getting ready

To begin with, ensure you are logged in to your Ubuntu client that has access to the `euca2ools` or Nova Client tools. These packages can be installed using the following command:

```
sudo apt-get update
sudo apt-get install euca2ools python-novaclient
```

How to do it...

Carry out the following steps to create a volume using `euca2ools`:

1. First, create the volume that we will attach to our instance. The size (`-s`) option is in gigabytes, so we will create one with 5 GB. The zone option (`-z`) will be `nova`, for our OpenStack setup.

    ```
    # Source in our ec2 credentials
    . ec2rc

    euca-create-volume -s 5 -z nova
    ```

2. You should see output similar to the following:

    ```
    VOLUME  vol-00000003  5  creating (cookbook, None, None, None)
    2011-12-11T14:02:29Z
    ```

3. To view the status of any volumes, run the `euca-describe-volumes` command. When the volume has been created, the status changes from `creating` to `available`.

    ```
    euca-describe-volumes
    ```

    You should see output similar to the following:

    ```
    VOLUME  vol-00000003  5  nova  available (cookbook, openstack1,
    None, None)  2011-12-11T14:02:29Z
    ```

    Note that this project has been created in `cookbook`, in the zone `nova`.

Carry out the following to create a volume using **Nova Client**:

1. First, create the volume that we will attach to our instance.

    ```
    # Source in our OpenStack Nova credentials
    . keystonerc

    nova volume-create --display_name volume1 5
    ```

2. On completion, the command simply returns with no output. To view our volumes using Nova Client, we run the following command:

    ```
    nova volume-list
    ```

3. This returns output similar to the following:

```
+----+-----------+--------------+------+-------------+-------------+
| ID |  Status   | Display Name | Size | Volume Type | Attached to |
+----+-----------+--------------+------+-------------+-------------+
| 1  | available | None         | 5    | None        |             |
| 2  | available | volume1      | 5    | None        |             |
+----+-----------+--------------+------+-------------+-------------+
```

How it works...

Creating nova-volumes for use within our project, cookbook, is very straightforward. Using euca2ools, we use the euca-create-volume tool, which takes the following syntax:

```
euca-create-volume -s size_Gb -z zone
```

This then creates the volume to be used in our environment with an ID in the form vol-00000000, on our nova-volume host.

With Nova Client, we use the create-volume option with the following syntax:

```
nova create-volume --display_name volume_name size_Gb
```

Here, volume_name can be any arbitrary name with no spaces.

We can see the actual LVM volumes on nova-volumes, using the usual LVM tools as follows:

```
sudo lvdisplay nova-volumes

--- Logical volume ---
LV Name                /dev/nova-volumes/volume-00000001
VG Name                nova-volumes
LV UUID                G62e3s-gXcX-v8F8-jmGI-DgcY-OONy-i0GSNl
LV Write Access        read/write
LV Status              available
# open                 0
LV Size                5.00 GiB
Current LE             1280
Segments               1
Allocation             inherit
Read ahead sectors     auto
- currently set to     256
Block device           252:0
```

Attaching volumes to instances

Now that we have a usable volume, we can attach this to any instance. We do this by using the `euca-attach-volume` command from `euca2ools` or the `nova volume-attach` command in Nova Client.

Getting ready

To begin with, ensure you are logged in to the Ubuntu client that has access to `euca2ools` or Nova Client tools. These packages can be installed using the following command:

```
sudo apt-get update
```

```
sudo apt-get-y install euca2ools python-novaclient
```

How to do it...

Carry out the following steps to attach a volume to an instance by using euca2ools:

1. If you have no instance running, spin one up. Once running, run the `euca-describe-instances` command and note the instance ID.

   ```
   # Source in our EC2 credentials
   . ec2rc
   ```

   ```
   euca-describe-instances
   ```

   The following output will be displayed

   ```
   RESERVATION  r-7r0wjd2o  cookbook  default
   INSTANCE  i-00000009  ami-00000002  172.16.1.1  10.0.0.3
   running  openstack (cookbook, openstack1)  0    m1.tiny
   2011-12-11T15:33:43Z  nova  aki-00000001  ami-00000000
   ```

2. Using the instance ID, we can attach the volume to our running instance, as follows:

   ```
   euca-attach-volume -i i-00000009 -d /dev/vdb vol-00000003
   ```

3. This will output the name of the volume when successful. To view this, log in to your running instance and view the volume that is now attached:

   ```
   sudo fdisk -l /dev/vdb
   ```

4. We should see 5 GB of space available for the running instance. At this moment, this is like adding a fresh disk to a system, so you need to format it for use and then mount it as part of your filesystem.

```
sudo mkfs.ext4 /dev/vdb
sudo mount /dev/vdb /mnt
df -h
```

We should now see the newly attached disk available at /mnt:

```
Filesystem      Size  Used Avail Use% Mounted on
/dev/vda        1.4G  602M  733M  46% /
devtmpfs        248M   12K  248M   1% /dev
none             50M  216K   50M   1% /run
none            5.0M     0  5.0M   0% /run/lock
none            248M     0  248M   0% /run/shm
/dev/vdb        5.0G  204M  4.6G   5% /mnt
```

 Only format the volume if this is the first time you have used it.

Carry out the following steps to attach a volume to an instance using Nova Client:

1. If you have no instance running, spin one up. Once running, run the nova list command and note the instance ID.

```
# Source in credentials
. keystonerc

nova list
```

The following output is generated:

```
+--------------------------------------+----------+--------+-----------------------------+
|                  ID                  |   Name   | Status |           Networks          |
+--------------------------------------+----------+--------+-----------------------------+
| ccd477d6-e65d-4f8d-9415-c150672c52bb | Server 9 | ACTIVE | vmnet=10.0.0.5, 172.16.1.1  |
+--------------------------------------+----------+--------+-----------------------------+
```

2. Using the instance ID, we can attach the volume to our running instance, as follows:

```
nova volume-attach ccd477d6-e65d-4f8d-9415-c150672c52bb 4 /dev/vdc
```

 /dev/vdc is specified here so as not to conflict with /dev/vdb, as the former refers to the same instance described previously.

3. The preceding command will output the name of the volume when successful. To view this, log in to your running instance and view the volume that is now attached:

```
sudo fdisk -l /dev/vdc
```

4. We should see 5 GB of space available for the running instance. At this moment, this is like adding a fresh disk to a system, so you need to format it for use and then mount it as part of your filesystem.

```
sudo mkfs.ext4 /dev/vdc
sudo mkdir /mnt1
sudo mount /dev/vdc /mnt1
df -h
```

We should now see the newly attached disk available at /mnt1:

```
Filesystem      Size  Used Avail Use% Mounted on
/dev/vda        1.4G  602M  733M  46% /
devtmpfs        248M   12K  248M   1% /dev
none             50M  216K   50M   1% /run
none            5.0M     0  5.0M   0% /run/lock
none            248M     0  248M   0% /run/shm
/dev/vdb        5.0G  204M  4.6G   5% /mnt
/dev/vdc        5.0G  204M  4.6G   5% /mnt1
```

How it works...

Attaching a nova-volume is no different from plugging in a USB stick on your own computer—we attach it, (optionally) format it, and mount it.

Under euca2ools, the command euca-attach-volume takes the following syntax:

```
euca-attach-volume -i instance_id -d device volume_id
```

instance_id is the ID returned from euca-describe-instances for the instance we want to attach the volume to. device is the name of the device within the instance that we will use to mount the volume. volume_id is the ID returned from euca-describe-volumes for the volume we want to use to attach.

Under Nova Client, the option volume-attach takes the following syntax:

```
nova volume-attach instance_id volume_id device
```

instance_id is the ID returned from nova list for the instance that we want to attach the volume to. volume_id is the name of the device within the instance that we will use to mount the volume that can be retrieved using nova volume-list. device is the device that will be created on our instance that we use to mount the volume.

Detaching volumes from an instance

As Nova Volumes are persistent storage and the best way of thinking of them is as a USB drive, this means you can only attach them to a single computer at a time. When you remove it from the computer, you can then move it to another one and attach it. The same principle works with Nova Volumes. To detach a volume, we use another euca2ools aptly named `euca-detach-volume`, or from Nova Client, the option `volume-detach`.

Getting ready

To begin with, ensure you are logged in to the Ubuntu client that has access to `euca2ools` or Nova Client tools. These packages can be installed using the following command:

```
sudo apt-get update
sudo apt-get-y install euca2ools python-novaclient
```

How to do it...

Carry out the following steps to detach a volume by using euca2ools:

1. First, we identify the volumes attached to running instances, by running the command `euca-describe-volumes`, as follows:

    ```
    euca-describe-volumes
    ```

2. This brings back the following output:

    ```
    VOLUME    vol-00000003   5     nova   in-use   2012-07-06T11:09:23.000Z
    ATTACHMENT   vol-00000003   i-00000009   /dev/vdb   attached   |
    VOLUME    vol-00000004   5     nova   in-use   2012-07-06T11:20:50.000Z
    ATTACHMENT   vol-00000004   i-00000009   /dev/vdc   attached
    ```

3. In a shell on the running instance that has the volume mounted, we must first unmount the volume as follows:

    ```
    sudo umount /mnt
    ```

4. Back on the Ubuntu client where euca2ools is installed, we can now detach this volume, as follows:

    ```
    euca-detach-volume -i i-00000009 vol-00000003
    ```

5. We are now free to attach this to another running instance, with data preserved.

Carry out the following steps to detach a volume using Nova Client:

1. First, we identify the volumes attached to running instances, by running the command `euca-describe-volumes`, as follows:

    `nova volume-list`

2. This brings back the following output:

```
+----+-----------+--------------+------+-------------+------------------------------------------+
| ID |  Status   | Display Name | Size | Volume Type |               Attached to                |
+----+-----------+--------------+------+-------------+------------------------------------------+
| 3  | available | volume1      | 5    | None        |                                          |
| 4  | in-use    | volume1      | 5    | None        | ccd477d6-e65d-4f8d-9415-c150672c52bb     |
+----+-----------+--------------+------+-------------+------------------------------------------+
```

3. In a shell on the instance that has the volume mounted, we must first unmount it as follows (if using the example before, this is on /mnt1):

    `sudo umount /mnt1`

4. Back on the Ubuntu client, where Nova Client is installed, we can now detach this volume as follows:

    `nova volume-detach ccd477d6-e65d-4f8d-9415-c150672c52bb 4`

5. We are now free to attach this to another running instance, with data preserved.

How it works...

Detaching `nova-volume` is no different to removing a USB stick from a computer. We first unmount the volume from our running instance. Then, we detach the volume from the running instance using `euca-detach-volume` from euca2ools or `nova volume-detach` from Nova Client.

`euca-detach-volume` has the following syntax:

`euca-detach-volume -i instance_id volume_id`

`instance_id` is the ID returned from `euca-describe-instances` for the instance we want to detach the volume from. `volume_id` is the ID returned from `euca-describe-volumes` for the volume we want to detach.

`nova volume-detach` has the following syntax:
`nova volume-detach instance_id volume_id`

`instance_id` is the ID from the **Attached to** column returned from `nova volume-list` for the instance we want to detach the volume from. `volume_id` is the ID returned from `euca-describe-volumes` for the volume we want to detach.

Deleting volumes

At some point, you will no longer need the volumes you have created. To remove the volumes from the system completely, so they are no longer available, we simply pull out another tool from euca2ools, `euca-delete-volume`, or invoke the `volume-delete` option from Nova Client.

Getting ready

Ensure you are logged in to the Ubuntu host where euca2ools is installed and have sourced in your OpenStack environment credentials.

How to do it...

To delete a volume using euca2ools, carry out the following steps:

1. First, we list the volumes available to identify the volume we want to delete, as follows:

    `euca-describe-volumes`

2. We now simply use the volume ID to delete this from the system, as follows:

    `euca-delete-volume vol-00000003`

3. On deletion, the volume you have deleted will be printed on screen.

To delete a volume using Nova Client, carry out the following steps:

1. First, we list the volumes available to identify the volume we want to delete, as follows:

    `nova volume-list`

2. We now simply use the volume ID to delete this from the system, as follows:

    `nova volume-delete 4`

3. On deletion, the volume you have deleted will be printed on screen.

How it works...

Deleting images removes the LVM volume from use within our system. To do this, we simply specify the name of the volume as a parameter to `euca-delete-volume`, if using euca2ools, or the ID as a parameter to `nova volume-delete` (when using Nova Client), first ensuring that the volume is not in use.

9
Horizon OpenStack Dashboard

In this chapter we will cover:

- ▶ Installing OpenStack Dashboard
- ▶ Keypair management in OpenStack Dashboard
- ▶ Security group management by using OpenStack Dashboard
- ▶ Launching instances by using OpenStack Dashboard
- ▶ Terminating instances by using OpenStack Dashboard
- ▶ Connecting to instances by using OpenStack Dashboard and VNC
- ▶ Adding new tenants by using OpenStack Dashboard
- ▶ User management by using OpenStack Dashboard

Introduction

Managing our OpenStack environment through a command-line interface allows us complete control of our cloud environment, but having a GUI that operators and administrators can use to manage their environments and instances makes this process easier. OpenStack Dashboard, known as Horizon, provides this GUI and is a web service that runs from an Apache installation, using Python's **Web Service Gateway Interface (WSGI)** and Django, a rapid development web framework.

With OpenStack Dashboard installed, we can manage all the core components of our OpenStack environment.

 Installation of OpenStack Dashboard under Ubuntu gives a slightly different look and feel than a stock installation of Dashboard. The functions remain the same, although Ubuntu adds an additional feature to allow the user to download environment settings for Juju.

Installing OpenStack Dashboard

Installation of OpenStack Dashboard is straightforward when using Ubuntu's package repository.

Getting ready

To begin with, ensure that you're logged in to our OpenStack Compute host or an appropriate server on the network that has access to our OpenStack environment.

How to do it...

To install OpenStack Dashboard, we simply install the required packages and dependencies by following the ensuing steps:

1. Install the required packages as follows:

   ```
   sudo apt-get update
   sudo apt-get -y install openstack-dashboard novnc nova-consoleauth
   nova-console
   ```

2. We can configure OpenStack Dashboard by editing the /etc/openstack-dashboard/local_settings.py file, thus:

   ```
   OPENSTACK_HOST = "172.16.0.1"
   OPENSTACK_KEYSTONE_URL = "http://%s:5000/v2.0" % OPENSTACK_HOST
   OPENSTACK_KEYSTONE_DEFAULT_ROLE = "Member"
   ```

3. Restart the Apache service to pick up our changes, as follows:

   ```
   sudo service apache2 restart
   ```

4. Now we need to configure Nova to use our VNC proxy service that can be used through our OpenStack Dashboard interface. To do so, add the following lines to `/etc/nova/nova.conf`:

```
--novnc_enabled=true
--novncproxy_base_url=
http://172.16.0.1:6080/vnc_auto.html
--vncserver_proxyclient_address=172.16.0.1
--vncserver_listen=172.16.0.1
```

5. Restart `nova-api` to pick up the changes:

```
sudo restart nova-api
sudo restart nova-compute
sudo service apache2 restart
```

How it works...

Installation of OpenStack Dashboard, Horizon, is simple when using Ubuntu's package repository. As it uses the Python RAD web environment, Django, and WSGI, OpenStack Dashboard can run under Apache. So, to pick up our changes, we restart our Apache 2 service.

We also include the VNC Proxy service. It provides us with a great feature to access our instances over the network, through the web interface.

Keypair management in OpenStack Dashboard

Keypairs allow users to connect SSH to our Linux instances, so users must have keypairs. Users have to manage keypairs through OpenStack Dashboard for their own setup. Usually, this is the first task a new user has to do when given access to our OpenStack environment.

Getting ready

Load a web browser, point it to our OpenStack Dashboard address at `http://172.16.0.1/`, and log in as the `demo` user with the password `openstack`.

How to do it...

Management of the logged-in user's keypairs is achieved with the steps discussed in the following sections.

Adding keypairs

Keypairs can be added by performing the following steps:

1. A new keypair can be added to our system by using the **Access & Security** tab, so click on it:

2. We will then be presented with a screen allowing us access to security settings and keypair management. Under **Keypairs**, there will be a list of keypairs that we can use to access our instances. To create a new keypair, click on the **Create Keypair** button:

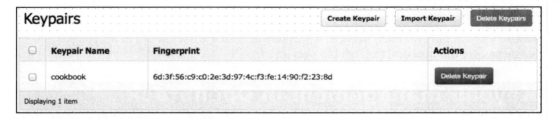

3. We will be presented with a screen that asks us to name the keypair, so name this appropriately (with no spaces), and then click on the **Create Keypair** button:

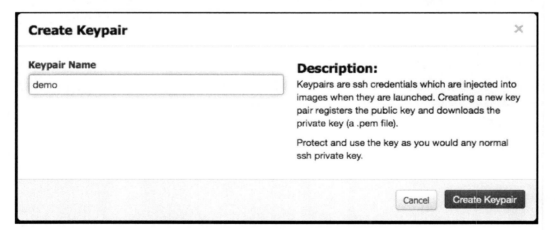

4. Once a keypair is created, we will be asked to save the private key portion of our keypair to disk. A private key cannot be recreated, so keep this safe and store it on the filesystem.

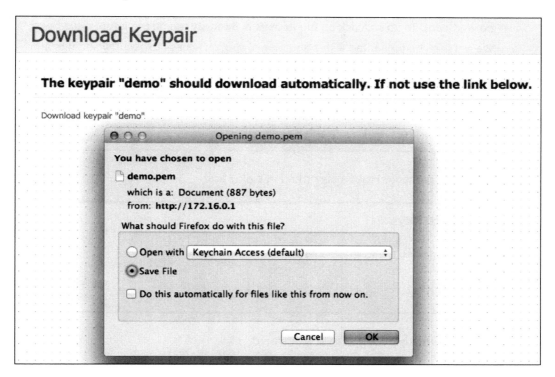

5. Click on the **Access & Security** tab to return to our list of keypairs. We will now see the newly created keypair listed. When launching instances, we can select this new keypair and only gain access to it by using the private key that we have stored locally:

Deleting keypairs

Keypairs can be deleted by performing the following steps:

1. When keypairs are no longer required, we can delete them from our OpenStack environment. To do so, click on the **Access & Security** tab on the left of our screen.

2. We will then be presented with a screen allowing us access to security settings and keypair management. Under **Keypairs**, there will be a list of keypairs that we can use to access our instances. To delete a keypair from our system, select the **Delete Keypair** button for the keypair that we want to delete:

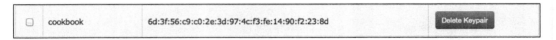

3. We will be presented with a confirmation dialog box:

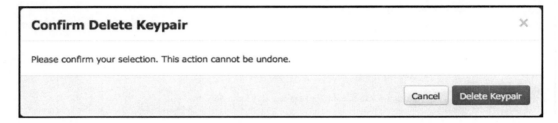

4. Once confirmed, the keypair will be deleted.

Importing Keypairs

To import keypairs, perform the following steps:

1. We can import keypairs that have been created in our traditional Linux- and Unix-based environments into our OpenStack setup. If you don't have one already, run the following from your Linux- or other Unix-based host.

    ```
    ssh-keygen -t rsa -N ""
    ```

2. This will produce two files on our client:
    - .ssh/id_rsa
    - .ssh/id_rsa.pub

3. The `.ssh/id_rsa` file is our private key and has to be protected, as it is the only key that matches the public portion of the keypair, `.ssh/id_rsa.pub`.

4. We can import this public key to use in our OpenStack environment, so that when an instance is launched, the public key is inserted into our running instance. To import the public key, ensure that you're at the **Access & Security** screen, and then under **Keypairs**, click on the **Import Keypair** button:

5. We will be presented with a screen that asks us to name our keypair and paste the contents of our public key. So name the keypair, and then copy and paste the contents of the public key into the space—for example, the contents of `.ssh/id_rsa.pub`. Once entered, click on the **Import Keypair** button:

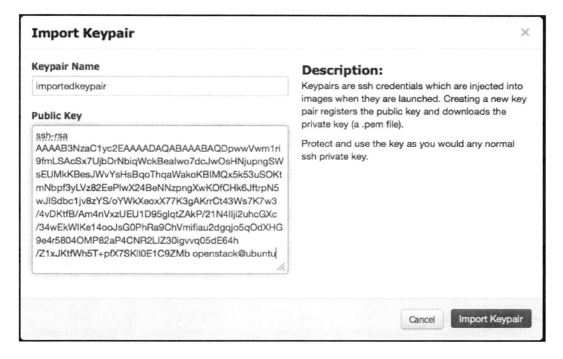

6. Once completed, we will be presented with the list of keypairs available to that user, including our imported keypair:

| Keypairs | | | Create Keypair | Import Keypair | Delete Keypairs |

	Keypair Name	Fingerprint	Actions
☐	demo	db:97:39:2e:19:55:32:17:3a:70:81:d4:e3:c7:bb:23	Delete Keypair
☐	importedkeypair	b8:63:1e:bc:ba:55:e6:b2:9f:1e:9d:c7:0d:1b:27:35	Delete Keypair

Displaying 2 items

How it works...

Keypair management is important, as it provides a consistent and secure approach for accessing our running instances. Allowing the user to create, delete, and import keypairs to use within his/her tenants allows them to create secure systems.

OpenStack Dashboard allows a user to create keypairs in a very simple way. The user must ensure, though, that the private key that he/she downloads is kept secure.

Deleting keypairs is very straightforward, but the user must remember that if he/she is deleting keypairs and there are running instances, the user will no longer be able to access the running system—every keypair created is unique, even if you name the keypairs the same.

Importing keypairs has the advantage that we can use our existing secure keypairs that we have been using outside of OpenStack within our new private cloud environment. This provides a consistent user experience when moving from one environment to another.

Security group management by using OpenStack Dashboard

Security groups are network rules that allow instances in one tenant (project) to be kept separate from other instances in another. Managing Security Group rules for our OpenStack instances is done as simply as possible with OpenStack Dashboard.

Getting ready

Load a web browser, point it to our OpenStack Dashboard address at `http://172.16.0.1/`, and log in as the `demo` user with the password `openstack`.

How to do it...

To administer security groups under OpenStack Dashboard, carry out the steps discussed in the following sections.

Creating a security group

To create a security group, perform the following steps:

1. A new keypair is added to our system by using the **Access & Security** tab, so click on it:

2. We will then be presented with a screen allowing us access to security settings and keypair management. Under **Security Groups**, there will be a list of security groups that can be used when we launch our instances. To create a new Security Group, click on the **Create Security Group** button:

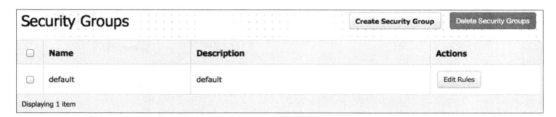

3. We will be presented with a screen that asks us to name the security group and provide a description. The name must have no spaces:

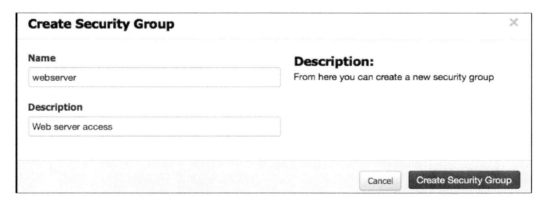

4. Once a new security group is created, the list of available security groups will appear on screen.

Editing security groups to add and remove rules

To add and remove rules, security groups can be edited by performing the following steps:

1. When we have created a new security group, or wish to modify the rules in an existing security group, we can click on the **Edit Rules** button for that particular security group:

2. We will then be asked to provide the rule information. As an example, we will add in a security group rule that allows HTTP and HTTPS access from anywhere. To do this, we choose the following:

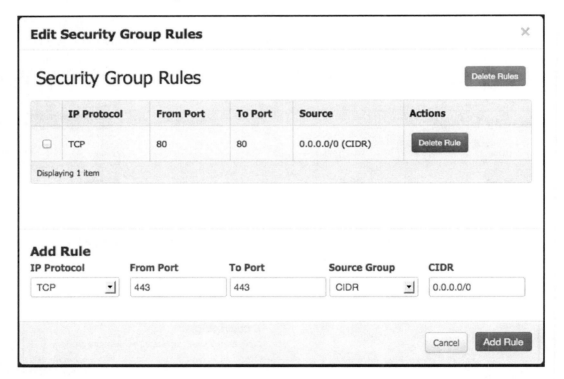

 Each time you add a rule, you will be sent back to the **Security Group** listing. Simply click on the **Edit Rules** button for the **webserver** group to add it again in both HTTP and HTTPS access.

3. Note that we can remove rules from here too. Simply select the rule that we no longer require and click on the **Delete Rule** button. We will be asked to confirm this removal.

Deleting security groups

Security groups can be deleted by performing the following steps:

1. Security groups are deleted by selecting the security group that we want to remove and clicking on the **Delete Security Groups** button:

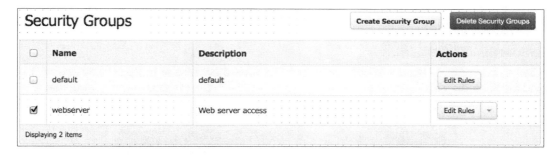

2. You will be asked to confirm this. Clicking on **OK**, removes the security group and associated access rules.

 You will not be able to remove a security group whilst an instance with that assigned security group is running.

How it works...

Security groups are important to our OpenStack environment, as they provide a consistent and secure approach for accessing our running instances. By allowing the users to create, delete, and amend security groups to use within their tenants allows them to create secure environments.

Security groups are associated with instances on creation, so we can't add a new security group to a running instance. We can, however, modify the rules assigned to a running instance. For example, suppose an instance was launched with only the Default security group. The default security group which we have set up, only has TCP port 22 and ability to ping the instance. If we require access to TCP port 80, we either have to add this rule to the default security group or relaunch the instance with a new security assigned to it, to allow TCP port 80.

 Modifications to security groups come into effect immediately, and any instance assigned with that security group will have those new rules associated with it.

Launching instances by using OpenStack Dashboard

Launching instances becomes a simple process, using OpenStack Dashboard. We simply select our chosen image, choose the size of the instance, and then launch it.

Getting ready

Load a web browser, point it to our OpenStack Dashboard address at `http://172.16.0.1/`, and log in as the `demo` user with the password `openstack` (as created in the *Adding users* recipe in *Chapter 3, Keystone OpenStack Identity Service*):

How to do it...

To launch an instance by using the OpenStack Dashboard interface, carry out the following steps:

1. Navigate to the **Images & Snapshots** tab and select an appropriate image to launch, for example, the **Ubuntu 12.04 i386 Server** image:

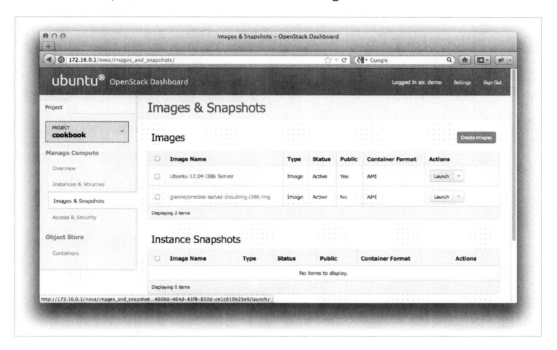

2. Click on the **Launch** button under the **Actions** column of the image to be launched.

3. A dialog box will appear requesting a name for the instance (for example, **horizon1**). Choose an instance type of **m1.tiny**. Select **demo** from the **Keypair** drop-down list. Then, check the **default** checkbox under **Security Groups**:

4. Once selected, we can click on the **Launch Instance** button.

5. We will be returned to the **Instances & Volumes** tab that shows the instance in a **Build** state, which will eventually change to **Active**:

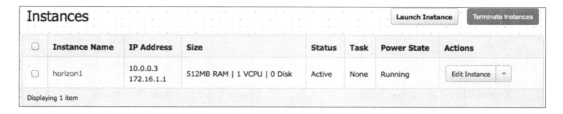

[If the display hasn't refreshed, click on the **Images & Volumes** tab to refresh the information manually.]

How it works...

Launching instances from Horizon—OpenStack Dashboard—is done in two stages:

1. Selecting the appropriate image from the **Images** tab.
2. Choosing the appropriate values to assign to the instance.

The **Instances** tab shows the running instances under our **cookbook** project.

[You can also see an overview of what is running in our environment by clicking on the **Overview** tab.]

Terminating instances by using OpenStack Dashboard

Terminating instances is very simple when using OpenStack Dashboard.

Getting ready

Load a web browser, point it to our OpenStack Dashboard address at `http://172.16.0.1/`, and log in as the `demo` user with the password `openstack`.

How to do it...

To terminate instances by using OpenStack Dashboard, carry out the following steps:

1. Select the **Instances & Volumes** tab and choose the instance to be terminated:

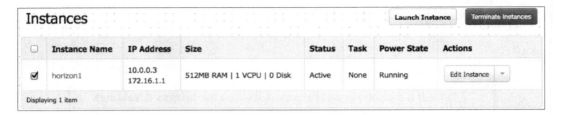

2. We will be presented with a confirmation screen. Click on **OK** to terminate the selected instance:

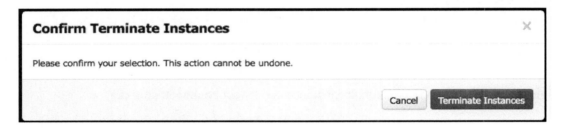

3. We will be presented with the **Instances & Volumes** screen with a confirmation that the instance has been terminated successfully.

How it works...

Terminating instances by using OpenStack Dashboard is easy. We simply select our running instance and click on the **Terminate Instances** button, which is highlighted when an instance is selected. After clicking on the **Terminate Instances** button, we will be asked to confirm this action to minimize the risk of accidentally terminating an instance.

Connecting to instances by using OpenStack Dashboard and VNC

OpenStack Dashboard has a very handy feature that allows a user to connect to our running instances through a VNC session within our web browser. This gives us the ability to manage our instance without invoking an SSH session separately.

Getting ready

Load up a web browser, point it to our OpenStack Dashboard address at `http://172.16.0.1/`, and log in as the `demo` user with the password `openstack`.

How to do it...

To connect to a running instance by using VNC through the web browser, carry out the following steps:

1. Select the **Instances & Volumes** tab and choose an instance to which we want to connect.

2. Next to the **Edit Instance** button is a down arrow, which reveals more options. Click on it:

3. Select the **VNC Console** option. This will take you to a console screen, which will allow you to log in to your instance:

Instance Detail: horizon1

Overview   Log   **VNC**

Instance VNC Console

If VNC console is not responding to keyboard input: click the grey status bar below.

Connected (unencrypted) to: QEMU (instance-0000000d)   Send CtrlAltDel

```
Ubuntu 12.04 LTS horizon1 tty1

horizon1 login: _
```

 Your instance must support local logins. Many Linux cloud images expect a user to authenticate by using SSH Keys.

How it works...

Connecting through our web browser uses a VNC proxy session, which was configured by using the nonce, nova-consoleauth, and nova-console packages, as described in the installation section. Only browsers that support WebSocket connections are supported. Generally, this can be any modern browser with HTML5 support.

Adding new tenants by using OpenStack Dashboard

OpenStack Dashboard is a lot more than just an interface to our instances. It allows an administrator to configure environments, users, and tenants.

Adding new tenants (projects) that users can be members of is achieved quite simply in OpenStack Dashboard. For a VLAN-managed environment, it also involves assigning an appropriate private network to that new tenant by using the console. To do this, we must log in to OpenStack Dashboard as a user with admin privileges and also log in to Shell on our OpenStack Controller API server.

Getting ready

Load a web browser, point it to our OpenStack Dashboard address at http://172.16.0.1/, and log in as the admin user with the password openstack. Log in to the same box, over SSH, where we can run the nova-manage command.

How to do it...

To add a new tenant to our OpenStack environment, carry out the following steps:

1. When we log in as a user with admin privileges, an extra tab called **Admin** appears. Clicking on this tab shows the **System Panel** options. This tab allows us to configure our OpenStack environment:

2. To manage tenants, click on the **Projects** option listed under **System Panel**:

3. Then we will be presented with a list of tenants in our OpenStack environment. To create a new tenant, click on the **Create New Project** button.

4. We will then be presented with a form that asks for the name of the tenant and a description. Enter `horizon` as our tenant, and enter a description:

5. Ensure that the tenant is enabled by placing a tick in the **Enabled** checkbox, and then click on the **Create Project** button.

6. We will be presented with the list of tenants that are now available and a message saying that the `horizon` tenant was created successfully and asking us to make a note of the new **Tenant ID**.

Only for a VLAN-managed network

If our OpenStack environment has been set up by using VlanManager in /etc/nova/nova.conf (the default when nothing is specified), run the following command in Shell on our OpenStack Controller API server:

```
sudo nova-manage network create --label=horizon
--num_networks=1 --network_size=64 --vlan=101
--bridge_interface=eth2 --project_id=900dae01996
343fb946b42a3c13a4140 --fixed_range_v4=10.2.0.0/8
```

This creates an IP range on a specific VLAN that we have associated with our horizon tenant. Once successful, our new tenant is available to use.

How it works...

OpenStack Dashboard is a feature-rich interface that complements the command-line options available to you when managing our OpenStack environment. This means we can simply create a tenant (Ubuntu's interface refers to this as a project) which users can belong to, within OpenStack Dashboard.

When creating new tenants under a VlanManager-configured OpenStack network, we assign an IP address range and specific VLAN ID to this tenant. If we assign a new VLAN, ensure you configure your switches accordingly, so that the private network can communicate by using this new VLAN ID. Note that we use the following parameters with the nova-manage command when configuring a network to match our new tenant:

- ▸ --label=horizon
- ▸ --vlan=101
- ▸ --project_id=900dae01996343fb946b42a3c13a4140

What we have done is name this private network appropriately, matching our tenancy. We have created a new VLAN so that traffic is encapsulated in a new VLAN, separating this traffic from other tenants. We finally specified the ID of the tenancy that was returned when we created the tenant through OpenStack Dashboard.

User management by using OpenStack Dashboard

OpenStack Dashboard gives us the ability to conduct user management through the web interface. This allows an administrator to easily create and amend users within an OpenStack environment. To manage users, you must log in as a user that is a member of the admin role.

Getting ready

Load a web browser, point it to our OpenStack Dashboard address at `http://172.16.0.1/`, and log in as the `admin` user with the password `openstack`.

How to do it...

User management under OpenStack Dashboard is achieved by carrying out the steps discussed in the following sections.

Adding Users

To add users, perform the following steps:

1. Under **Admin System Panel**, click on the **Users** option to bring back a list of users on the system:

	ID	User Name	Email	Enabled	Actions
☐	026c9ab70adb4c51adc173354bbe56d4	admin	root@localhost	True	Edit ▾
☐	028c189ca12347a493de6399596672f5	nova	nova@localhost	True	Edit ▾
☐	869d38e9eeb743c0a3c5ddd99d4f1d71	swift	swift@localhost	True	Edit ▾
☐	942f855bfd6f4a0b8ef45529260261eb	glance	glance@localhost	True	Edit ▾
☐	bd2b79cdb85443749041c2bf63b8fdf9	demo	demo@localhost	True	Edit ▾
☐	e6d3d754959c4bfb9b2feb53467aa1d5	keystone	keystone@localhost	True	Edit ▾

Displaying 6 items

2. To create a new user, select the **Create User** button.

3. We will be presented with a form that asks for username details. Enter the name of a user, the e-mail address of that user, and the password for that user. In the example shown in the following screenshot, we create a user named `test`, set `openstack` as the password, and assign that user to the `horizon` tenant:

4. We will then be returned to the list of users that are part of our OpenStack environment. Then we will see a message saying that the user was created successfully.

Deleting users

To delete users, perform the following steps:

1. Under **Admin System Panel**, click on the **Users** option to bring back a list of users on the system.

2. We will be presented with a list of users in our OpenStack cloud setup. Next to the **Edit** button for the user that we want to remove, you can find a drop-down menu. Select this to reveal an option called **Delete User**:

3. Selecting this brings up a confirmation dialog box. Clicking on the **Delete User** button will remove the user from the system:

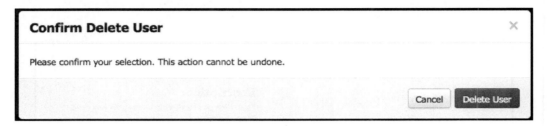

Updating user details and passwords

To update user details and passwords, perform the following steps:

1. Under **Admin System Panel**, click on the **Users** option to bring back a list of users on the system.

2. To change a user's password, e-mail address, or primary project (tenant) click on the **Edit** button for that user.

3. This brings up a dialog box asking for the relevant information. When the information is filled up, click on the **Update User** button:

Adding users to tenants

To add users to tenants, perform the following steps:

1. Under **Admin System Panel**, click on the **Projects** option to bring back a list of tenants on the system:

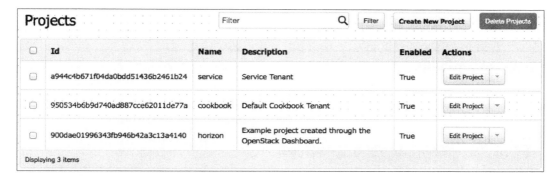

2. To add a user to a tenant, for example `horizon`, click on the drop-down list next to the **Edit Project** button to reveal further options:

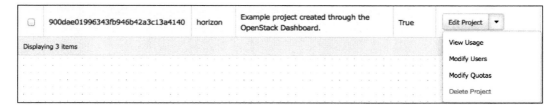

3. Click on the **Modify Users** option to bring up a list of users associated with a tenant as well as a list of users we can add to that tenant:

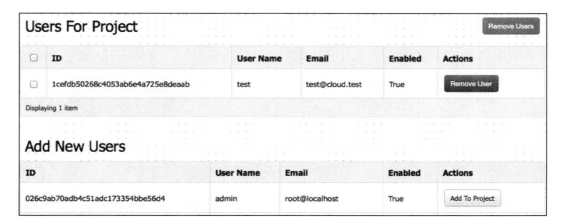

4. To add a new user to the list, simply click on the **Add To Project** button for that user:

bd2b79cdb85443749041c2bf63b8fdf9	demo	demo@localhost	True	Add To Project

5. We will then be asked to assign the role to that user in this tenant. Once the role is selected, simply click on the **Add** button:

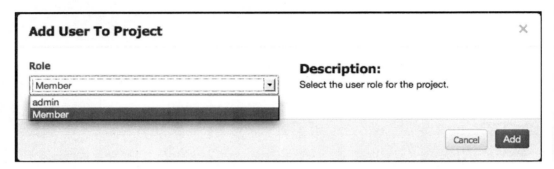

6. Then, we will be presented with a success message saying that our new user has been added to the `horizon` tenant. This user can now launch instances in different tenants when he/she logs in.

Removing users from tenants

To remove users from tenants, perform the following steps:

1. Under **Admin System Panel**, click on the **Projects** option to bring back a list of tenants on the system.

2. To remove a user from a tenant, for example `horizon`, click on the drop-down list next to the **Edit Project** button, to reveal further options.

3. Click on the **Modify Users** option to bring up a list of users associated with a tenant as well as a list of users we can add to that tenant:

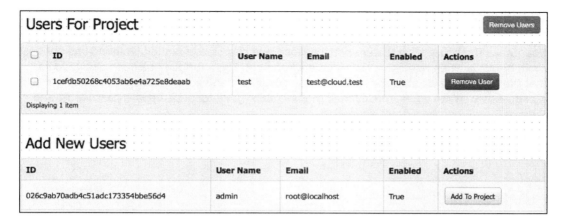

4. To remove a user from this tenant, click on the **Remove User** button for that particular user:

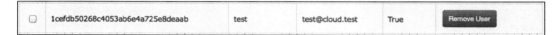

5. This brings back a dialog box that asks us to confirm our action. Clicking on the **Remove User** button removes that user from the tenant:

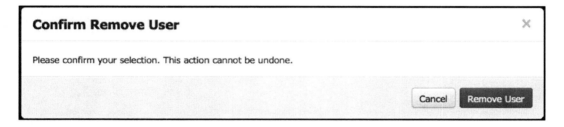

How it works...

OpenStack Dashboard is a feature-rich interface that complements the command-line options available to us when managing our cloud environment. The interface has been designed so that the functions available are as intuitive as possible to the administrator. This means that we can easily create users, modify their membership within tenants, update passwords, and remove them from the system altogether.

OpenStack Networking 10

In this chapter, we will cover:

- ▸ Configuring Flat networking
- ▸ Configuring Flat networking with DHCP
- ▸ Configuring VLAN Manager networking
- ▸ Configuring per-project (tenant) IP ranges
- ▸ Automatically assigning fixed networks to tenants
- ▸ Modifying a tenant's fixed network
- ▸ Manually associating floating IPs to instances
- ▸ Manually disassociating floating IPs from instances
- ▸ Automatically assigning floating IPs

Introduction

OpenStack supports three modes of networking in the current Essex release. These are Flat networking, Flat networking with DHCP, and VLAN Manager. The latter, VLAN Manager, is the default in OpenStack and allows for a multi-tenant environment where each of those separate tenants is assigned an IP address range and VLAN tag that ensures project separation. In the Flat networking modes, isolation between tenants is done at the Security Group level. In all of the available modes, OpenStack presents two networks associated with an instance: a private address range and a public address range. The private address, also referred to as the fixed IP address, is the address an instance gets assigned for the lifetime of that instance. The public address, also referred to as the floating IP address, is an address an instance gets that makes that instance available to the public, (or in many private cloud installations, routed to the rest of your network). This public (floating) address can be associated with or disassociated from an instance at any time, meaning that you can assign any particular IP on your public (floating) range to any instance. **Network Address Translation** (**NAT**) handles the communication flow of traffic to and from the instances, as it traverses the public and private network spaces.

Configuring Flat networking

In Flat networking, the IP addresses for our instances are injected from a defined subnet of IP addresses at launch. To make this work, a network bridge is configured the same on each compute and network host in our cloud environment.

 Only Linux distributions that keep their network information under /etc/network/interfaces support Flat networking.

Getting ready

To begin with, ensure you're logged into the OpenStack API server.

If using the openstack1 host created in *Chapter 1, Starting OpenStack Compute,* we will have three interfaces in our virtual instance:

 ▶ eth0 is a NAT to the host running VirtualBox

 ▶ eth1 is our floating (public) network (172.16.0.0/16)

 ▶ eth2 is our fixed (private) network (10.0.0.0/8)

In a physical production environment, that first interface wouldn't be present and references to this NATed eth0 in the following section can be ignored.

How to do it...

To configure our OpenStack environment to use Flat networking, carry out the following steps:

1. OpenStack requires bridging in order for any of the network modes to work. The bridge tools are installed as dependencies when installing the OpenStack nova-network package, but if they aren't installed you can issue the following commands:

    ```
    sudo apt-get update
    sudo apt-get -y install bridge-utils
    ```

2. We first need to configure our network bridge (br100) by editing /etc/network/interfaces, as follows:

    ```
    # The primary network interface
    auto eth0
    iface eth0 inet dhcp

    # eth1 public
    auto eth1
    ```

```
iface eth1 inet static
        address 172.16.0.1
        netmask 255.255.0.0
        network 172.16.0.0
        broadcast 172.16.255.255

# eth2 private
auto br100
iface br100 inet manual
        bridge_ports eth2
        bridge_stp   off
        bridge_maxwait 0
        bridge_fd       0
        up ifconfig eth2 up
```

3. We then restart our network service to pick up the changes, as follows:

   ```
   sudo /etc/init.d/networking restart
   ```

4. We now configure OpenStack Compute to use the new bridged interface as part of our flat network. Add the following lines to /etc/nova/nova.conf:

   ```
   --network_manager=nova.network.manager.FlatManager
   --flat_network_bridge=br100
   --flat_interface=eth2
   --public_interface=eth1
   ```

5. Restart the required OpenStack Compute services to pick up the changes:

   ```
   sudo restart nova-compute
   sudo restart nova-network
   ```

6. We now create a private (fixed) network that OpenStack Compute can use, as follows:

   ```
   sudo nova-manage network create
       --fixed_range_v4=10.0.1.0/24 --label flat
       --bridge br100
   ```

7. With this in place, we now have a bridge from our eth2 interface and our internal network assigned to our instances. To ensure this works in a multi-network device host, run the following command to enable IP forwarding:

   ```
   sudo sysctl -w net.ipv4.ip_forward=1
   ```

8. We can now create our *floating* public range, which we will use to connect to our running instances, as follows:

   ```
   sudo nova-manage floating create --ip_range=172.16.1.0/24
   ```

9. When an instance spawns now, an address is injected from our address space into our instance. We can then access this, as before, by assigning a public floating IP to this instance, which associates this IP address with our instance's private IP address.

How it works...

`FlatManager` networking is useful for small proof-of-concept environments. They only work for Linux systems that support networking set in `/etc/network/interfaces` and are limited to a single network and project.

In order to make `FlatManager` work, we must manually configure our hosts with the same bridging, which is set to `br100`, as specified in `/etc/nova/nova.conf`:

```
--flat_network_bridge=br100
```

When our instance spawns, it will be given an address in the range that we have specified: 10.0.1.0 - 10.0.1.254, which we specified with the following command:

```
nova-manage network create --fixed_range_v4=ip_range --label label
    --bridge bridge
```

Note that we also don't assign an IP address to the interface that acts as our bridge—in our case, `eth2`.

Configuring Flat networking with DHCP

In Flat networking with DHCP, the IP addresses for our instances are assigned from a running DHCP service on the OpenStack Compute host. This service is provided by `dnsmasq`. As with Flat networking, a bridge must be configured manually in order for this to function.

Getting ready

To begin with, ensure you're logged in to the OpenStack API server.

If using the `openstack1` host created in *Chapter 1, Starting OpenStack Compute*, we will have three interfaces in our virtual instance:

- `eth0` is a NAT to the host running VirtualBox
- `eth1` is our floating (public) network (`172.16.0.0/16`)
- `eth2` is our fixed (private) network (`10.0.0.0/8`)

In a physical production environment, that first interface wouldn't be present, and references to this NATed `eth0` in the following section can be ignored.

How to do it...

To configure our OpenStack environment to use Flat networking with DHCP, carry out the following steps:

1. OpenStack requires bridging in order for any of the network modes to work. The bridge tools are installed as dependencies when installing the OpenStack `nova-network` package, but if they aren't installed you can issue the following commands:

   ```
   sudo apt-get update
   sudo apt-get -y install bridge-utils
   ```

2. We first need to configure our network bridge (`br100`) by editing `/etc/network/interfaces`, as follows:

   ```
   # The primary network interface

   auto eth0
   iface eth0 inet dhcp
   # eth1 public
   auto eth1
   iface eth1 inet static
           address 172.16.0.1
           netmask 255.255.0.0
           network 172.16.0.0
           broadcast 172.16.255.255

   # eth2 private
   auto br100
   iface br100 inet manual
           bridge_ports eth2
           bridge_stp    off
           bridge_maxwait 0
           bridge_fd      0
           up ifconfig eth2 up
   ```

3. We then restart our network service to pick up the changes, as follows:

   ```
   sudo /etc/init.d/networking restart
   ```

4. We now configure OpenStack Compute to use the new bridged interface as part of our flat network. Add the following lines to `/etc/nova/nova.conf`:

   ```
   -dhcpbridge_flagfile=/etc/nova/nova.conf
   --dhcpbridge=/usr/bin/nova-dhcpbridge
   --network_manager=nova.network.manager.FlatDHCPManager
   --flat_network_dhcp_start=10.0.1.2
   --flat_network_bridge=br100
   --flat_interface=eth2
   --flat_injected=False
   --public_interface=eth1
   ```

5. Restart the required OpenStack Compute services, to pick up the changes:

```
sudo restart nova-compute
sudo restart nova-network
```

6. In order to separate private ranges per project (tenant), we get the ID of our tenant, that we will use when creating the network. On a client machine with the keystone client installed, run the following command:

```
keystone tenant-list
```

7. We now create a private (fixed) network—that OpenStack Compute can use—for that particular tenant, as follows:

```
sudo nova-manage network create
    --fixed_range_v4=10.0.1.0/24
    --label cookbook --bridge br100
    --project 950534b6b9d740ad887cce62011de77a
```

8. We can now create our *floating* public range that we will use to connect to our running instances. We do this as follows:

```
sudo nova-manage floating create --ip_range=172.16.1.0/24
```

9. With this in place, we now have a bridge from our eth2 network and our internal network assigned to our instances. To ensure this works in a multi-network device host, run the following command to enable IP forwarding:

```
sudo sysctl -w net.ipv4.ip_forward=1
```

10. When an instance spawns now, a private address is injected from our fixed address range into our instance. We then access this as before, by assigning a public floating IP to this instance, which associates this floating IP address with our instance's fixed IP address.

How it works...

FlatDHCPManager networking is a common option for networking, as it provides a flat network that is only limited by the IP address range assigned. It doesn't require a Linux operating system and the /etc/network/interfaces file in order to operate correctly through the use of standard DHCP for assigning addresses.

In order to make FlatDHCPManager work, we manually configure our hosts with the same bridging, which is set to br100, as specified in /etc/nova/nova.conf:

```
--flat_network_bridge=br100
```

Once set up, we configure our network range, where we can specify in our /etc/nova/ nova.conf configuration file the start of this range that our instances get when they start:

```
--flat_network_dhcp_start=10.0.1.2
```

When creating the fixed (private) range using `nova-manage network create`, we assign this fixed range to a particular tenant (project). This allows us to have specific IP ranges that are isolated from different projects in a multi-tenant environment.

When our instance boots up, our `dnsmasq` service that is running on our `nova-network` host assigns an address from its `dhcp` pool to the instance.

Also note that we don't assign an IP address to the interface that we connect to our bridge, in our case `eth2`. We simply bring this interface up so we can bridge to it (and therefore forward traffic to the instance interfaces that are bridged to it).

Configuring VLAN Manager networking

VLAN Manager networking is the default networking mode in OpenStack. When VLAN mode is configured, each project (or tenancy) has its own VLAN and network assigned to it. Any intermediary physical switches must however support 802.1q VLAN tagging, for this to operate.

 Virtual switches in our sandbox environment support VLAN tagging.

Getting ready

To begin with, ensure you're logged in to the OpenStack API server.

If using the `openstack1` host created in *Chapter 1, Starting OpenStack Compute*, we will have three interfaces in our virtual instance:

- `eth0` is a NAT to the host running VirtualBox
- `eth1` is our floating (public) network (`172.16.0.0/16`)
- `eth2` is our fixed (private) network (`10.0.0.0/8`)

In a physical production environment, that first interface wouldn't be present, and references to this NATed `eth0` in the following section can be ignored.

How to do it...

1. OpenStack requires bridging in order for any of the network modes to work. The bridge tools are installed as dependencies when installing the OpenStack `nova-network` package, but if they aren't installed you can issue the following commands. As we are also configuring VLANs, the required package to support VLANs must also be installed:

```
sudo apt-get update
sudo apt-get -y install bridge-utils vlan
```

2. The networking on our host is as follows:

```
# The primary network interface
auto eth0
iface eth0 inet dhcp

# eth1 public
auto eth1
iface eth1 inet static
        address 172.16.0.1
        netmask 255.255.0.0
        network 172.16.0.0
        broadcast 172.16.255.255


# eth2 private
auto eth2
iface eth2 inet manual
        up ifconfig eth2 up
```

3. We then restart our network service to pick up the changes, as follows:

```
sudo /etc/init.d/networking restart
```

4. By default, if we don't specify a Network Manager in our `/etc/nova/nova.conf` file, OpenStack Compute defaults to VLAN networking. To explicitly state this, so there are no ambiguities, we put the following in `/etc/nova/nova.conf` specifying our VLAN details:

```
--network_manager=nova.network.manager.VlanManager
--vlan_start=100
--vlan_interface=eth2
--public_interface=eth1
--dhcpbridge_flagfile=/etc/nova/nova.conf
--dhcpbridge=/usr/bin/nova-dhcpbridge
```

5. Restart the required OpenStack Compute services, to pick up the changes:

```
sudo restart nova-compute
sudo restart nova-network
```

6. In order to separate private ranges per project (tenant), we get the ID of our tenant that we will use when creating the network. On a client machine with the `keystone` client installed, run the following command:

```
. keystonerc
keystone project-list
```

7. We now create a private network that OpenStack can use, which we are assigning to a project, as follows:

```
sudo nova-manage network create
    --fixed_range_v4=10.0.3.0/24
    --label cookbook --vlan=100
    --project 950534b6b9d740ad887cce62011de77a
```

8. Once created, we can configure our public network address space, which we will use to connect to our instances:

```
sudo nova-manage floating create --ip_range=172.16.1.0/24
```

9. When we launch an instance now, the private address is assigned to the VLAN interface. We can assign floating IP addresses to this instance, and they get forwarded to the instance's internal private IP address.

How it works...

VLAN Manager networking is the default and, for a private cloud environment in networks accustomed to VLANs, this option is the most flexible. It allows for per-project and secure networking by using VLANs. If you do not have a `--network_manager` flag in your `/etc/nova/nova.conf` file, OpenStack Compute will default to `VlanManager`.

Creating the network is no different in any of the managers; in this instance, with `VlanManager`, the private network is assigned to a VLAN that is specified in the `--vlan=100` option. We then associate this network and VLAN with our `cookbook` project, by specifying the ID of that tenant, using the `--project` option.

On our OpenStack Compute host, this creates an interface named `vlan100`, which is the tagged interface to `eth2`, as specified in `--vlan_interface` from `/etc/nova/nova.conf`.

Configuring per-project (tenant) IP ranges

Projects in Nova are a way of keeping user's cloud resources separate. In a project, there are a number of images, instances, and its own network resources assigned to it. When we create a project, we assign it its own VLAN with its own private and public ranges. For example, we may wish to create a development tenancy that is separate from the performance testing tenancy and live tenancies.

Getting ready

To begin with, ensure you're logged in to the OpenStack API server (our OpenStack VirtualBox Virtual Machine, `openstack1`, created in *Chapter 1*, *Starting OpenStack Compute*).

How to do it...

In order to configure per-project (tenant) IP ranges, carry out the following steps:

1. First, on our `keystone` client, list the current projects, as follows:

```
# Use the admin token
export ENDPOINT=172.16.0.1
export SERVICE_TOKEN=ADMIN
export SERVICE_ENDPOINT=http://${ENDPOINT}:35357/v2.0
keystone tenant-list
```

This returns a list of projects in our example.

2. Now, let's create another project named `development`; the project user will be `demo`. We do this as follows:

```
keystone tenant-create --name=development
```

An example of running the previous command is shown as follows:

```
+-------------+------------------------------------+
|  Property   |               Value                |
+-------------+------------------------------------+
| description | None                               |
| enabled     | True                               |
| id          | bfe40200d6ee413aa8062891a8270edb   |
| name        | development                        |
+-------------+------------------------------------+
```

3. This will return a project ID. Now let's create a fixed IP range for this project. We will create a fixed range of `10.0.4.0/24`. To allocate this to our project, along with a new VLAN ID associated with this network, enter the following command:

```
sudo nova-manage network create
    --label=development --fixed_range_v4=10.0.4.0/24
    --project_id=bfe40200d6ee413aa8062891a8270edb
    --vlan=101
```

How it works...

Creating IP address ranges for projects is done as part of creating new projects (tenants). We first create the project, which returns an ID that we use when creating that network, using the following syntax:

```
sudo nova-manage network create --label=project_name
    --fixed_range_v4=ip_range --bridge_interface=interface
    --project_id=id --vlan=vlan_id
```

Automatically assigning fixed networks to tenants

When using `VlanManager` to separate tenants, we can manually assign VLANs and network ranges to them by creating a secure multi-tenant environment. We can, however, have OpenStack manage this association for us, so that when we create a project it automatically gets assigned these details.

Getting ready

To begin with, ensure you are logged in to the OpenStack API server as well as a client that can access the `keystone` environment.

How to do it...

1. Carry out the following steps to configure networking in OpenStack to automatically assign new tenants' individual VLANs and private (fixed) IP in the file `/etc/nova/nova.conf`, and ensure there is a flag called `--vlan_start` with a VLAN ID, for example:

   ```
   --vlan_start=100
   ```

2. We can now create a range of networks, each with 256 addresses available, by issuing the following command:

   ```
   sudo nova-manage network create
       --num_networks=10 --network_size=256
       --fixed_range_v4=10.0.0.0/8 --label=auto
   ```

3. This creates 10 networks, with 256 IP addresses starting from 10.0.0.0/24 to 10.0.9.0/24 and starting from VLAN ID `100` to VLAN ID `110`.

> You can specify an alternative VLAN start ID on the command line by adding in the `--vlan=id` option, where `id` is a number.

How it works...

By specifying the `--num_networks` option and specifying the `--network_size` option (the number of IPs in each of the created networks), we can tell our OpenStack environment to create multiple networks within the range specified by `--fixed_range_v4`. When projects are created now, rather than having to manually associate an address range with a tenant, they are automatically assigned a VLAN, starting from the `--vlan_start` ID, as specified in `/etc/nova/nova.conf`.

Modifying a tenant's fixed network

To ensure that our OpenStack environment is able to separate traffic from one tenant to another, we assign different fixed ranges to each. When a fixed network is no longer required, or we want to assign a particular tenant to a specific network, we can use the `nova-manage` command to modify these details.

Getting ready

To begin with, ensure you're logged in to the OpenStack API server as well as to a client that can access the `keystone` environment.

How to do it...

To assign a particular network to a tenant, carry out the following steps:

1. On a client that has access to the `keystone` command, run the following commands to list the projects available:

```
# Use the admin token
export ENDPOINT=172.16.0.1
export SERVICE_TOKEN=ADMIN
export SERVICE_ENDPOINT=http://${ENDPOINT}:35357/v2.0
keystone tenant-list
```

An example of running the previous commands is as follows:

```
+----------------------------------+-------------+---------+
|                id                |    name     | enabled |
+----------------------------------+-------------+---------+
| 900dae01996343fb946b42a3c13a4140 | horizon     | True    |
| 950534b6b9d740ad887cce62011de77a | cookbook    | True    |
| a944c4b671f04da0bdd51436b2461b24 | service     | True    |
| bfe40200d6ee413aa8062891a8270edb | development | True    |
| fd5a85c21c244144aa961658f659b020 | another     | True    |
+----------------------------------+-------------+---------+
```

2. To view the list of networks and ranges available, issue the following command on an OpenStack API host:

```
sudo nova-manage network list
```

An example of running the previous commands is as follows:

```
id      IPv4                   IPv6              start address  DNS1           DNS2               VlanID
        project        uuid
1       10.0.0.0/24            None              10.0.0.3       None           None               100
        950534b6b9d740ad887cce62011de77a        3eB035e3-73df-477d-9368-30bffa7d459b
2       10.0.1.0/24            None              10.0.1.3       None           None               101
        900dae01996343fb946b42a3c13a4140        ba168358-2865-40a1-b226-c82ba754a1c3
3       10.0.2.0/24            None              10.0.2.3       None           None               102
        fd5a85c21c244144aa961658f659b020        9455a709-2681-47ae-9508-f606382a7737
4       10.0.3.0/24            None              10.0.3.3       None           None               103
        None           695cc325-bfba-48e6-8bec-122ec3a21177
```

3. The output shown lists network ranges and their associated project IDs. From this, we can see we have 10.0.3.0/24 not assigned to a project (where it says **None** under the project column). To assign this network range to the `development` tenant, we issue the following commands:

   ```
   sudo nova-manage network modify
        --project=bfe40200d6ee413aa8062891a8270edb
        --fixed_range=10.0.3.0/24
   ```

4. When we view the output now for that network range, we will have this project ID assigned to it and any instances spawned under this tenant will be assigned an address in this range.

How it works...

When configuring tenants in our OpenStack environment, it is recommended (although not a requirement) to have their own private (fixed) range assigned to them. This allows for those instances in a particular tenant to be kept separated through their different ranges along with appropriately set security group rules.

The syntax to modify a network is as follows:

```
nova-manage network modify --project=project_id
     --fixed_range=ip_range
```

Manually associating floating IPs to instances

When an instance boots, it is assigned a private IP address. This IP range is only accessible within our virtual environment's network. To access this instance to serve the rest of the network or the public, we need to assign it a floating IP, which is the range we configure when we set up public IP ranges.

There are two ways to allocate floating IPs to instances: either automatically, as the instance is spawned, or manually through our client tools. In both cases, our tenancy must have a range of floating IPs assigned to it so they can be allocated.

Getting ready

While on the OpenStack API host, for example, `openstack1`, run the following command to list any floating ranges we have assigned:

```
sudo nova-manage floating list
```

This should list the IP range we originally set up when we first installed our `openstack1` server.

```
None   172.16.1.1   None   nova   eth1
None  172.16.1.2   None   nova   eth1
...
```

To allocate a floating IP to an instance, ensure you're logged in to a client that is running euca2ools or Nova Client.

How to do it...

To assign a floating (public) IP address to an instance using euca2ools, carry out the following steps:

1. To allocate one of the floating IP addresses available to our project, we run the following command:

    ```
    euca-allocate-address
    ```

2. An address will appear from the pool of IPs we have available, for example, `172.16.1.1`.

3. To associate this address to an instance, we issue the following commands:

    ```
    euca-associate-address -i i-00000002 172.16.1.1
    ```

4. We are now able to communicate with that instance using this assigned floating IP address.

To assign a floating (public) IP address to an instance using Nova Client, carry out the following steps:

1. To allocate one of the floating IP addresses available to our project, we run the following command:

    ```
    nova floating-ip-create
    ```

2. An address will appear from the pool of IPs we have available, for example `172.16.1.1`.

3. To associate this address to an instance, we issue the following command:

```
nova add-floating-ip 6c79552c-7006-4b74-a037-ebe9707cc9ce
    172.16.1.1
```

We are now able to communicate with that instance using this assigned floating IP address.

How it works...

Instances are not instantly accessible outside of the OpenStack host unless a public IP address is attached to it. Manually associating an address consists of the following two steps:

1. Allocating an address from the available IP range.
2. Associating the address with an instance.

This is an important concept, as it allows you to control the allocation of IP addresses as well as allocating specific addresses to specific instances, which is very much like Amazon's Elastic IP feature.

Manually disassociating floating IPs from instances

In our cloud environment, we have the ability to add and remove access to and from the instance publicly by adding or removing a floating IP address to or from it. This flexibility allows us to move services seamlessly between instances. To the outside world it would appear to be the same instance, as their access to it via that IP has not changed to them.

Getting ready

To begin with, ensure you are logged in to a client machine running euca2ools or Nova Client.

How to do it...

To disassociate a public (floating) address from an instance using euca2ools, carry out the following steps:

1. We first list the instances in our environment, to identify the instance we wish to remove the public IP address from, as follows:

   ```
   euca-describe-instances
   ```

2. Once we have identified the instance we wish to disassociate the IP from, we execute the following command:

   ```
   euca-disassociate-address 172.16.1.1
   ```

3. This instantly removes the association between this address and the instance.

 If we no longer require that floating IP address for our project, we can remove it from our project's pool by issuing the following command: `euca-release-address 172.16.1.1`.

To disassociate a public (floating) address from an instance using **Nova Client**, carry out the following:

1. We first list the instance in our environment, to identify the instance we wish to remove the public IP address from, as follows:

```
nova list
```

2. Once we have identified the instance we wish to disassociate the IP from, we execute the following command:

```
nova remove-floating-ip 2abf8d8d-6f45-42a5-9f9f-
    63b6a956b74f 172.16.1.1
```

3. This instantly removes the association with this address from the instance.

 If we no longer require that floating IP address for our project, we can remove it from our project's pool by issuing the following command: `nova floating-ip-delete 172.16.1.1`

How it works...

Removing a floating IP address is very straightforward. When using euca2ools, we use the `euca-disassociate-address` command or, when using Nova Client, we use the `remove-floating-ip` option to the `nova` command.

Automatically assigning floating IPs

When an instance boots, it is assigned a private IP address. This private IP address is only accessible within our virtual environment's network. To access this instance to serve the rest of the network or the public, we need to assign it a floating IP, which is the range we configure when we set up public IP ranges.

Automatically assigning floating IPs to instances gives us the ability, in our environment, to have access to all instances on our network. Although there are times when we might want to manually assign addresses (for example, where we have a limited number of IPs assigned to a tenancy), the convenience of having this done for you is very beneficial and makes our OpenStack environment operate much closer to how Amazon EC2 operates.

Getting ready

To begin with, ensure you are logged in to the OpenStack API server. We will also be using the client machine, so log in to your client that is running euca2ools or Nova Client.

How to do it...

To ensure each of the instances gets a public (floating) IP address assigned to it when it is launched, carry out the following steps:

1. While on our OpenStack API host, run the following command to list any floating ranges we have assigned:

   ```
   sudo nova-manage floating list
   ```

   An example of the output when listing the floating IPs is shown as follows, truncated for brevity:

   ```
   None  172.16.1.1  None  nova  eth1
   None  172.16.1.2  None  nova  eth1
   ...
   ```

2. The values indicate we have a floating range available for use. Rather than using client tools to assign addresses to instances, a flag in our /etc/nova/nova.conf file ensures our instances are always allocated an address:

   ```
   --auto_assign_floating_ip
   ```

3. With this added to our nova.conf configuration file, we restart our nova-network and nova-compute services, to pick up the change:

   ```
   sudo restart nova-network
   sudo restart nova-network
   ```

4. When an instance spawns, it will automatically be assigned a public floating IP address that we can instantly use to gain access.

How it works...

Instances aren't instantly accessible outside of the OpenStack host unless a public IP address is assigned to them. Configuring our OpenStack environment so that each instance is assigned an address on launch makes the instances instantly accessible.

11
In the Datacenter

In this chapter, we will cover:

- ▶ Installing MAAS for bare-metal provisioning
- ▶ Using MAAS for bare-metal provisioning of hosts
- ▶ Installing and configuring Juju
- ▶ Installing OpenStack services using Juju
- ▶ Increasing OpenStack Compute capacity
- ▶ MySQL clustering using Galera
- ▶ Configuring HA Proxy for MySQL Galera load balancing
- ▶ Increasing resilience of OpenStack services
- ▶ Bonding network interfaces for redundancy

Introduction

OpenStack is a suite of software designed to offer scale-out cloud environments deployed in datacenters around the world. Managing installation of software in a remote location is different (and sometimes challenging), compared to being able to install software locally, and so tools and techniques have been developed to ease this task. Design considerations of how to deal with hardware and software failure must also be taken into consideration in operational environments. Identifying **single points of failure** (**SPOF**) and adding ways of making them resilient ensures our OpenStack environment remains available when something goes wrong.

This chapter introduces some methods and software to help manage OpenStack in production datacenters.

Installing MAAS for bare-metal provisioning

There are a number of ways, such as Cobbler and Kickstart, to provision an operating system such as Ubuntu to bare-metal. Ubuntu provides a convenient tool for bare-metal provisioning of servers in our datacenter that they call **MAAS**, which stands for **Metal-as-a-Service**. This tool allows us to simply set up a network boot environment that then allows us to allocate services to it, for example, OpenStack services, such as Compute or Dashboard.

Getting ready

We need to identify a server on the network that will be running the MAAS services, such as PXE Boot and TFTP Daemon services. Log in to this server to install the MAAS services. This server will need Internet access to pull in the required Ubuntu packages.

How to do it...

To install MAAS for the installation of Ubuntu on servers on our network, carry out the following steps:

1. Install the actual MAAS package, which itself will pull in dependent components. We do this as follows:

   ```
   sudo apt-get update
   sudo apt-get -y install maas
   ```

2. Once installed, create a super-user account, as follows:

   ```
   sudo maas createsuperuser
   ```

   An example of running the previous command is as follows:

   ```
   Username (Leave blank to use 'root'): admin
   E-mail address: root@mycloudnetwork.com
   Password:
   Password (again):
   Superuser created successfully.
   ```

3. When that's done, we need to configure DHCP as follows:

   ```
   sudo apt-get -y install maas-dhcp
   ```

4. During the installation, we will be asked to fill in details for our network. Assuming our network is 172.16.0.0/16 and that we will run and set up our hosts in the range 172.16.0.11 to 172.16.0.200, we define the range with:

   ```
   Set the network range for DHCP Clients:
   172.16.0.11,172.16.0.200
   ```

5. Next, we configure the gateway of the hosts when they receive an IP address. In this example, we're assuming this is 172.16.0.250.

    ```
    Set Default Gateway for DHCP Clients:
    172.16.0.250
    ```

6. Enter the domain of your network (or optionally leave it blank):

    ```
    internal.mycloudnetwork.com
    ```

7. Once complete, this will configure and run dnsmasq to provide these services to our hosts from our MAAS server.

8. With MAAS with DHCP configured, we now need to import the ISOs, for use within our environment, that our hosts can use to boot and install. We do this with the following command:

    sudo maas-import-isos

9. After a short while, the ISOs will be downloaded, ready for use.

How it works...

MAAS provides PXE boot services that reduce the complexity with network boot bare-metal environments. Installation is very easy with these packages, with the appropriate configuration done at installation time.

The main command-line tool used is called maas, and we use this to create an administrator user that is used to create further accounts if required.

With everything configured, we then perform a pull of the ISOs from ubuntu.com. This job is run weekly, but we must first kick this off manually, once installed.

Using MAAS for bare-metal provisioning of hosts

MAAS allows us to provision hosts on our network from bare-metal, meaning from power-on, the hosts are installed appropriately for our use.

Getting ready

The MAAS server has a web interface that we use to set up our hosts. Identify the server that has MAAS installed.

How to do it...

Once MAAS is installed, we can use it to provision servers on our network by carrying out the following steps:

1. Open up a web browser and point it your MAAS server. For example, if you installed MAAS on 172.16.0.250, point it at the following address `http://172.16.0.250/MAAS`.

2. This will present you with a username and password screen. Enter the details you used when you ran the `maas createsuperuser` command.

3. Once logged in, you will be presented with a basic screen saying **0** nodes in the deployment. Clicking on the text by MAAS allows you to change the name.

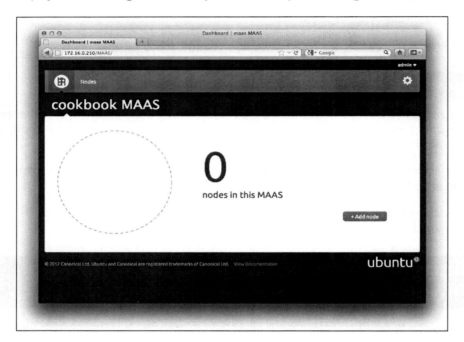

4. With this setup, we network boot (PXE boot) a node that will communicate with the MAAS server, providing us with a list of boot options. From the list of options, choose the **maas-enlist** option, which will bootstrap the node, register the node with our MAAS server, and then power itself off.

5. The MAAS web interface will now change to showing **1 nodes in this MAAS**. Click on the **Nodes** menu option.

6. You will see a list of nodes associated with MAAS as the MAC addresses seen on the node. Click on the listed node to be presented with a screen that details some more information about it and the actions associated with it. The state of the machine should say **Declared**.

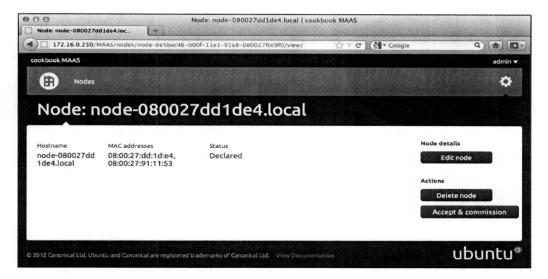

7. Click on the **Accept & commission** button. This will change the status to **Commissioning**.

8. The MAAS server can automatically power on servers using Wake-On-LAN/Avahi. If not, power the node back on again and PXE boot a second time. This will configure the node so that it can be commissioned by MAAS and then power itself off again.

9. On viewing our MAAS screen now, we see that the node status screen has changed to green and MAAS is telling us there is **1 node queued**.

10. Using the **Node** menu, browse to the node that is available to us, and then click on **Start node**.

11. If the node does not power on again, manually start it and PXE boot the node a third time. This will then start an installation of Ubuntu 12.04 on this node.

How it works...

Using MAAS is done in a few stages. The first is to notify MAAS of the node that will be installed using MAAS, by enlisting it with the service. This sends some information over to MAAS, which will identify it (specifically the MAC addresses of the interfaces on the node). Once MAAS is aware of the node, we can start the node—which MAAS can boot automatically using **Wake-On-Lan** (**WOL**)—which will then bootstrap the node that is ready for an OS installation. Once bootstrapped, we can perform a final PXE boot that will then install the operating system for us, ready for further work—particularly Juju.

Installing and configuring Juju

Ubuntu provides a tool named Juju that allows us to not only install packages, but to also install and configure the services by way of *charms*. Charms are a collection of scripts and descriptions on how to install and configure that service. For example, a charm for, say Wordpress, will install the Wordpress PHP files, as well as allow us to attach the Wordpress installation to a MySQL backend, or attach to a load balancer through relationships with those other services.

Getting ready

Log in to a shell on the MAAS server.

How to do it...

Carry out the following steps to install and configure Juju on our MAAS host:

1. First, we need to install the Juju tools. We do this as follows:

    ```
    sudo apt-get update
    sudo apt-get -y install juju
    ```

2. Once installed, we need to get the MAAS API key for our admin user set up under MAAS. To do this, we navigate to the **Preferences** link in the MAAS web interface and copy the key (or alternatively generate a new one and take a copy of that).

3. We are now ready to configure our Juju environment. To do this, we create a file named ~/.juju/environments.yaml, as follows:

    ```
    environments:
        maas:
            type: maas
            maas-server: 'http://172.16.0.250:80/MAAS'
            maas-oauth:
            'tcWxFpwbWqyeBFDd4P:HTCSqrsw7XQKBcvm8n:
            bp67u5TkSLu2wf2b7wUS2ckLjwELCZED'
            admin-secret: 'nothing'
            default-series: precise
    ```

4. Finally, Juju requires SSH keys to be configured to allow it to access the deployed nodes. To create the keys, issue the following command:

```
ssh-keygen -t rsa -N ""
```

How it works...

Juju is a very powerful tool to allow you to manage your environments very easily using simple commands. Since Ubuntu 12.04, Juju is part of the distribution and works in tandem with MAAS to allow us to provision bare-metal services using Juju commands.

By configuring Juju to work with MAAS in this way, we can launch new machines with configured services by instructing MAAS to power on servers and to install that service once the relevant operating system has been installed. This, in our case, will be Ubuntu 12.04, precisely as dictated by the `default-series` configuration option.

Ensure that we have the correct MAAS API key, where it is states `maas-oauth`.

Finally, putting in our public SSH key into MAAS allows us to use our Juju environment using SSH keys.

Installing OpenStack services using Juju

With Juju installed and configured to work with MAAS, we're ready to configure Juju to install our OpenStack environment.

At this point, it is assumed you have *at least nine servers available*, with two separate network cards in each to deploy OpenStack to, in order to provision an OpenStack environment using Juju and MAAS. This is because Juju installs each service to a new server.

Getting ready

Log in to a shell on the MAAS server.

How to do it...

To install OpenStack using Juju, carry out the following steps:

1. Create the file `.juju/openstack.cfg`, with the following contents:

```
keystone:
     admin-password: "openstack"
nova-cloud-controller:
     network-manager: "FlatDHCPManager"
nova-volume:
```

```
# This must be a free block device that is writable on the
# nova-volume host.
block-device: "xvdb"
overwrite: "true"
```

2. Once that is done, we bootstrap the environment, which sets up an initial administration server that is able to orchestrate the deployment of services:

```
juju bootstrap
```

 It might take a while for a node to fully bootstrap as it installs and pulls down required packages. Check with **juju status -v**, for an update on whether the bootstrap node has finished installing.

3. In our MAAS web GUI, the status screen will change the node we have bootstrapped to blue, to show this is successful, and the status of the node will change to **Allocated to Admin**.

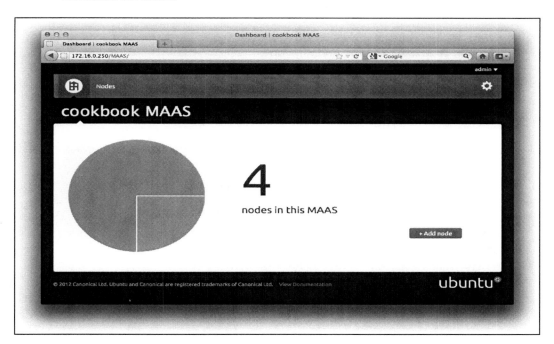

4. Once this is in place, we can deploy the OpenStack environment. First, we'll deploy the MySQL and RabbitMQ services, referencing the local charms we have downloaded:

```
juju deploy mysql
juju deploy rabbitmq-server
```

5. After this, we install Keystone, Nova Cloud Controller (`nova-api`), and the Nova Volume services, specifying the configuration file to pass as an argument to the installation that we created earlier:

```
juju deploy --config=.juju/openstack.cfg keystone
juju deploy --config=.juju/openstack.cfg nova-cloud-
    controller
juju deploy --config=.juju/openstack.cfg nova-volume
```

6. And finally, we finish this off with the following service installations:

```
juju deploy nova-compute
juju deploy glance
juju deploy openstack-dashboard
```

7. With all the packages deployed, we now need to establish the relationships between the services. We continue to use the `juju` commands to do this. We first connect Keystone to MySQL, as follows:

```
juju add-relation keystone mysql
```

8. Next, we can connect `nova-cloud-controller` to the supporting services of MySQL, RabbitMQ, Glance, and Keystone.

```
juju add-relation nova-cloud-controller mysql
juju add-relation nova-cloud-controller rabbitmq
juju add-relation nova-cloud-controller glance
juju add-relation nova-cloud-controller keystone
```

9. We continue connecting `nova-volume` to MySQL and RabbitMQ, as follows:

```
juju add-relation nova-volume mysql
juju add-relation nova-volume rabbitmq
```

10. Then, we can connect `nova-compute` to the required services:

```
juju add-relation nova-compute mysql
juju add-relation nova-compute rabbitmq
juju add-relation nova-compute glance
juju add-relation nova-compute keystone
juju add-relation nova-compute:network-manager nova-cloud-
    controller:network-manager
```

11. Then, we can connect Glance to its required supporting services of MySQL and Keystone:

```
juju add-relation glance mysql
juju add-relation glance keystone
```

12. Finally, we connect Horizon OpenStack Dashboard to Keystone:

```
juju add-relation openstack-dashboard keystone
```

13. Congratulations! Our environment has been deployed. To discover the node that has the OpenStack Dashboard installed, we execute the following command that will return the address we need to use to put in our web browser:

```
juju status openstack-dashboard
```

How it works...

Juju is a powerful tool for deploying environments and services. With Juju, we're able to utilize the power of `apt` with the ability to link services together known as "relations" in Juju terminology.

We first set up a configuration file that we can refer to when installing some components of OpenStack. This adds an important level of flexibility to our Juju use.

With the configuration of OpenStack ready, we are now ready to begin using Juju. The first step is to bootstrap the environment. This sets up a server that is used to provision our environment. Following this, we install the services one by one. Currently, Juju only supports installation of services onto their own nodes—so every Juju deployment step utilizes a new node.

With the services deployed, we simply define the relationships between the services—which is another term for connecting the services together. For example, we connect our `keystone` server with the MySQL server. We also connect `keystone` to `compute`, `glance`, and so on, as they all rely on OpenStack Identity Service. Similarly, the services that rely on `mysql` are all connected together. This continues until all relationships have been set up.

Once completed, given that Juju decides where to install the services, we need to discover which node has the OpenStack Dashboard installed. To do this, we simply ask for status information about `openstack-dashboard`, which returns the URL for us to use.

Increasing OpenStack Compute capacity

Adding extra Compute capacity is very simple with OpenStack. You essentially add in as many compute nodes as required, each having the same configuration file that tells OpenStack of its existence.

Adding Compute capacity using Juju is simply achieved by enlisting a new server into MAAS, and then running the following commands:

```
juju deploy nova-compute
juju add-relation nova-compute mysql
juju add-relation nova-compute rabbitmq
juju add-relation nova-compute glance
juju add-relation nova-compute keystone
juju add-relation nova-compute:network-manager nova-cloud-
    controller:network-manager
```

If Juju is not configured, add Compute hosts manually using the package manager, `apt`, and carry out the steps in the following section.

Getting ready

Ensure that Ubuntu is installed on the new node and networking has been configured appropriately. Log in to a shell on this new node that will become the extra Compute resource that we are adding to our OpenStack Compute cluster.

How to do it...

To increase OpenStack Compute capacity, carry out the following steps:

1. Configure the server as you would for the rest of your OpenStack environment. This includes the same OS, disk layout (and any mount points), and networking configuration.

2. Once this has been done, we install the packages on this new node, as follows:
    ```
    sudo apt-get update
    sudo apt-get -y install nova-compute nova-network nova-api
    ```

3. Ensure that the servers are time-synced and configured appropriately:
    ```
    sudo apt-get  -y install ntp
    # configure
    sudo service ntpd start
    ```

4. From an existing OpenStack node, copy over the /etc/nova directory to our new Compute node:
    ```
    # On an existing host, copy /etc/nova to new host
        (openstackX)
    cd /etc
    sudo scp -r nova/ openstackX:/tmp
    ```

```
# On new host (openstackX) host
sudo mv /tmp/nova /etc
sudo chown -R nova:nova /etc/nova
```

5. Finally, start up the new Compute services, as follows:

```
sudo start nova-compute
sudo start nova-api
sudo start nova-network
```

6. To check that our new host is ready to accept new services, log in to the OpenStack Controller node, where `nova-manage` is available, and issue the following command:

```
sudo nova-manage service list
```

7. The new host and its services, with **:-)** as the status, shows that the new node is ready.

How it works...

Scaling out OpenStack Compute using Juju is a very simple process. Manually adding in hosts is equally as straightforward, as each OpenStack host is configured with the same `nova.conf` configuration files. We simply install the services, configure the service (by copying over existing configuration files, as they reference the same RabbitMQ, MySQL, Keystone services, and so on), and ensure that the servers are time-synced. When we start up the services (for example, adding a row into the relevant table), they contact the supporting services, which in turn makes the other services aware of their existence. The scheduler will then take advantage of this new node to launch instances.

MySQL clustering using Galera

OpenStack can be backed by a number of database backends, and one of the most common options is MySQL. There are a number of ways to make MySQL more resilient and available. The following approach uses a load balancer to front a multi-read/write master with *Galera*, taking care of the synchronous replication required in such a setup. The advantage of this is that we are adding resilience in the event of a database node failure, as each node is getting ready.

We'll be using a free online configuration tool from `SeveralNines.com` to configure a 3-node, multi-master MySQL setup with Galera, monitored using the free cluster management interface, `cmon`, using a fourth node. This implies we have four servers available, running Ubuntu (other platforms are supported) with enough memory and disk space for our environment and at least two CPUs available.

How to do it...

To cluster MySQL using Galera, carry out the following steps:

MySQL and Galera configuration

1. We first use a web browser from our desktop and head over to `http://www.severalnines.com/galera-configurator/`, where we will input some information about our environment to produce the script required to install our Galera-based MySQL cluster.

 This is a third-party service asking for details pertinent to our environment. Do not include passwords for the environment that this will be deployed to. The process downloads scripts and configuration files that should be edited to suit before execution with real settings.

2. The first screen asks for general settings, as follows:
   ```
   Cloud Provider: none/on-premise
   Operating System: Ubuntu/Debian
   Platform: Linux 64-bit (x86_64)
   Number of Galera Servers: 3+1
   MySQL Server password (root user): openstack
   Port Number: 3306
   Config directory: /etc/
   OS User: galera
   CMON DB password (cmon user): cmon
   ```

3. Next, we'll configure server properties (configure as appropriate):
   ```
   System Memory (MySQL Servers): (at least 512Mb)
   WAN: no
   Skip DNS Resolve: yes
   Database Size < 8Gb
   MySQL Usage: Medium write/high read
   Number of cores: 2
   Innodb_buffer_pool_size: (at least 358) Mb
   Innodb_file_per_table: checked
   ```

4. Next, we'll configure the nodes and addresses, as follows:
   ```
   ClusterControl Server: 172.16.0.20
   System Memory: (at least 512Mb)
   Datadir: <same as for mysql>
   Installdir: /usr/local
   ```

```
Web server(apache) settings
Apache User: www-data
WWWROOT: /var/www/
```

```
Galera Servers
```

The following table lists the IP address, data directory, and installation directory for the servers:

Server-id	IP-address	Datadir	Installdir
1	172.16.0.21	/var/lib/mysql/	/usr/local/
2	172.16.0.22	same as mentioned earlier	same as mentioned earlier
3	172.16.0.23	same as mentioned earlier	same as mentioned earlier

5. The final step asks for an e-mail address to send the configuration and deployment script to. Once a valid e-mail address has been entered, press the **Generate Deployment Scripts** button.

Node preparation

1. Each node is configured such that the user used to run the setup routine (the OS user as configured in step 2 in the previous section) can SSH to each node—including itself—and run commands through `sudo` without being asked for a password. To do this, we first create the user's SSH key as follows:

```
ssh-keygen -t rsa -N ""
```

2. We now need to copy this to each of our nodes, including the node we're on now (so that it can SSH to itself):

```
# copy ssh key to 172.16.0.20, 172.16.0.21, 172.16.0.22
# and 172.16.0.23
for a in {20..23}
do
   ssh-copy-id -i .ssh/id_rsa.pub galera@172.16.0.${a}
done
```

3. This will ask for the password of the `galera` user on each of the nodes, but following this, we shouldn't be prompted. To test, simply do the following, which should get executed without intervention:

```
for a in {20..23}
do
   ssh galera@172.16.0.${a} ls
done
```

4. We now need to ensure the `galera` user can execute commands using `sudo` without being asked for a password. To do this, we execute the following *on all nodes*:

```
echo "galera  ALL=(ALL:ALL) NOPASSWD:ALL" | sudo tee -a
    /etc/sudoers.d/galera
# Then fix the permissions to prevent future warnings
sudo chmod 0440 /etc/sudoers.d/galera
```

Installation

1. From the e-mail that has been sent, download the attached gzipped tarball, and copy it over to the first of our nodes that we specified in the configuration as the ClusterControl Server (for example, 172.16.0.20).

2. Log in to the ClusterControl Server as the `OS user` specified in step 2 of the MySQL and Galera Configuration section (for example, `galera`):

```
ssh galera@172.16.0.20
```

3. Unpack the tarball copied over and change to the install directory in the unpacked archive, as follows:

```
tar zxf s9s-galera-2.0.0.tar.gz
cd s9s-galera-2.0.0/mysql/scripts/install
```

4. Once in this directory, we simply execute the `deploy.sh` script:

```
bash ./deploy.sh 2>&1 |tee cc.log
```

5. A question will be asked regarding the ability to shell to each node. Answer `Y` to this. Installation will then continue, which will configure MySQL with Galera as well as `cmon`, to monitor the environment.

6. After a period of time, once installation has completed, we point our web browser to the ClusterControl server to finalize the setup at the address specified, for example, `http://172.16.0.20/cmon/setup.php`, and change the cmon server listening address to be 172.16.0.20.

Configuration of database cluster for OpenStack

1. Once the cluster has been set up, we can now create the databases, users, and privileges required for our OpenStack environment, as we would do for any other OpenStack installation. To do this, we can use the web administration interface provided by the SeveralNines' ClusterControl interface.

2. The first step is to point your web browser to the ClusterControl server dashboard, for example, `http://172.16.0.20/cmon/`.

3. Select the cluster (**default_repl_1**) that will then list the nodes in our cluster. A menu will appear on the right side of the screen. Select the **Schema mgmt** link, as shown in the following screenshot:

4. Under **Schema Management**, we can create and drop databases, create and delete users, and grant and revoke privileges. For OpenStack, we need to create three users and three databases, with appropriate privileges. First, we create the nova database. To do this, click on the **Privileges** button.

5. The screen will change to one that allows us to create databases, users, and assign privileges. Create a database named nova, by clicking on the **Create Database** button.

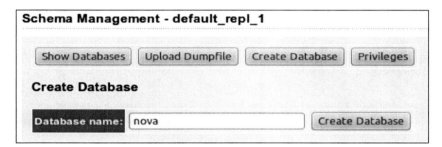

6. Repeat the process to create the keystone and glance databases.

7. Once done, we can now create a user named nova, who is allowed to access our database cluster from any host (using the MySQL wildcard character %) with a password of openstack:

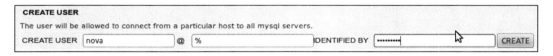

8. Repeat the process for a keystone and a glance user.

9. We end up with a number of users with passwords entered into our MySQL cluster that we can use when configuring OpenStack services that require access to MySQL.

> Click on the **Privileges** button again to refresh the screen to see the user just created.

10. We now assign privileges to these users. To do this for the nova user, we select the following entries:

    - **ALL PRIVILEGES**
    - **ON nova.***
    - **TO 'nova'@'%'**

    as shown in the following screenshot:

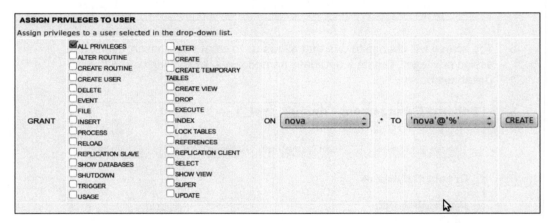

11. Repeat the process for the keystone and glance users and their respective databases.

12. We now have all our databases, users, and privileges set up, ready for our OpenStack environment.

USERs and GRANTs

The following USERs and GRANTs have been created. You can replay the actions in case a server was down when you executed the GRANT.

Users created from ClusterControl

Command	Username	Executed on	Date Issued	Action
CREATE USER	nova@%	synced by Galera	2012-05-28 13:48:48	DROP USER
CREATE USER	glance@%	synced by Galera	2012-05-28 13:49:27	DROP USER
CREATE USER	keystone@%	synced by Galera	2012-05-28 13:49:55	DROP USER
CREATE USER	root@%	synced by Galera	2012-05-28 13:51:42	DROP USER

GRANTS issued from ClusterControl

Command	Executed on	Date Issued	Action
GRANT ALL PRIVILEGES ON nova.* TO 'nova'@'%'	synced by Galera	2012-05-28 13:48:59	REVOKE
GRANT ALL PRIVILEGES ON glance.* TO 'glance'@'%'	synced by Galera	2012-05-28 13:49:36	REVOKE
GRANT ALL PRIVILEGES ON keystone.* TO 'keystone'@'%'	synced by Galera	2012-05-28 13:50:13	REVOKE
GRANT ALL PRIVILEGES ON *.* TO 'root'@'%'	synced by Galera	2012-05-28 13:51:59	REVOKE

How it works...

Galera replication is a *synchronous multi-master* plugin for InnoDB. It has the advantage that any client can write to any node in the cluster and not suffer from write conflicts or a data replication lag. There are some caveats to a Galera-backed MySQL cluster that must be considered though. Any database write is only as fast as the slowest node, to maintain synchronicity. As the number of nodes in a Galera cluster increases, the time to write to the database can increase. And finally, given that each node maintains a copy of the database on its local storage, it isn't as space-efficient as using a cluster based on shared storage.

Setting up a highly available MySQL cluster with Galera for data replication is easily achieved using the freely available online configuration tool from SeveralNines. By following the process, we end up with four nodes, of which three are assigned to running MySQL with Galera and the fourth allows us to manage the cluster.

With the automatic routine installation complete, we can create our databases and users and can assign privileges using the ClusterControl interface, without needing to think about any replication issues. In fact, we can create these by attaching to any one of the three MySQL servers we would normally treat independently, and the data will automatically sync to the other nodes.

For OpenStack, we create three databases (nova, glance, and keystone) and assign appropriate users and privileges to these databases. We can then use this information to put into the appropriate configuration files for OpenStack.

Configuring HA Proxy for MySQL Galera load balancing

With our MySQL Galera cluster configured, each of the nodes is able to take traffic, and the writes are seamlessly replicated to other nodes in the cluster. We could use any of the MySQL node addresses and place them in our configuration files, but if that node failed, we would not have a database to attach to and our OpenStack environment would fail. A solution to this is to front the MySQL cluster using load balancing. Given that any of the nodes are able to take reads and writes, with data consistency, load balancing is a great solution.

The steps in the following section configure a highly available 2-node HA Proxy setup that we can use as a MySQL endpoint to place in our OpenStack configuration files. In production, if load balancing is desired, it is recommended that dedicated HA load balancers be used.

Getting ready

Configure two servers, both running Ubuntu 12.04, that are configured on the same network as our OpenStack environment and MySQL Galera cluster. In the following steps, the two nodes will be on IP addresses 172.16.0.20 and 172.16.0.21, with a floating IP address (that has been set up using `keepalived`) of 172.16.0.30. This address is used when we configure database connections in our OpenStack configuration files.

How to do it...

To configure HA Proxy for MySQL Galera load balancing, carry out the following steps:

Installation of HA Proxy for MySQL

1. As we are setting up identical servers to act in a pair, we will configure a single server first, and then repeat the process for the second server. We first install HA Proxy using the usual `apt-get` process, as follows:

    ```
    sudo apt-get update
    sudo apt-get -y install haproxy
    ```

2. With HA Proxy installed, we'll simply configure this first proxy server appropriately for our MySQL Galera cluster. To do this, we edit the `/etc/haproxy/haproxy.cfg` file with the following contents:

    ```
    global
            log 127.0.0.1    local0
            log 127.0.0.1    local1 notice
            #log loghost     local0 info
            maxconn 4096
            #chroot /usr/share/haproxy
    ```

```
            user haproxy
            group haproxy
            daemon
            #debug
            #quiet

    defaults
            log global
            mode http
            option tcplog
            option dontlognull
            retries 3
            option redispatch
            maxconn 4096
            timeout connect 50000ms
            timeout client 50000ms
            timeout server 50000ms

    listen  mysql 0.0.0.0:3306
            mode tcp
            balance roundrobin
            option tcpka
            option mysql-check user haproxy
            server galera1 172.16.0.21:3306 weight 1
            server galera2 172.16.0.22:3306 weight 1
            server galera3 172.16.0.23:3306 weight 1
```

3. Save and exit the file and start up HA Proxy, as follows:

   ```
   sudo sed -i 's/^ENABLED.*/ENABLED=1/' /etc/defaults/haproxy
   sudo service haproxy start
   ```

4. Before we can use this HA Proxy server to access our three MySQL nodes, we must create the user specified in the haproxy.cfg file that is used to do a very simple check to see if MySQL is up. To do this, we add a user into our cluster that is simply able to connect to MySQL. Using the ClusterControl interface, or using the mysql client and attaching to any of the MySQL instances in our cluster, create the user haproxy with no password set that is allowed access from the IP address of the HA Proxy server.

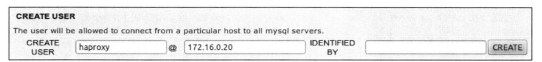

5. At this point, we can use a MySQL client and point this to the HA Proxy address.

6. Having a single HA Proxy server sitting in front of our multi-master MySQL cluster makes the HA Proxy server our single point of failure. To overcome this, we repeat the previous steps for our second HA Proxy server, and then we use a simple solution provided by `keepalived` for **VRRP (Virtual Redundant Router Protocol)** management. To do this, we need to install `keepalived` on our HA Proxy servers. Like before, we will configure one server then repeat the steps for our second server. We do this as follows:

```
sudo apt-get update
sudo apt-get -y install keepalived
```

7. To allow running software to bind to an address that does not physically exist on our server, we add in an option to `sysctl.conf`, to allow this. Add the following line to `/etc/sysctl.conf`:

```
net.ipv4.ip_nonlocal_bind=1
```

8. To pick up the change, issue the following command:

```
sudo sysctl -p
```

9. We can now configure `keepalived`. To do this, we create a `/etc/keepalived/keepalived.conf` file with the following contents:

```
vrrp_script chk_haproxy {
        script "killall -0 haproxy" # verify the pid exists or not
        interval 2          # check every 2 seconds
        weight 2            # add 2 points if OK
}

vrrp_instance VI_1 {
        interface eth1      # interface to monitor
        state MASTER
        virtual_router_id 51  # Assign one ID for this route
        priority 101        # 101 on master, 100 on backup
        virtual_ipaddress {
            172.16.0.30     # the virtual IP
        }
        track_script {
            chk_haproxy
        }
}
```

10. We can now start up `keepalived` on this server, by issuing the following command:

```
sudo service keepalived start
```

11. With `keepalived` now running on our first HA Proxy server, which we have designated as the `MASTER` node, we repeat the previous steps for our second HA Proxy server with only two changes to the `keepalived.conf` file (`state BACKUP` and `priority 100`) to give the complete file on our second host the following contents:

```
vrrp_script chk_haproxy {
        script "killall -0 haproxy" # verify the pid exists or not
        interval 2        # check every 2 seconds
        weight 2          # add 2 points if OK
}

vrrp_instance VI_1 {
        interface eth1    # interface to monitor
        state BACKUP
        virtual_router_id 51  # Assign one ID for this route
        priority 100      # 101 on master, 100 on backup
        virtual_ipaddress {
            172.16.0.30   # the virtual IP
        }
        track_script {
            chk_haproxy
        }
}
```

12. Start up `keepalived` on this second node, and they will be acting in co-ordination with each other. So if you powered off the first HA Proxy server, the second will pick up the floating IP address, 172.16.0.30, after two seconds, and new connections can be made to our MySQL cluster without disruption.

OpenStack Configuration using a floating IP address

With both HA Proxy servers running the same HA Proxy configuration, and with both running `keepalived`, we can use the `virtual_ipaddress` address (our floating IP address) configured as the address that we would then connect to and use in our configuration files. In OpenStack, we would change the following to use our floating IP address of 172.16.0.30:

```
/etc/nova/nova.conf
--sql_connection=mysql://nova:openstack@172.16.0.30/nova

/etc/keystone/keystone.conf
[sql]
connection = mysql://keystone:openstack@172.16.0.30/keystone

/etc/glance/glance-registry.conf
sql_connection = mysql://glance:openstack@172.16.0.30/glance
```

How it works...

HA Proxy is a very popular and useful proxy and load balancer that makes it ideal for fronting a MySQL cluster to add load-balancing capabilities. It is simple to set up the service to front MySQL.

The first requirement is to listen on the appropriate port, which for MySQL is 3306. The `listen` line in the configuration files here also specifies it will listen on all addresses by using `0.0.0.0` as the address, but you can bind this to a particular address by specifying this to add an extra layer of control in our environment.

To use MySQL, the mode must be set to `tcp` and we set `keepalived` with the `tcpka` option, to ensure long-lived connections are not interrupted and closed when a client opens up a connection to our MySQL servers.

The load balance method used is `roundrobin`, which is perfectly suitable for a multi-master cluster where any node can perform reads and writes.

We add in a basic check to ensure our MySQL servers are marked `off-line` appropriately. Using the inbuilt `mysql-check` option (which requires a user to be set up in MySQL to log in to the MySQL nodes and quit), when a MySQL server fails, the server is ignored and traffic passes to a MySQL server that is alive. Note that it does not perform any checks for whether a particular table exists—though this can be achieved with more complex configurations using a check script running on each MySQL server and calling this as part of our checks.

The final configuration step for HA Proxy is listing the nodes and the addresses that they listen on, which forms the load balance pool of servers.

Having a single HA Proxy acting as a load balancer to a highly available multi-master cluster is not recommended, as the load balancer then becomes our single point of failure. To overcome this, we can simply install and configure `keepalived`, which gives us the ability to share a floating IP address between our HA Proxy servers. This allows us to use this floating IP address as the address to use for our OpenStack services.

Increasing resilience of OpenStack services

OpenStack has been designed for highly scalable environments where it is possible to avoid single point of failures (SPOFs), but you must build this into your own environment. For example, Keystone is a central service underpinning your entire OpenStack environment, so you would build multiple instances into your environment. Glance is another service that is a key to the running of your OpenStack environment. By setting up multiple instances running these services, controlled with Pacemaker and Corosync, we can enjoy an increase in resilience to failure of the nodes running these services.

This recipe represents two nodes running both Glance and Keystone, controlled by Pacemaker with Corosync in active/passive mode, that allows for a failure of a single node. In a production environment, it is recommended that a cluster consist of at least three nodes to ensure resiliency and consistency in the case of a single node failure.

Getting ready

We must first create two servers configured appropriately for use with OpenStack. As these two servers will just be running Keystone and Glance, only a single network interface and address on the network that our OpenStack services communicate on will be required. This interface can be bonded for added resilience.

How to do it...

To increase the resilience of OpenStack services, carry out the following steps:

First node (openstack1)

1. Once Ubuntu has been installed with an address in our OpenStack environment that our other OpenStack services can use to communicate, we can proceed to install Pacemaker and Corosync, as follows:

```
sudo apt-get update
sudo apt-get -y install pacemaker corosync
```

2. It's important that our two nodes know each other by address and hostname, so enter their details in /etc/hosts to avoid DNS lookups, as follows:

```
172.16.0.1 openstack1.cloud.test openstack1
172.16.0.2 openstack2.cloud.test openstack2
```

3. Edit the /etc/corosync/corosync.conf file so the interface section matches the following:

```
interface {
      # The following values need to be set based on your
environment
      ringnumber: 0
      bindnetaddr: 172.16.0.0
      mcastaddr: 226.94.1.1
      mcastport: 5405
}
```

 Corosync uses *multi-cast*. Ensure the values don't conflict with any other multi-cast-enabled services on your network.

4. The `corosync` service isn't set to start by default. To ensure it starts, edit the `/etc/default/corosync` service and set `START=yes`, as follows:

```
sudo sed -i 's/^START=no/START=yes/g' /etc/default/corosync
```

5. We now need to generate an authorization key to secure the communication between our two hosts:

```
sudo corosync-keygen
```

6. You will be asked to generate some random entropy by typing at the keyboard. *If you are using an SSH session*, rather than a console connection, you won't be able to generate the entropy using a keyboard. To do this remotely, launch a new SSH session, and in that new session, while the `corosync-keygen` command is waiting for entropy, run the following:

```
while /bin/true; do dd if=/dev/urandom of=/tmp/100 bs=1024
    count=100000; for i in {1..10}; do cp /tmp/100
    /tmp/tmp_$i_$RANDOM; done; rm -f /tmp/tmp_*
    /tmp/100; done
```

7. When the `corosync-keygen` command has finished running and an `authkey` file has been generated, simply press *Ctrl+C* to copy this random entropy creation loop.

Second node (openstack2)

1. We now need to install Pacemaker and Corosync on our second host, `openstack2`. We do this as follows:

```
sudo apt-get update
sudo apt-get install pacemaker corosync
```

2. We also ensure that our `/etc/hosts` file has the same entries for our other host, as before:

```
172.16.0.1 openstack1.cloud.test openstack1
172.16.0.2 openstack2.cloud.test openstack2
```

3. The `corosync` service isn't set to start by default. To ensure that it starts, edit the `/etc/default/corosync` service and set `START=yes`:

```
sudo sed -i 's/^START=no/START=yes/g' /etc/default/corosync
```

4. We also ensure that our `/etc/hosts` file has the same entries for our other host, as before:

```
172.16.0.1 openstack1.cloud.test openstack1
172.16.0.2 openstack2.cloud.test openstack2
```

First node (openstack1)

With the `/etc/corosync/corosync.conf` file modified and the `/etc/corosync/` `authkey` file generated, we copy this to the other node (or nodes) in our cluster, as follows:

```
scp /etc/corosync/corosync.conf /etc/corosync/authkey
    openstack@172.16.0.2:
```

Second node (openstack2)

We can now put the same `corosync.conf` file as used by our first node, and the generated `authkey` file, into `/etc/corosync`:

```
sudo mv corosync.conf authkey /etc/corosync
```

Start the Pacemaker and Corosync services

1. We are now ready to start the services. On both nodes, issue the following commands:

   ```
   sudo service pacemaker start
   sudo service corosync start
   ```

2. To check that our services have started fine and our cluster is working, we can use the `crm_mon` command to query the cluster status, as follows:

   ```
   sudo crm_mon -1
   ```

3. This will return output similar to the following:

   ```
   ============
   Last updated: Tue Jun 12 21:07:05 2012
   Last change: Tue Jun 12 21:06:10 2012 via crmd on
       openstack1
   Stack: openais
   Current DC: openstack1 - partition with quorum
   Version: 1.1.6-9971ebba4494012a93c03b40a2c58ec0eb60f50c
   2 Nodes configured, 2 expected votes
   0 Resources configured.
   ============


   Online: [ openstack1 openstack2 ]
   ```

First node (openstack1)

1. We can validate the configuration using the `crm_verify` command, as follows:

```
sudo crm_verify -L
```

2. This will bring back an error mentioning **STONITH** (Shoot The Other Node In The Head). STONITH is used to maintain quorum when there are at least three nodes configured. It isn't required in a 2-node cluster. As we are only configuring a 2-node cluster, we disable STONITH.

```
sudo crm configure property stonith-enabled=false
```

3. Verifying the cluster using `crm_verify` again will now show errors:

```
sudo crm_verify -L
```

4. Again, as this is only a 2-node cluster, we also disable any notion of quorum, using the following command:

```
sudo crm configure property no-quorum-policy=ignore
```

5. On the first node, we can now configure our services and set up a floating address that will be shared between the two servers. In the following command, we've chosen 172.16.0.10 as the floating IP address. To do this, we use the `crm` command again to configure this floating IP address, which we will call `FloatingIP`.

```
sudo crm configure primitive FloatingIP
    ocf:heartbeat:IPaddr2 params ip=172.16.0.10
    cidr_netmask=32 op monitor interval=30s
```

6. On viewing the status of our cluster, using `crm_mon`, we can now see that the `FloatingIP` address has been assigned to our `openstack1` host:

```
sudo crm_mon -1
```

7. This outputs something similar to the following example:

```
============
Last updated: Tue Jun 12 21:23:07 2012
Last change: Tue Jun 12 21:06:10 2012 via crmd on
    openstack1
Stack: openais
Current DC: openstack1 - partition with quorum
Version: 1.1.6-9971ebba4494012a93c03b40a2c58ec0eb60f50c
2 Nodes configured, 2 expected votes
1 Resources configured.
============

Online: [ openstack1 openstack2 ]

    FloatingIP    (ocf::heartbeat:IPaddr2):    Started openstack1
```

8. We can now use this address to connect to our first node and, when we power that node off, that address will be sent to our second node after 30 seconds of no response from the first node.

Keystone across 2 nodes with FloatingIP

1. If Keystone is not installed on this first host, install it and configure it appropriately, as if we are configuring a single host (See *Chapter 3, Keystone OpenStack Identity Service*). Ensure the `keystone` database is backed by a database backend such as MySQL.

2. With Keystone running on this host, we should be able to query Keystone using both its own IP address (172.16.0.1) and the floating IP (172.16.0.10) from a client that has access to the OpenStack environment.

```
# Assigned IP
export OS_USERNAME=admin
export OS_PASSWORD=openstack
export OS_TENANT_NAME=cookbook
export OS_AUTH_URL=http://172.16.0.1:5000/v2.0/
keystone user-list
# FloatingIP
export OS_AUTH_URL=http://172.16.0.10:5000/v2.0/
keystone user-list
```

3. On the second node, install and configure Keystone, configured such that Keystone is pointing at the same database backend.

```
sudo apt-get update
sudo apt-get install keystone python-mysqldb
```

4. Copy over the `/etc/keystone/keystone.conf` file from the first host, put it in place on the second node, and then restart the Keystone service. There is no further work required, as the database population with endpoints and users has already been done on the first node.

```
sudo stop keystone
sudo start keystone
```

5. We can now interrogate the second Keystone service on its own IP address.

```
# Second Node
export OS_AUTH_URL=http://172.16.0.2:5000/v2.0/
keystone user-list
```

Glance across 2 nodes with FloatingIP

1. In order to have Glance able to run across multiple nodes, it must be configured with a shared storage backend (such as *Swift*) and be backed by a database backend (such as MySQL). On the first host, install and configure Glance, as described in *Chapter 7, Glance OpenStack Image Service*.

2. On the second node, simply install the required packages to run Glance, which is backed by MySQL and Swift:

```
sudo apt-get install glance python-swift
```

3. Copy over the configuration files in /etc/glance to the second host, and start the glance-api and glance-registry services on both nodes, as follows:

```
sudo start glance-api
sudo start glance-registry
```

4. We can now use either the *Glance* server to view our images, as well as the FloatingIP address that is assigned to our first node.

```
# First node
glance -I admin -K openstack -T cookbook -N
    http://172.16.0.1:5000/v2.0 index
# Second node
glance -I admin -K openstack -T cookbook -N
    http://172.16.0.2:5000/v2.0 index
# FloatingIP
glance -I admin -K openstack -T cookbook -N
    http://172.16.0.10:5000/v2.0 index
```

Configuring Pacemaker for use with Glance and Keystone

1. With Keystone and Glance running on both nodes, we can now configure Pacemaker to take control of this service, so that we can ensure Keystone and Glance are running on the appropriate node when the other node fails. To do this, we first disable the upstart jobs for controlling Keystone and Glance services. To do this, we create upstart override files for these services (on both nodes). Create /etc/init/keystone.override, /etc/init/glance-api.override, and /etc/init/glance-registry.override with just the keyword, manual, in.

2. We now grab the OCF agents that are able to control our Keystone and Glance services. *We must do this on both our nodes.*

```
wget https://raw.github.com/madkiss/keystone
    /ha/tools/ocf/keystone
wget https://raw.github.com/madkiss/glance/
    ha/tools/ocf/glance-api
wget https://raw.github.com/madkiss/glance/
    ha/tools/ocf/glance-registry
sudo mkdir -p /usr/lib/ocf/resource.d/openstack
```

```
sudo cp keystone glance-api glance-registry
   /usr/lib/ocf/resource.d/openstack
sudo chmod 755 /usr/lib/ocf/resource.d/openstack/*
```

3. We should now be able to query these new OCF agents, which will return these three OCF agents:

```
sudo crm ra list ocf openstack
```

4. We can now configure Pacemaker to use these agents to control our Keystone service. To do this, we run the following set of commands:

```
sudo crm cib new conf-keystone
sudo crm configure property stonith-enabled=false
sudo crm configure property no-quorum-policy=ignore
sudo crm configure primitive p_keystone
   ocf:openstack:keystone \
   params config="/etc/keystone/keystone.conf" \
   os_auth_url="http://localhost:5000/v2.0/" \
 os_password="openstack" \
   os_tenant_name="cookbook" \
   os_username="admin" \
   user="keystone" \
   client_binary="/usr/bin/keystone" \
   op monitor interval="30s" timeout="30s"
sudo crm cib use live
sudo crm cib commit conf-keystone
```

5. We then issue a similar set of commands for the two Glance services, as follows:

```
sudo crm cib new conf-glance-api
sudo crm configure property stonith-enabled=false
sudo crm configure property no-quorum-policy=ignore
sudo crm configure primitive p_glance_api ocf:openstack:glance-api
\
   params config="/etc/glance/glance-api.conf" \
   os_auth_url="http://localhost:5000/v2.0/" \
   os_password="openstack" \
   os_tenant_name="cookbook" \
   os_username="admin" \
   user="glance" \
   client_binary="/usr/bin/glance" \
   op monitor interval="30s" timeout="30s"
sudo crm cib use live
sudo crm cib commit conf-glance-api
```

```
sudo crm cib new conf-glance-registry
sudo crm configure property stonith-enabled=false
sudo crm configure property no-quorum-policy=ignore
sudo crm configure primitive p_glance_registry
ocf:openstack:glance-registry \
    params config="/etc/glance/glance-registry.conf" \
    os_auth_url="http://localhost:5000/v2.0/" \
    os_password="openstack" \
    os_tenant_name="cookbook" \
    os_username="admin" \
    user="glance" \
    op monitor interval="30s" timeout="30s"
sudo crm cib use live
sudo crm cib commit conf-glance-registry
```

6. We can verify that we have our Pacemaker configured correctly, by issuing the following command:

```
sudo crm_mon -1
```

7. This brings back something similar to the following:

```
Last updated: Tue Jun 12 22:55:25 2012
Last change: Tue Jun 12 21:06:10 2012 via crmd on
    openstack1
Stack: openais
Current DC: openstack1 - partition with quorum
Version: 1.1.6-9971ebba4494012a93c03b40a2c58ec0eb60f50c
2 Nodes configured, 2 expected votes
4 Resources configured.
============

Online: [ openstack1 openstack2 ]

 FloatingIP    (ocf::heartbeat:IPaddr2):  Started openstack1
 p_keystone    (ocf::openstack:keystone):
     Started openstack1
 p_glance_api  (ocf::openstack:glance_api):
     Started openstack1
 p_glance_registry  (ocf::openstack:glance_registry):
     Started openstack1
```

Here's what to do if you receive an error similar to the following:

```
Failed actions:
    p_keystone_monitor_0 (node=ubuntu2, call=3, rc=5,
    status=complete): not installed
```

Issue the following to clear the status and then view the status again:

```
sudo crm_resource -P
sudo crm_mon -1
```

8. We are now able to configure our client so that it uses the FloatingIP address of 172.16.0.10 for both Glance and Keystone services. With this in place, we can bring down the interface on our first node and still have our Keystone and Glance services available on this FloatingIP address.

We now have Keystone and Glance running on two separate nodes, where a node can fail and the services will still be available.

How it works...

Making OpenStack services highly available is a complex subject, and there are a number of ways to achieve this. Using Pacemaker and Corosync is a very good solution to this problem. It allows us to configure a floating IP address assigned to the cluster that will attach itself to the appropriate node (using Corosync), as well as control services using agents, so the cluster manager can start and stop services as required, to provide a highly available experience to the end user.

By installing both Keystone and Glance on two separate nodes (each configured appropriately with a remote database backend such as MySQL and Glance), having the images available using a shared filesystem or cloud storage solution means we can configure these services with Pacemaker to allow Pacemaker to monitor them. If unavailable on the active node, Pacemaker can start those services on the passive node.

Configuration of Pacemaker is predominantly done with the crm tool. This allows us to script the configuration but, if invoked on its own, allows us to invoke an interactive shell that we can use to edit, add, and remove services as well as query the status of the cluster. This is a very powerful tool to control an equally powerful cluster manager.

With both nodes running Keystone and Glance, and with Pacemaker and Corosync running and accessible on the floating IP provided by Corosync, we configure Pacemaker to control the running of the Keystone and Glance services by using an OCF agent written specifically for this purpose. The OCF agent uses a number of parameters that will be familiar to us—whereby they require the same username, password, tenant, and endpoint URL that we would use in a client to access that service.

A timeout of 30 seconds was set up for both the agent and when the floating IP address moves to another host.

Bonding network interfaces for redundancy

Running multiple services across multiple machines and implementing appropriate HA methods ensures a high degree of tolerance to failure within our environment, but if it's the physical network that fails and not the service, outages will occur if traffic cannot flow to and from that service. Adding in NIC bonding (also known as teaming or link aggregation) can help alleviate these issues by ensuring traffic flows through diverse routes and switches as appropriate.

Getting ready

NIC bonding requires co-ordination between system administrators and the network administrators, who are responsible for the switches. There are various methods available for NIC bonding. The method presented here is the *active-passive* mode, which describes that traffic will normally flow through a single switch, leaving the other teamed NIC to take no traffic until it is required.

How to do it...

Setting up NIC bonding in Ubuntu 12.04 requires an extra package installation to allow for bonding.

1. We install this in the usual manner, as follows:

   ```
   sudo apt-get update
   sudo apt-get -y install ifenslave
   ```

2. With this installed, we simply configure networking as normal in Ubuntu but add in the required elements for bonding. To do this, we edit the /etc/network/ interfaces file with the following contents (for active-passive mode bonding)—here we're bonding eth1 and eth2 to give us bond0:

   ```
   auto eth1
   iface eth1 inet manual
           bond-master bond0
           bond-primary eth1 eth2

   auto eth2
   iface eth2 inet manual
           bond-master bond0
           bond-primary eth1 eth2

   auto bond0
   iface bond0 inet static
           address 172.16.0.101
   ```

```
netmask 255.255.0.0
network 172.16.0.0
broadcast 172.16.255.255
bond-slaves none
bond-mode 1
bond-miimon 100
```

3. To ensure that the correct bonding mode is used, we add the following contents into /etc/modprobe.d/bonding.conf:

```
alias bond0 bonding
options bonding mode=1 miimon=100
```

4. We can now restart our networking, which in turn will bring up our bonded interface with the required IP address, as specified:

sudo service networking restart

How it works...

Bonding network interfaces in Ubuntu to cater to switch failure is relatively straightforward, providing co-ordination with how the switches are set up and configured. With different paths to different switches configured, and each network interface going to separate switches, a high level of fault tolerance to network-level events such as a switch failure can be achieved.

To do this, we simply configure our bonding in the traditional /etc/network/interfaces file under Ubuntu, but we specify which NICs are teamed with which bonded interface. Each bonded interface configured has at least a unique pair of interfaces assigned to it, and then we configure that bonded interface, bond0, with the usual IP address, netmask, and so on. We tag a few options specifically to notify Ubuntu that this is a bonded interface of a particular mode.

To ensure the bonding module that gets loaded as part of the kernel has the right mode assigned to it, we configure the module in /etc/modprobe.d/bonding.conf. When the bonding module loads along with the network interface, we end up with a server that is able to withstand isolated switch failures.

See also

▶ See https://help.ubuntu.com/community/LinkAggregation, for more information

12
Monitoring

In this chapter, we will cover:

- ▸ Monitoring Compute services with Munin
- ▸ Monitoring instances using Munin and Collectd
- ▸ Monitoring the storage service using StatsD/Graphite
- ▸ Monitoring MySQL with Hyperic

Introduction

There are a number of ways to monitor computer systems and their services but the same principles remain. Adequate monitoring and alerting of services is the only way to ensure we know there's a problem before our customers. From SNMP traps to agents running on machines specific to the services running, configuration of monitoring is an essential step in production deployments of OpenStack. This chapter introduces some tools that can be used to monitor services within our OpenStack environment.

Monitoring Compute services with Munin

Munin is a network and system monitoring application that outputs graphs through a web interface. It comprises of a master server that gathers the output from the agents running on each of our hosts.

Getting ready

We will be configuring Munin on a server that has access to the OpenStack Compute environment hosts. Ensure this server has enough RAM, disk, and CPU capacity for the environment you are running. As a bare minimum in a test environment, it is possible to run this on a VM with 1vCPU, 1.5 GB of RAM, and 8 GB of disk space.

How to do it...

To set up Munin with OpenStack, carry out the following steps:

1. Install Munin.
2. Configure the Munin nodes.
3. Configure OpenStack plugins for Munin.

Munin Master Server

The Munin Master node is the server that provides us with the web interface to view the collected information about the nodes in our network and must be installed first, as follows:

1. Configure a server with the Ubuntu 12.04 64-bit version, with access to the servers in our OpenStack environment.

2. Install Munin from the Ubuntu repositories:

```
sudo apt-get update
sudo apt-get -y install apache2
sudo apt-get -y install munin munin-plugins-extra
sudo service apache2 restart
```

3. By default, the Apache configuration for Munin only allows access from 127.0.0.1. To allow access from our network, we edit /etc/apache2/conf.d/munin and allow the server(s) or network(s) that can access Munin. For example, to allow access from 192.168.1.0/24, we add the following Access line in:

```
Allow from 192.168.1.
```

4. We reload the Apache service to pick up this change. We do this as follows:

```
sudo service apache2 reload
```

5. At this stage, we have a basic installation of Munin that is gathering statistics for the running machine where we have just installed Munin. This can be seen if you load up a web browser and browse to http://server/munin.

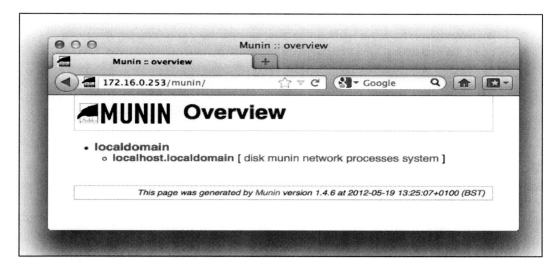

6. Configuration of Munin Master is done in the /etc/munin/munin.conf file. Here, we tell Munin where our OpenStack hosts, which are specified as FQDNs, are. Munin groups these hosts under the same domain. For example, to add in two OpenStack hosts that have the addresses 172.16.0.1 (openstack1) and 172.16.0.2 (openstack2), we add the following section into the munin.conf file:

```
[openstack1.cloud.test]
    address 172.16.0.1
    use_node_name yes

[openstack2.cloud.test]
    address 172.16.0.2
    use_node_name yes
```

We can now proceed to configure the nodes openstack1 and openstack2.

Munin nodes

With the Munin Master server installed, we can now configure the Munin nodes. These have an agent on them, called munin-node, that the master uses to gather the information and present to the user.

1. We first need to install the munin-node package on our OpenStack hosts. So, for each one, we execute the following:

```
sudo apt-get update
sudo apt-get -y install munin-node munin-plugins-extra
```

2. Once installed, we need to configure this so that our Munin Master host is allowed to get information from the node. To do this, we edit the `/etc/munin/munin-node.conf` file and add in an `allow` line. To allow our Master on IP address 172.16.0.253, we add the following entry:

```
allow ^172\.16\.0\.253$
```

3. Once that line is in, we can restart the `munin-node` service to pick up the change.

```
sudo restart munin-node
```

Monitoring OpenStack Compute services

With Munin Master installed, and having a couple of nodes with graphs showing up on the Master, we can add in plugins to pick up the OpenStack services and graph them. To do this, we check out some plugins from GitHub.

1. We first ensure we have the `git` client available to us on our OpenStack nodes:

```
sudo apt-get update
sudo apt-get -y install git
```

2. We can now check out the OpenStack plugins for Munin as they're not yet available in the `munin-plugins-extra` package:

```
git clone https://github.com/munin-monitoring/contrib.git
```

3. This checks out contributed code and plugins to a directory named `contrib`. We copy the relevant plugins for the OpenStack services into the Munin plugins directory, as follows:

```
cd contrib/plugins
sudo cp nova/* /usr/share/munin/plugins/
sudo cp keystone/* /usr/share/munin/plugins
sudo cp glance/* /usr/share/munin/plugins
```

4. `Munin-node` comes with a utility that allows us to enable appropriate plugins on our hosts automatically. We run the following commands to do this:

```
sudo munin-node-configure --suggest
sudo -i # get root shell
munin-node-configure --shell 2>&1 | egrep -v "^\#" | sh
```

5. The Keystone and Glance plugins don't get picked up automatically, so we add these to the plugins' directory, manually, with `symlinks`:

```
cd /etc/munin/plugins
sudo ln -s /usr/share/munin/plugins/keystone_stats
sudo ln -s /usr/share/munin/plugins/glance_size
sudo ln -s /usr/share/munin/plugins/glance_status
```

6. We also need to add in an extra configuration file to sit alongside the OpenStack plugins, called /etc/munin/plugin-conf.d/openstack.

```
[nova_*]
user nova

[keystone_*]
user keystone

[glance_*]
user glance
```

7. With the appropriate plugins configured, we restart the munin-node service, as follows, to pick up the change:

    sudo restart munin-node

8. When the Master server refreshes, we see OpenStack services as options and graphs we can click through to.

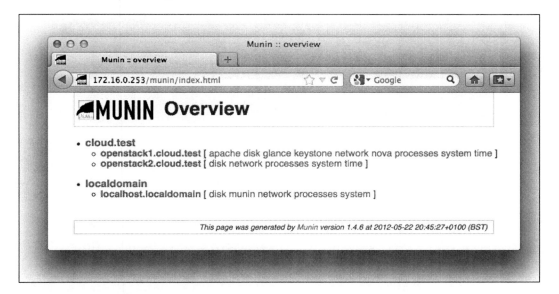

How it works...

Munin is an excellent, open source networked, resource-monitoring tool that can help analyze resource trends and identify problems with our OpenStack environment. Configuration is very straightforward, with out of the box configuration providing lots of very useful graphs from **RRD (Round Robin Database)** files. By adding in a few extra configuration options and plugins, we can extend Munin to monitor our OpenStack environment.

Once Munin has been installed, we have to do a few things to configure it to produce graphed statistics for our environment:

1. Configure the Master Munin server with the nodes we wish to get graphs from. This is done in the /etc/munin/munin.conf file by using the tree-like structure domain/host address sections.

2. We then configure each node with the munin-node service. The munin-node service has its own configuration file where we set the IP address of our master Munin server. This authorizes the master server, with this IP address, to retrieve the collected data from this node. This is set in the allow line in the /etc/munin/munin.conf file.

3. Finally, we configure appropriate plugins for the services that we want to monitor. With the OpenStack plugins installed, we can monitor the Compute, Keystone, and Glance services and obtain statistics on the number of instances running, the number of floating IPs assigned, allocated, and used, and so on.

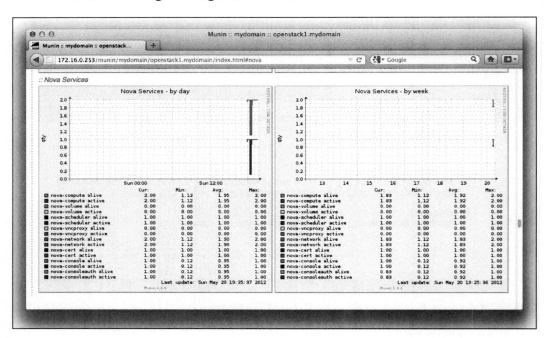

Monitoring instances using Munin and Collectd

The health of the underlying infrastructure operating our on-premise cloud solution is important, but of equal importance is to understand the metrics given by the Compute instances themselves. For this, we can get metrics sent from them by using a monitoring tool called Collectd, and we can leverage Munin for an overall view of our running virtual instances.

How to do it...

To set Munin and Collectd up, carry out the following steps:

Munin

We can configure Munin to look at more than just the CPU, memory, and disk space of the host, by invoking the `libvirt` plugin to query values within the running instances on our Compute hosts.

1. The `libvirt munin` plugin is conveniently provided by the Ubuntu repositories, so we grab these in the usual way:

    ```
    sudo apt-get update
    sudo apt-get -y install munin-libvirt-plugins
    ```

2. Once downloaded, we then configure the `munin libvirt` plugins on the Compute host:

    ```
    cd /etc/munin/plugins
    sudo ln -s /usr/share/munin/plugins/libvirt-blkstat
    sudo ln -s /usr/share/munin/plugins/libvirt-ifstat
    sudo ln -s /usr/share/munin/plugins/libvirt-cputime
    sudo ln -s /usr/share/munin/plugins/libvirt-mem
    ```

3. With the plugins in place, we now need to configure them. This is done by placing a file in `/etc/munin/plugin-conf.d/libvirt`, with the following contents:

    ```
    [libvirt*]
    user root
    env.address qemu:///system
    env.tmpfile /var/lib/munin/plugin-state/libvirt
    ```

4. Once this is done, we restart the `munin-node` service, and we will see an additional category show up in Munin, named **virtual machines**, where we can then see how much of the system resources are being consumed on the host.

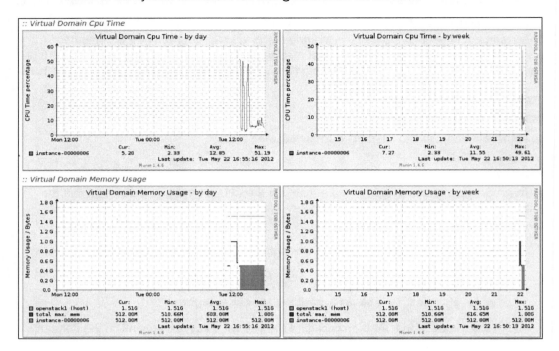

Collectd

Collectd is set up in three parts. There is a `collectd` server that listens over UDP for data sent from clients. There is the client `collectd` service that sends the data to the `collectd` server. Finally, there is a web interface to Collectd, named `collectd-web`, that allows for easy viewing of the graphs sent from `collectd`.

Collectd server

1. We first install `collectd` and the required Perl resources in the usual way from Ubuntu's repositories:

```
sudo apt-get update
sudo apt-get -y install collectd libjson-perl
```

2. Once installed, we configure the service to listen on a port of our choosing. The configuration of `collectd` is done in `/etc/collectd/collectd.conf`. In the following configuration, we listen on UDP port 12345:

```
Hostname "servername"
Interval   10
ReadThreads 5

LoadPlugin network
<Plugin network>
  Listen "*" "12345"
</Plugin>

LoadPlugin cpu
LoadPlugin df
LoadPlugin disk
LoadPlugin load
LoadPlugin memory
LoadPlugin processes
LoadPlugin swap
LoadPlugin syslog
LoadPlugin users
LoadPlugin interface
<Plugin interface>
    Interface "eth0"
</Plugin>
LoadPlugin tcpconns

LoadPlugin rrdtool
<Plugin "rrdtool">
  CacheFlush 120
  WritesPerSecond 50
</Plugin>

Include "/etc/collectd/filters.conf"
Include "/etc/collectd/thresholds.conf"
```

3. We restart the service to pick up these changes:

```
sudo service collectd restart
```

Collectd Client

1. The `collectd` client and server both use the same package, so we install the client in the same way.

   sudo apt-get update
   sudo apt-get -y install collectd libjson-perl

2. The configuration file for the guest is the same as for the server, but we specify different options. Edit `/etc/collectd/collectd.conf` with the following contents:

```
FQDNLookup true
Interval  10
ReadThreads 5
LoadPlugin network
<Plugin network>
  Server "172.16.0.253" "12345"
</Plugin>
LoadPlugin cpu
LoadPlugin df
LoadPlugin disk
LoadPlugin load
LoadPlugin memory
LoadPlugin processes
LoadPlugin swap
LoadPlugin syslog
LoadPlugin users
LoadPlugin interface
<Plugin interface>
  Interface "eth0"
</Plugin>
```

3. Restart the `collectd` service to pick up this change:

   sudo service collectd restart

Collectd-web

1. At this point, data is being sent over to the `collectd` server (at address 172.16.0.253). To view this data, we install another package that can interpret the RRD files and present them in an easy-to-use web interface. We first download the `collectd-web` tarball from the following URL:

   `http://collectdweb.appspot.com/download/`

2. We then unpack the archive, as follows:

   tar zxvf collectd-web_0.4.0.tar.gz

3. Then, we copy everything over to the web server `DocumentRoot` directory:

   ```
   sudo cp -a ./collectd-web /var/www
   ```

4. Create or modify the `/etc/collectd/collection.conf` file with the following contents:

   ```
   datadir: "/var/lib/collectd/"
   libdir: "/usr/lib/collectd/"
   ```

5. We then run the `standalone` server that will listen locally for requests from Apache:

   ```
   cd /var/www/collectd-web
   sudo nohup python runserver.py &
   ```

6. After this we edit the `vhost` file that controls the `DocumentRoot` of our Apache setup (on Ubuntu, this is `/etc/apache2/sites-enabled/000-default`) to ensure that `.htaccess` files are understood with the `AllowOverride all` configuration:

   ```
   <Directory /var/www/>
        Options Indexes FollowSymLinks MultiViews
        AllowOverride all
        Order allow,deny
        allow from all
   </Directory>
   ```

7. We can now simply reload Apache to pick up the changes, as follows:

   ```
   sudo service apache2 reload
   ```

8. Now, we point our web browser to our installation, for example, `http://172.16.0.253/collectd-web`, to view the `collectd` stats from the listed servers.

How it works...

Munin has plugins for various monitoring activities, including `libvirt`. As `libvirt` is used to manage the running instances on our Compute nodes, they hold an array of information that we can send to Munin to allow us to get a better understanding of what is happening in and on our OpenStack Compute hosts and instances.

Collectd is regarded as one of the standard ways of collecting resource information from servers and instances. It can act as a server and a client and, as such, we use the same installation binaries on both our monitoring host and guests. The difference is in the configuration file, `/etc/collectd/collectd.conf`. For the server, we specify that we listen on a specific port using the following lines in the server's configuration file:

```
<Plugin network>
  Listen "*" "12345"
</Plugin>
```

For the client configuration, we specify where we want the data sent to, using the following lines in the client's configuration file:

```
<Plugin network>
  Server "172.16.0.253" "12345"
</Plugin>
```

To bring the two together in a convenient interface to `collectd`, we install the `collectd-web` interface that has a standalone service that is used in conjunction with Apache to provide us with the interface.

Monitoring the storage service using StatsD/Graphite

When monitoring the OpenStack Storage service, Swift, we are looking at gathering key metrics from within the storage cluster in order to make decisions on its health. For this, we can use a small piece of middleware named `swift-informant`, together with StatsD and Graphite, to produce near real-time stats of our cluster.

Getting ready

We will be configuring StatsD and Graphite on a server that has access to the OpenStack Storage proxy server. Ensure this server has enough RAM, disk, and CPU capacity for the environment you are running.

How to do it...

To install StatsD and Graphite, carry out the following steps:

Prerequisites

For this, we will be configuring a new Ubuntu 12.04 server. Once Ubuntu has been installed, we need to install some prerequisite packages.

```
sudo apt-get update
sudo apt-get -y install git python-pip gcc python2.7-dev apache2
    libapache2-mod-python python-cairo python-django
    libapache2-mod-wsgi python-django-tagging
```

Graphite

1. Installation of Graphite is achieved using the Python Package Index tool, `pip`:

    ```
    sudo pip install carbon
    sudo pip install whisper
    sudo pip install graphite-web
    ```

2. Once installed, we can configure the installation. Example configuration files for Graphite are found in /opt/graphite/conf. We rename these to their respective conf files:

```
cd /opt/graphite/conf
sudo mv carbon.conf.example carbon.conf
sudo mv storage-schemas.conf.example storage-schemas.conf
```

3. We now create the vhost file for Apache that will load the Graphite frontend. Create /etc/apache2/sites-available/graphite with the following contents:

```
<VirtualHost *:80>
        ServerName 172.16.0.253
        DocumentRoot "/opt/graphite/webapp"
        ErrorLog /opt/graphite/storage/log/webapp/error.log
        CustomLog /opt/graphite/storage/log/webapp/access.log
        common

        # I've found that an equal number of processes & threads
        # tends
        # to show the best performance for Graphite (ymmv).
        WSGIDaemonProcess graphite processes=5 threads=5
        display-name='%{GROUP}' inactivity-timeout=120
        WSGIProcessGroup graphite
        WSGIApplicationGroup %{GLOBAL}
        WSGIImportScript /opt/graphite/conf/graphite.wsgi
        process-group=graphite application-group=%{GLOBAL}

        WSGIScriptAlias / /opt/graphite/conf/graphite.wsgi

        Alias /content/ /opt/graphite/webapp/content/
        <Location "/content/">
                SetHandler None
        </Location>

        Alias /media/ "/usr/lib/python2.7/dist-packages/django/
        contrib/admin/media/"
        <Location "/media/">
                SetHandler None
        </Location>

        # The graphite.wsgi file has to be accessible by apache.
        # It won't be visible to clients
        # because of the DocumentRoot though.
        <Directory /opt/graphite/conf/>
                Order deny,allow
                Allow from all
        </Directory>
</VirtualHost>
```

4. We enable this website using the `a2ensite` utility:

```
sudo a2ensite graphite
```

5. We now need to enable the WSGI file for Graphite:

```
sudo mv graphite.wsgi.example graphite.wsgi
```

6. Various areas need to change their ownership to that of the process running the Apache web server:

```
sudo chown -R www-data:www-data /opt/graphite/storage/log/
sudo touch /opt/graphite/storage/index
sudo chown www-data:www-data /opt/graphite/storage/index
```

7. We can now restart Apache to pick up these changes:

```
sudo service apache2 restart
```

8. The Graphite service runs with a SQLite database backend, so we need to initialize this.

```
cd /opt/graphite/webapp/graphite
sudo python manage.py syncdb
```

9. This will ask for some information, as displayed next:

```
You just installed Django's auth system, which means you don't
have any superusers defined.
Would you like to create one now? (yes/no): yes
Username (Leave blank to use 'root'):
E-mail address: user@somedomain.com
Password:
Password (again):
Superuser created successfully.
Installing custom SQL ...
Installing indexes ...
No fixtures found.
```

10. We also need to ensure that Apache can write to this, too:

```
sudo chown -R www-data:www-data /opt/graphite/storage
```

11. Finally, we start the services, thus:

```
cd /opt/graphite
sudo bin/carbon-cache.py start
```

StatsD

1. StatsD runs using `node.js`, so we have to install it first, using packages from Ubuntu's repositories:

   ```
   sudo apt-get update
   sudo apt-get -y install nodejs
   ```

2. We then check out the StatsD code from Git:

   ```
   git clone https://github.com/etsy/statsd.git
   ```

3. Configuring StatsD is done by modifying an example configuration file:

   ```
   cd statsd
   cp exampleConfig.js Config.js
   ```

4. We need to modify the `Config.js` file to change the `graphiteHost:` parameter to `localhost`, as we're running Graphite on the same host as StatsD:

   ```
   {
     graphitePort: 2003
   , graphiteHost: "localhost"
   , port: 8125
   }
   ```

5. To start the service, we issue the following command:

   ```
   nohup node stats.js Config.js &
   ```

swift-informant

We are now ready to configure the OpenStack Swift proxy server to include the `swift-informant` middleware in the pipeline. This is done by configuring the `/etc/swift/proxy-server.conf` file.

1. We first download and install the middleware by running the following commands:

   ```
   git clone https://github.com/pandemicsyn/swift-
       informant.git
   cd swift-informant
   sudo python setup.py install
   ```

2. Once installed, we modify the pipeline in `/etc/swift/proxy-server.conf` to specify a filter named `informant`:

   ```
   [pipeline:main]
   pipeline =  informant healthcheck cache swift3 s3token
       tokenauth keystone proxy-server
   ```

3. We then add in the informant filter section, specifying the address of our StatsD server, in the `statsd_host` section, as follows:

```
[filter:informant]
use = egg:informant#informant
statsd_host = 172.16.0.9
# statsd_port = 8125
# standard statsd sample rate 0.0 <= 1
# statsd_sample_rate = 0.5
# list of allowed methods, all others will generate a
    "BAD_METHOD" event
# valid_http_methods = GET,HEAD,POST,PUT,DELETE,COPY
# send multiple statsd events per packet as supported by
    statsdpy
# combined_events = no
# prepends name to metric collection output for easier
    recognition, e.g. company.swift.
# metric_name_prepend =
```

4. Once done, we simply restart our OpenStack proxy service:

   `sudo swift-init proxy-server restart`

5. Load up your web browser and point it to your Graphite web installation, to see the graphs get populated in real time.

How it works...

Gaining insight into what our OpenStack Storage cluster is doing can be achieved by including a piece of middleware in the pipeline of our OpenStack Storage proxy server, named `swift-informant`, along with StatsD and Graphite. StatsD is a `node.js` service that listens for statistics sent to it in UDP packets. Graphite takes this data and gives us a real-time graph view of our running services.

Installation and configuration is done in stages. We first install and configure a server that will be used for StatsD and Graphite. Graphite can be installed using Python's Package Index (using the `pip` tool), and for this, we install three pieces of software: `carbon` (the collector), `whisper` (fixed-size RRD service), and the Django Web Interface, `graphite-web`. Using the `pip` tool installs these services to the `/opt` directory of our server.

Once the server for running Graphite and StatsD has been set up, we can configure the OpenStack Storage proxy service, so that statistics are then sent to the Graphite and StatsD server. With the appropriate configuration in place, the OpenStack Storage service will happily send events, via UDP, to the StatsD service.

Configuration of the Graphite interface is done in an Apache `vhost` file that we place in Ubuntu's Apache `sites-available` directory. We then enable this for our installation.

Note that vhost needs to be configured appropriately for our environment—specifically the path to the DJANGO_ROOT area—as part of our Python installation. For Ubuntu 12.04, this is /usr/lib/python2.7/dist-packages/django to give us the following in our vhost file:

```
Alias /media/ "/usr/lib/python2.7/dist-
    packages/django/contrib/admin/media/"
```

We then ensure that the Graphite **WSGI** (**Web Service Gateway Interface**) file is in place at the appropriate path, as specified by the WSGIScriptAlias directive at /opt/graphite/conf/graphite.wsgi.

Once in place, we ensure that our filesystem has the appropriate permissions to allow Graphite to write various logs and information as it's running.

When this has been done, we simply restart Apache to pick up the changes.

With the Graphite web interface configured, we initialize the database; for this installation we will make use of a SQLite database resource. This is achieved by running the syncdb option with the Graphite manage.py script in the /opt/graphite/webapp/graphite directory. This asks us to create a superuser called user for the system, to manage it later.

Once this has been done, we can start the collector service, carbon, which starts the appropriate services that will listen for data being sent to it.

With all that in place, we simply move our efforts to the OpenStack Storage proxy service, where we checkout the swift-informant middleware to be inserted into the pipeline of our proxy service.

Monitoring MySQL with Hyperic

Database monitoring can be quite complex, and, depending on your deployment or experience, monitoring may already be set up. For those that don't have existing monitoring of a MySQL service, *Hyperic* from *SpringSource* is an excellent tool to set up monitoring and alerting for MySQL. The software comes in two editions—an Open Source edition—suitable for smaller installations—and an Enterprise edition with paid for support. The steps in the following section are for the Open Source edition.

 Hyperic can monitor many aspects of our OpenStack environment including system load, network statistics, Memcached, and RabbitMQ status.

Getting ready

We will be configuring Hyperic on an Ubuntu 12.04 server that has access to the MySQL server in our OpenStack environment. Ensure this server has enough RAM, disk, and CPU capacity for the environment you are running. Log in as a normal user to download and install the software.

How to do it...

To install Hyperic, carry out the following steps:

Hyperic server

1. We can find the Hyperic server installation package at the following URL:

   ```
   http://www.springsource.com/landing/hyperic-open-
   source-download
   ```

2. Fill in the details, and you will be presented with two links. One is for the server, and the other for the agent. Download both.

3. On the server that will be running the Hyperic server, we unpack the Hyperic server installation package as follows:

   ```
   tar zxvf hyperic-hq-installer-4.5-x86-64-linux.tar.gz
   ```

4. Once unpacked, change to the directory:

   ```
   cd hyperic-hq-installer-4.5
   ```

5. The default install area for Hyperic is /home/hyperic, so we create this and ensure our unprivileged user can write to it:

   ```
   sudo mkdir -p /home/hyperic
   sudo chown openstack /home/hyperic
   ```

6. Once this area is ready, we can run the setup script to install Hyperic:

   ```
   ./setup.sh
   ```

7. During the installation, a message will pop up asking us to open up another terminal on our server as the root user to execute a small script, as shown in the following screenshot:

   ```
   ****
   Now login to another terminal as root and execute this script:
       /home/openstack/hyperic-hq-installer-4.5/installer/data/hqdb/tune-os.sh
   This script sets up the proper shared memory settings to run the built-in database.
   Press Enter after you run the script to continue this installation.
   ****
   ```

8. In another terminal, log in as root and execute the previous step.

9. Return to the original shell and continue the installation. Eventually, the installation will complete. We can now start the Hyperic HQ service with the following command:

   `/home/hyperic/server-4.5/bin/hq-server.sh start`

10. First-time start up can be quite slow, but eventually you will be able to point your web browser at the address the installation has presented to you, which will be `http://server:7080/`.

11. Log in with user `hqadmin` and password `hqadmin`.

Nodes

Each node that we want to monitor in Hyperic needs an agent installed, which then gets configured to talk back to the Hyperic server.

1. Copy the agent `tarball` to the server that we'll be monitoring in Hyperic.

2. Unpack the agent as follows:

   `tar zxvf hyperic-hq-agent-4.5-x86-64.tar.gz`

3. Change to the unpacked directory:

   `cd hyperic-hq-agent-4.5`

4. Start the agent, which will ask for information about the Hyperic server installation. Specify the server address, port, username (`hqadmin`), and password (`hqadmin`). When asked for the IP to use, specify the address that Hyperic can use to communicate with the server.

   `bin/hq-agent.sh start`

   The output from running the previous command is as follows:

```
Starting HQ Agent...
[ Running agent setup ]
What is the HQ server IP address: 172.16.0.9
Should Agent communications to HQ always be secure [default=no]:
What is the HQ server port     [default=7080]:
- Testing insecure connection ... Success
What is your HQ login [default=hqadmin]:
What is your HQ password:
What IP should HQ use to contact the agent [default=127.0.1.1]: 172.16.0.1
What port should HQ use to contact the agent [default=2144]:
- Received temporary auth token from agent
- Registering agent with HQ
- HQ gave us the following agent token
    1337604028694-3863173946525631442-3528732157517579451
- Informing agent of new HQ server
- Validating
- Successfully setup agent
```

5. This completes the installation of the agent.

6. Once done, the new node will appear in Hyperic, with auto-discovered services listed.

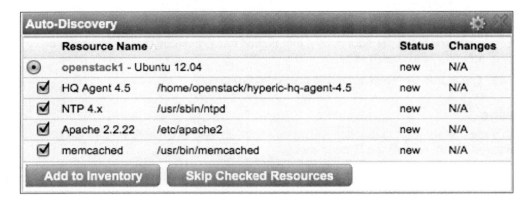

7. Click on the **Add to Inventory** button to accept these to be added to Hyperic, and you will see our new node listed with the services that have been discovered.

Monitoring MySQL

To monitor MySQL, carry out the following steps:

1. Monitoring MySQL involves the agent understanding how to authenticate with MySQL. We first add in the MySQL service to our host by selecting the host that has recently been added. This takes us to the main screen for that host, where we can click through services that are being monitored.

2. We then click on the **Tools Menu** option and select **New Server**.

3. This takes us to a screen where we can add in a label for the new service and the service type.

```
Name: openstack1 MySQL
Server Type: MySQL 5.x
Install Path: /usr
```

4. Clicking on **OK** takes us to the configuration screen for this new service. At the bottom of the page, there is a section named **Configuration Properties**. Click on the **EDIT...** button for this section.

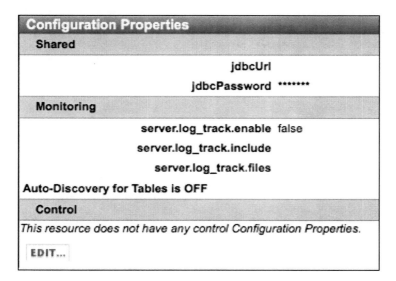

5. We can now specify the username, password, and connect string, to connect to the running MySQL instance.

```
JDBC User: root
JDBC Password: openstack
```

These are the credentials for a user in MySQL that can see all databases. Check the **Auto-Discover Tables** option and leave the rest of the options at their default values, unless you need to change the address that the agent will connect to for MySQL.

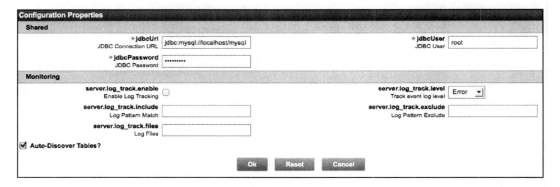

6. By clicking on **OK** and then browsing back to the host, we will now have a monitoring option named `openstack1 MySQL`, as specified in step 3. The agent will then collect statistics about our MySQL instance.

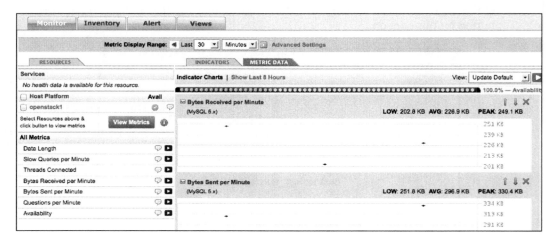

How it works...

Hyperic uses agents to collect information and sends this back to the Hyperic server, where we can view statistics about the environment and configure alerting based on thresholds. The agent is very flexible and can be configured to monitor many more services than just MySQL.

Configuration of the agent is done through the Hyperic server's interface, where a running node's service is known as a "server". Here, we can configure usernames, ports, and passwords, to allow the agent to successfully communicate with that service. For MySQL, this is providing the agent with the correct username, password, and address for the familiar jdbc (Java Database Connector) connect string.

There's more...

In your datacenter, you may have a MySQL cluster rather than a single server, where a view of the cluster *as a whole* is of equal (if not more) importance to that of the individual nodes. An example cluster monitoring suite that has both free and enterprise options is named CMON and is available at SeveralNines (http://www.severalnines.com/resources/cmon-cluster-monitor-mysql-cluster).

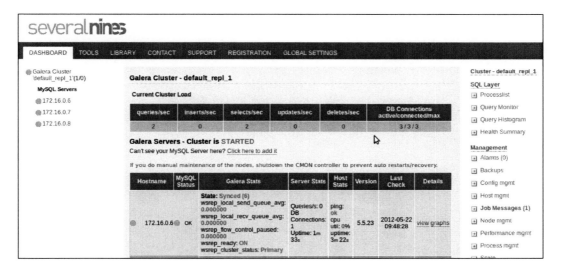

13
Troubleshooting

In this chapter, we will cover:

- ▸ Checking OpenStack Compute Services
- ▸ Understanding logging
- ▸ Troubleshooting OpenStack Compute Services
- ▸ Troubleshooting OpenStack Storage Service
- ▸ Troubleshooting OpenStack Authentication
- ▸ Submitting bug reports
- ▸ Getting help from the community

Introduction

OpenStack is a complex suite of software that can make tracking down issues and faults quite daunting to beginners and experienced system administrators alike. While there is no single approach to troubleshooting systems, understanding where OpenStack logs vital information or what tools are available to help track down bugs will help resolve issues we may encounter. It should also be expected that we won't be able to solve all issues without further help. Gathering the required information so that the OpenStack community can identify bugs and suggest fixes is important in ensuring those bugs or issues are dealt with quickly and efficiently.

Checking OpenStack Compute Services

OpenStack provides tools to check various parts of Compute Services, and we'll use common system commands to check whether our environment is running as expected.

Getting ready

To check our OpenStack Compute host we must log in to that server, so do this now before following the given steps.

How to do it...

To check that Nova is running the required services, we invoke the `nova-manage` tool and ask it various questions of the environment as follows:

- To check the OpenStack Compute hosts are running OK:

  ```
  sudo nova-manage service list
  ```

  You will see the following output. The **:-)** icons are indicative that everything is fine.

Binary	Host	Zone	Status	State	Updated_At
nova-scheduler	openstack1	nova	enabled	:-)	2012-08-09 09:22:21
nova-compute	openstack1	nova	enabled	:-)	2012-08-09 09:22:22
nova-network	openstack1	nova	enabled	:-)	2012-08-09 09:22:21
nova-cert	openstack1	nova	enabled	:-)	2012-08-09 09:22:21
nova-consoleauth	openstack1	nova	enabled	:-)	2012-08-09 09:22:24
nova-console	openstack1	nova	enabled	:-)	2012-08-09 09:22:21

- If Nova has a problem:

  If you see **XXX** where the **:-)** icon should be, then you have a problem.

nova-compute	openstack2	nova	enabled	XXX	2012-06-28 21:10:51
nova-network	openstack2	nova	enabled	XXX	2012-06-28 21:10:51

Troubleshooting is covered at the end of the book, but if you do see **XXX** then the answer will be in the logs at `/var/log/nova/`.

 If you get intermittent **XXX** and **:-)** icons for a service, first check if the clocks are in sync.

- Checking Glance:

  Glance doesn't have a tool to check, so we can use some system commands instead.

  ```
  ps -ef | grep glance
  netstat -ant | grep 9292.*LISTEN
  ```

These should return process information for Glance to show it is running and `9292` is the default port that should be open in the `LISTEN` mode on your server ready for use.

- ▸ Other services that you should check:

  - ❑ `rabbitmq`:

    sudo rabbitmqctl status

The following is an example output from `rabbitmqctl` when everything is running OK:

```
Status of node rabbit@openstack1 ...
[{pid,1473},
 {running_applications,[{rabbit,"RabbitMQ","2.7.1"},
                        {os_mon,"CPO  CXC 138 46","2.2.7"},
                        {sasl,"SASL  CXC 138 11","2.1.10"},
                        {mnesia,"MNESIA  CXC 138 12","4.5"},
                        {stdlib,"ERTS  CXC 138 10","1.17.5"},
                        {kernel,"ERTS  CXC 138 10","2.14.5"}]},
 {os,{unix,linux}},
 {erlang_version,"Erlang R14B04 (erts-5.8.5) [source] [64-bit] [smp:2:2] [rq:2] [async-threads:30]
[kernel-poll:true]\n"},
 {memory,[{total,32213736},
         {processes,11210448},
         {processes_used,11197944},
         {system,21003288},
         {atom,1124441},
         {atom_used,1120346},
         {binary,98968},
         {code,11134417},
         {ets,6860208}]},
 {vm_memory_high_watermark,0.39999999979675105},
 {vm_memory_limit,787211878}]
...done.
```

  - ❑ ntp (Network Time Protocol, for keeping nodes in sync):

    ntpq -p

It should return output regarding contacting NTP servers, for example:

```
     remote           refid      st t when poll reach   delay   offset  jitter
==============================================================================
+gromit.nocabal. 130.149.17.8     2 u  746 1024  377   74.528    2.364  26.894
-89.163.176.82   78.47.234.59     3 u 1042 1024  377   83.911   -1.137   4.877
*server2.as2.ch  129.69.1.153     2 u  543 1024  377   63.878    2.439  21.667
+ntp1.wtnet.de   130.149.17.21    2 u  231 1024  377   71.860    8.728  69.687
+europium.canoni 193.79.237.14    2 u 1021 1024  377   45.399    5.765  11.399
```

  - ❑ MySQL Database Server:

    MYSQL_PASS=openstack
    mysqladmin -uroot -p$MYSQL_PASS status

This will return some statistics about MySQL, if it is running:

```
Uptime: 2730109  Threads: 7  Questions: 15586157  Slow queries: 0  Opens: 73  Flush tables: 1
 Open tables: 66  Queries per second avg: 5.708
```

How it works...

We have used some basic commands that communicate with OpenStack Compute and other services to show they are running. This elementary level of troubleshooting ensures you have the system running as expected.

Understanding logging

Logging is important in all computer systems, but the more complex the system, the more you rely on being able to spot problems to cut down on troubleshooting time. Understanding logging in OpenStack is important to ensure your environment is healthy and is able to submit relevant log entries back to the community to help fix bugs.

Getting ready

Log in as the `root` user onto the appropriate servers where the OpenStack services are installed.

How to do it...

OpenStack produces a large number of logs that help troubleshoot our OpenStack installations. The following details outline where these services write their logs.

OpenStack Compute Services Logs

Logs for the OpenStack Compute services are written to `/var/log/nova/`, which is owned by the `nova` user, by default. To read these, log in as the `root` user. The following is a list of services and their corresponding logs:

- `nova-compute`: `/var/log/nova/nova-compute.log`

  Log entries regarding the spinning up and running of the instances

- `nova-network`: `/var/log/nova/nova-network.log`

  Log entries regarding network state, assignment, routing, and security groups

- `nova-manage`: `/var/log/nova/nova-manage.log`

  Log entries produced when running the `nova-manage` command

- `nova-scheduler`: `/var/log/nova/nova-scheduler.log`

  Log entries pertaining to the scheduler, its assignment of tasks to nodes, and messages from the queue

- nova-objectstore: /var/log/nova/nova-objectstore.log

  Log entries regarding the images

- nova-api: /var/log/nova/nova-api.log

  Log entries regarding user interaction with OpenStack as well as messages regarding interaction with other components of OpenStack

- nova-cert: /var/log/nova/nova-cert.log

  Entries regarding the nova-cert process

- nova-console: /var/log/nova/nova-console.log

  Details about the nova-console VNC service

- nova-consoleauth: /var/log/nova/nova-consoleauth.log

  Authentication details related to the nova-console service

- nova-dhcpbridge: /var/log/nova/nova-dhcpbridge.log

  Network information regarding the dhcpbridge service

OpenStack Dashboard logs

OpenStack Dashboard (Horizon) is a web application that runs through Apache by default, so any errors and access details will be in the Apache logs. These can be found in /var/log/apache2/*.log, which will help you understand who is accessing the service as well as the report on any errors seen with the service.

OpenStack Storage logs

OpenStack Storage (Swift) writes logs to syslog by default. On an Ubuntu system, these can be viewed in /var/log/syslog. On other systems, these might be available at /var/log/messages.

Logging can be adjusted to allow for these messages to be filtered in syslog using the log_level, log_facility, and log_message options. Each service allows you to set the following:

```
set log_name        Default: name of service
set log_facility    Default: LOG_LOCAL0
set log_level       Default: INFO
set log_requests    Default: True
```

If you change any of these options, you will need to restart that service to pick up the change.

Log-level settings in OpenStack Compute services

Many OpenStack services allow you to control the chatter in the logs by setting different log output settings. Some services, though, tend to produce a lot of DEBUG noise by default.

This is controlled within the configuration files for that service. For example, the *Glance Registry* service has the following settings in its configuration files:

```
[DEFAULT]
# Show more verbose log output (sets INFO log level output)
verbose = True

# Show debugging output in logs (sets DEBUG log level output)
debug = False
```

Moreover, many services are adopting this facility. In production, you would set debug to False and optionally keep a fairly high level of INFO requests being produced, which may help with the general health reports of your OpenStack environment.

How it works...

Logging is an important activity in any software, and OpenStack is no different. It allows an administrator to track down problematic activity that can be used in conjunction with the community to help provide a solution. Understanding where the services log, and managing those logs to allow someone to identify problems quickly and easily, are important.

Troubleshooting OpenStack Compute Services

OpenStack Compute services are complex, and being able to diagnose faults is an essential part of ensuring the smooth running of the services. Fortunately, OpenStack Compute provides some tools to help with this process, along with tools provided by Ubuntu to help identify issues.

How to do it...

Troubleshooting OpenStack Compute services can be a complex issue, but working through problems methodically and logically will help you reach a satisfactory outcome. Carry out the following steps when encountering the different problems presented.

Cannot ping or SSH to an instance

1. When launching instances, we specify a security group. If none is specified, a security group named `default` is used. These mandatory security groups ensure security is enabled by default in our cloud environment, and as such, we must explicitly state that we require the ability to ping our instances and SSH to them. For such a basic activity, it is common to add these abilities to the `default` security group.

2. Network issues may prevent us from accessing our cloud instances. First, check that the compute instances are able to forward packets from the public interface to the bridged interface.

   ```
   sysctl -A | grep ip_forward
   ```

3. `net.ipv4.ip_forward` should be set to 1. If it isn't, check that `/etc/sysctl.conf` has the following option uncommented:

   ```
   net.ipv4.ip_forward=1
   ```

4. Then, run the following, to pick up the change:

   ```
   sudo sysctl -p
   ```

5. Other network issues could be routing problems. Check that we can communicate with the OpenStack Compute nodes from our client and that any routing to get to these instances has the correct entries.

6. We may have a conflict with IPv6, if IPv6 isn't required. If this is the case, try adding `--use_ipv6=false` to your `/etc/nova/nova.conf` file, and restart the `nova-compute` and `nova-network` services. We may also need to disable IPv6 in the operating system, which can be achieved using something like the following line in `/etc/modprobe.d/ipv6.conf`:

   ```
   install ipv6 /bin/true
   ```

7. Reboot your host.

Viewing the Instance Console log

You can view the console information for an instance using a number of methods:

- When using the command line, issue the following commands:

   ```
   # euca2ools
   euca-get-console i-00000001
   # nova client
   nova console-log 4b8776eb-77b5-48eb-9ec4-f4b6c6e3bdaa
   ```

▶ When using Horizon, carry out the following steps:

    1. Navigate to the list of instances and select an instance.

    2. You will be taken to an **Overview** screen. Along the top of the **Overview** screen is a **Log** tab. This is the console log for the instance.

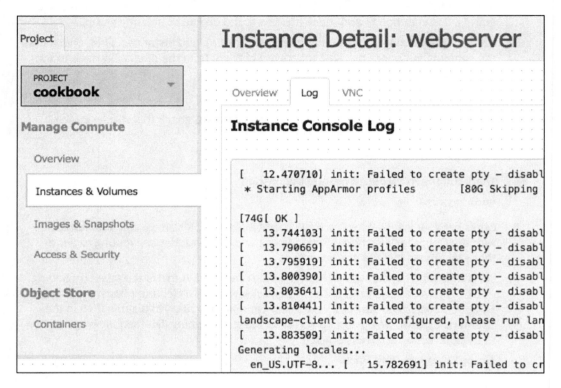

▶ When viewing the logs directly on a `nova-compute` host, look for the following file:

The console logs are owned by `root`, so only an administrator can do this. They are placed at `/var/lib/nova/instances/<instance_id>/console.log`.

Instance fails to download meta information

If an instance fails to communicate to download the extra information that can be supplied to the instance `meta-data`, we can end up in a situation where the instance is up but you're unable to log in, as the SSH key information is injected using this method.

Viewing the console log will show output like in the following screenshot:

```
2011-04-27 09:10:33,828 - DataSourceEc2.py[WARNING]: 09:10:33 [37/120]: url error [[Errno 101] Network is unreachable]
2011-04-27 09:11:06,839 - DataSourceEc2.py[WARNING]: 09:11:06 [70/120]: url error [[Errno 101] Network is unreachable]
2011-10-21 09:11:56,851 - DataSourceEc2.py[CRITICAL]: giving up on md after 120 seconds
```

Ensure the following:

1. nova-api is running on the host (in a multi_host environment, ensure there's a nova-api and a nova-network node running on the nova-compute host).

2. Perform the following iptables check on the nova-network node that is running nova-compute:

   sudo iptables -L -n -t nat

   We should see a line in the output like in the following screenshot:

```
Chain nova-network-PREROUTING (1 references)
target     prot opt source               destination
DNAT       tcp  --  0.0.0.0/0            169.254.169.254      tcp dpt:80 to:172.16.0.1:8775
```

3. If not, restart your nova-network services and check again.

4. Sometimes there are multiple copies of dnsmasq running, which can cause this issue. Ensure that there is only one instance of dnsmasq running:

   ps -ef | grep dnsmasq

   This will bring back two process entries, the parent dnsmasq process and a spawned child (verify by the PIDs). If there are any other instances of dnsmasq running, kill the dnsmasq processes. When killed, restart nova-network, which will spawn dnsmasq again without any conflicting processes.

Instance launches, stuck at "Booting" or "Pending"

Sometimes, a little patience is needed before assuming the instance has not booted, because the image is copied across the network to a node that has not seen the image before. At other times though, if the instance has been stuck in booting or a similar state for longer than normal, it indicates a problem. The first place to look will be for errors in the logs. A quick way of doing this is from the controller server and by issuing the following command:

sudo nova-manage logs error

A common error that is usually present is related to AMQP being unreachable. These can be ignored unless the errors are currently appearing.

This command brings back any log line with the ERROR as log level, but you will need to view the logs in more detail to get a clearer picture.

A key log file, when troubleshooting instances are not booting properly, will be available at /var/log/nova/nova-compute.log. Look here at the time you launch the instance and the ID.

Check `/var/log/nova/nova-network.log` for any reason why instances aren't being assigned IP addresses. It could be issues around DHCP preventing address allocation.

Error codes such as 401, 403, 500

The majority of the OpenStack services are web services, meaning the responses from the services are well defined.

40X refers to a service that is up but responding to an event that is produced by some user error. For example, a 401 is an authentication failure, so check the credentials used when accessing the service.

50X errors mean a connecting service is unavailable or has caused an error that has caused the service to interpret a response to cause a failure. Common problems here are services that have not started properly, so check for running services.

If all avenues have been exhausted when troubleshooting your environment, reach out to the community, using the mailing list or IRC, where there is a raft of people willing to offer their time and assistance.

Listing all instances across all hosts

From the OpenStack controller node, you can execute the following command to get a list of the running instances in the environment:

```
sudo nova-manage vm list
```

This is useful in identifying any failed instances and the host on which it is running. You can then investigate further.

How it works...

Troubleshooting OpenStack Compute problems can be quite complex, but looking in the right places can help solve some of the more common problems. Unfortunately, like troubleshooting any computer system, there isn't a single command that can help identify all the problems that you may encounter, but OpenStack provides some tools to help you identify some problems. Having an understanding of managing servers and networks will help troubleshoot a distributed cloud environment such as OpenStack.

There's more than one place where you can go to identify the issues, as they can stem from the environment to the instances themselves. Methodically working your way through the problems though will help lead you to a resolution.

Troubleshooting OpenStack Storage Service

OpenStack Storage Service (Swift) is built for highly available storage, but there will be times where something will go wrong, from authentication issues to failing hardware.

How to do it...

Carry out the following steps when encountering the problems presented.

Authentication issues

Authentication issues in Swift occur when a user or a system has been configured with the wrong credentials. A Swift system that has been supported by OpenStack Authentication Service (Keystone) will require you to perform authentication steps against Keystone manually as well as view logs during the transactions. Check the Keystone logs for evidence of user authentication issues for Swift.

The user will see the following message with authentication issues:

```
Auth GET failed: http://172.16.0.1:5000/v2.0/tokens 401 Not Authorized
```

If Swift is working correctly but Keystone isn't, skip to the *Troubleshooting OpenStack Authentication* recipe.

Swift can add complexity to authentication issues when ACLs have been applied to containers. For example, a user might not have been placed in an appropriate group that is allowed to perform that function on that container. To view a container's ACL, issue the following command on a client that has the Swift tool installed:

```
swift -V 2.0 -A http://keystone_server:5000/v2.0 -U tenant:user -K
password stat container
```

The **Read ACL:** and **Write ACL:** information will show which roles are allowed to perform those actions.

To check a user's roles, run the following set of commands on the Keystone server:

```
# Administrator Credentials
export OS_USERNAME=admin
export OS_PASSWORD=openstack

export OS_AUTH_URL=http://172.16.0.1:5000/v2.0

export OS_TENANT_NAME=cookbook

# Get User ID

keystone user-list

# Get Tenant ID
```

```
keystone tenant-list
# Use the user-id and tenant-id to get the roles for
# that user in that tenant
keystone -I admin -K openstack -N http://172.16.0.1:5000/v2.0/ -T
cookbook role-list --user user-id --tenant tenant-id
```

Now compare with the ACL roles assigned to the container.

Handling drive failure

When a drive fails in an OpenStack Storage environment, you must first ensure the drive is unmounted so Swift isn't attempting to write data to it. Replace the drive and rebalance the rings. This is covered in more detail in the *Detecting and replacing failed hard drives* recipe in *Chapter 6, Administering OpenStack Storage*.

Handling server failure and reboots

The OpenStack Storage service is very resilient. If a server is out of action for a couple of hours, Swift can happily work around this server being missing from the ring. Any longer than a couple of hours though, and the server will need removing from the ring. To do this, follow the steps mentioned in the *Removing nodes from a cluster* recipe in *Chapter 6, Administering OpenStack Storage*.

How it works...

The OpenStack Storage service, Swift, is a robust object storage environment, and as such, handles a relatively large number of failures within this environment. Troubleshooting Swift involves running client tests, viewing logs, and in the event of failure, identifying what the best course of action is.

Troubleshooting OpenStack Authentication

OpenStack Authentication Service (Keystone) is a complex service, as it has to deal with underpinning the authentication and authorization for the complete cloud environment. Common problems include misconfigured endpoints, incorrect parameters being stored, and general user authentication issues, which involve resetting passwords or providing further details to the end user.

Getting ready

Administrator access is required to troubleshoot Keystone, so we first configure our environment, so that we can simply execute the relevant Keystone commands.

```
# Administrator Credentials
export OS_USERNAME=admin
export OS_PASSWORD=openstack
export OS_AUTH_URL=http://172.16.0.1:5000/v2.0
export OS_TENANT_NAME=cookbook
```

How to do it...

Carry out the following steps when encountering the problems presented.

Misconfigured endpoints

Keystone is the central service that directs authenticated users to the correct service, so it's vital that the users be sent to the correct location. Symptoms include HTTP 500 error messages in various logs regarding the services that are being accessed, and clients timing out trying to connect to network services that don't exist. To verify your endpoints in each region, perform the following command:

```
keystone endpoint-list
```

We can drill down into specific service types with the following command. For example, to show adminURL for the compute service type in all regions.

```
keystone endpoint-get --service compute --endpoint_type adminURL
```

An alternative to listing the endpoints in this format is to list the catalog, which outputs the details in a more human-readable way:

```
keystone catalog
```

This provides a convenient way of seeing the endpoints configured.

Authentication issues

From time to time, users will have trouble authenticating against Keystone due to forgotten or expired details or unexpected failure within the authentication system. Being able to identify such issues will allow you to restore the service or allow the user to continue using the environment.

The first place to look will be the relevant logs. This includes the /var/log/nova logs, the /var/log/glance logs (if related to images), as well as the /var/log/keystone logs.

Troubleshooting accounts might include missing accounts, so view the users on the system using the following command:

```
keystone user-list
```

After displaying the user list to ensure an account exists for the user, we can get further information on a particular user by issuing, for example, the following command, after retrieving the user ID of a particular user:

```
keystone user-get 68ba544e500c40668435aa6201e557e4
```

This will display output similar to the following screenshot:

```
+-----------+------------------------------------+
| Property  |               Value                |
+-----------+------------------------------------+
| email     | kevin@example.com                  |
| enabled   | True                               |
| id        | 68ba544e500c40668435aa6201e557e4   |
| name      | kevinj                             |
| tenantId  | 1a50d87215ba444f8c62b42cb6b9de6f   |
+-----------+------------------------------------+
```

This allows us to verify that the user has a valid account in a particular tenant.

If a user's password needs resetting, we can execute the following command after getting the user ID, to set a user's password to (for example) `openstack`:

```
keystone user-password-update --pass openstack
68ba544e500c40668435aa6201e557e4
```

If it turns out a user has been set to disabled, we can simply re-enable the account with the following command:

```
keystone user-update --enabled true 68ba544e500c40668435aa6201e557e4
```

There could be times when the account is working but problems exist on the client side. Before looking at Keystone for the issue, ensure your environment is set up correctly, in other words, set the following environment variables:

```
export OS_USERNAME=kevinj
export OS_PASSWORD=openstack

export OS_AUTH_URL=http://172.16.0.1:5000/v2.0

export OS_TENANT_NAME=cookbook
```

How it works...

User authentication issues can be client- or server-side, and when some basic troubleshooting has been performed on the client, we can use Keystone commands to find out why someone's user journey has been interrupted. With this, we are able to view and update user details, set passwords, set them into the appropriate tenants, and disable or enable them, as required.

Submitting bug reports

OpenStack is a hugely successful open source, public and private cloud framework. It has gained this momentum by individuals and organizations downloading and contributing to it. By using the software in a vast array of environments and scenarios, and running the software on a myriad of hardware configurations, you will invariably encounter bugs. In an open source project, the best thing we can now do is tell the developers about it so they can develop or suggest a solution for us.

How to do it...

The OpenStack project is available through LaunchPad. LaunchPad is an open source suite of tools that helps people and teams to work together on software projects and is accessible at `http://launchpad.net/`, so the first step is to create an account.

Creating an account on LaunchPad

1. Creating an account on LaunchPad is easy. First, head over to `https://login.launchpad.net/+new_account` (or navigate from the home page to the **Login/Register** link).

2. Fill in your name, e-mail address, and password details, as shown in the following screenshot:

3. We will then be sent an e-mail with a link to complete the registration. Click on this to be taken to a confirmation page.

4. We will then be taken to an account page, but no further details need to be entered here.

Submitting bug reports through LaunchPad

Now that we have an account on LaunchPad, we can submit bug reports. The following links take us directly to the bug report sections of those projects:

- **Nova**: `https://bugs.launchpad.net/nova/+filebug`
- **Swift**: `https://bugs.launchpad.net/swift/+filebug`
- **Glance**: `https://bugs.launchpad.net/glance/+filebug`
- **Keystone**: `https://bugs.launchpad.net/keystone/+filebug`
- **Dashboard**: `https://bugs.launchpad.net/horizon/+filebug`
- **Quantum**: `https://bugs.launchpad.net/quantum/+filebug`

On submitting a short summary, a search is made to see if a similar bug exists. If it does, click on the bug and then ensure you click on the **This bug affects X people. Does this bug affect you?** link. If multiple people report that they are affected by a bug, its status changes from *reported by a single person* to *confirmed*, helping the Bug Triage team with their work. Please ensure you add any relevant additional information to the bug report, in support of the issues you are facing.

If the bug doesn't exist, we will be presented with a form that has a one-liner **Summary** field and a free-form textbox in which to put in the required information.

On submitting bugs, try to follow these rules:

- Include the OS platform, architecture, and software package versions
- Give step-by-step details on how to recreate the bug
- Enter what you expected to happen
- Enter what actually happened instead
- Be precise—developers like precision

Useful commands to help complete a bug report

The following is a list of useful commands that will help you in the completion of the bug report:

- OS System Version: `lsb_release -r`
- Architecture: `uname -i`
- Package version:

```
dpkg -l | grep name_of_package
dpkg -s name_of_package | grep Version
```

Pasting logs

Sometimes, there will be a need to submit logging information to support your bug report. This information can be quite lengthy, so rather than including the text from such logs, within the bug report, it is encouraged to use a text paste service, which will provide you with a unique URL that you can use to reference the information within your bug report. For this purpose, you can use the service at `http://paste.openstack.org/`.

 Ensure you sanitize any data that you paste in public. This includes removing any sensitive data such as IPs, usernames, and passwords.

Once a bug is submitted, an e-mail will be sent to the e-mail address used to register with LaunchPad, and any subsequent updates in relation to the bug will be sent to this e-mail address, allowing us to track its progress all the way through to a fix being released.

How it works...

OpenStack is developed by a relatively small number of people, compared to the number of people in the community that end up downloading and using the software. This means the software gets used in scenarios that developers can't feasibly test or just didn't see as possible at the time. The net result is that bugs often come out during this time. Being able to report these bugs is vital, and this is why open source software development is so hugely successful in creating proven and reliable software.

OpenStack's development lives on LaunchPad, so all bug tracking and reporting is done using this service. This provides a central tool for the global community and allows end users to communicate with the relevant projects to submit bugs.

Submitting bugs is a vital element in an open source project. It allows you to shape the future of the project as well as be part of the ecosystem that is built around it.

It is important to give as much information as possible to the developers when submitting bugs. Be precise and ensure that the steps to recreate the bug are easy to follow and provide an explanation of the environment you are working in, to allow the bug to be recreated. If it can't be recreated, it can't be fixed.

See also

> ▶ You can find out more information about the OpenStack community at
> `http://www.openstack.org/community/`

Getting help from the community

OpenStack would not be where it is today without the ever-growing community of businesses, sponsors, and individuals. As with many large OSS projects, support is fantastic, meaning round-the-clock attention to requests for help, which can sometimes exceed the best efforts of paid-for support.

How to do it...

There are a number of ways to reach out for support from the excellent OpenStack community. They are:

IRC Support

Internet Relay Chat has been the mainstay of the Internet since the beginning, and collaboration from developers and users can be found on the Freenode IRC network.

OpenStack has a channel (or a room) on the Freenode IRC network called `#openstack`.

There are two ways of accessing IRC, either through the web interface or by using an IRC client:

► **IRC access using a web browser**

1. Accessing the `#openstack` channel, using a web browser, can be achieved at `http://webchat.freenode.net/`.

2. Enter `#openstack` as the channel.

3. Choose a username for yourself.

4. Complete the CAPTCHA and you will be placed into the `#openstack` channel.

► **IRC access using an IRC client**

1. Download a suitable IRC client for your operating system (for example, Xchat).

2. When loading up your client, choose a username (and enter a password if you have registered your username) and connect to the Freenode network (`irc.freenode.net`).

3. When connected, type the following command to join #openstack:

   /j #openstack

4. We will now be in the `#openstack` channel.

Mailing list

Subscribing to the mailing list allows you to submit and respond to queries where an instant response might not be required and is useful if you need your question to reach more members than the relatively smaller number that is on IRC.

To subscribe to the mailing list, head over to `https://launchpad.net/openstack`, where you will see an option to subscribe to the mailing list.

 You will need to create a LaunchPad ID and be a member of the OpenStack project (see the *Submitting bug reports* recipe on submitting bugs on how to do this).

Pasting logs

When asking for help, it usually involves copying logs from your environment and sharing them with the community. To help facilitate this, a web service has been created that allows you to paste the log entries that can be referred to in an IRC chat or in an e-mail without having to paste them directly. This can be found at `http://paste.openstack.org/`. When you create a new paste, you are given a unique URL that you can then refer to for the information instead.

 Ensure you sanitize any data that you paste in public. This includes removing any sensitive data such as IPs, usernames, and passwords.

How it works...

The OpenStack community is what makes OpenStack what it is. It is made up of developers, users, testers, companies, and individuals with a vested interest in ensuring OpenStack's success. There are a number of useful places to ask for help when it comes to community support. This includes IRC and the mailing list.

You are encouraged to post and respond to requests in IRC and on the mailing list, as there are likely to be many people wanting the same questions answered. There will also be the development and project teams wanting to understand what is causing issues so they can help address them.

See also

 ▶ You can find out more information about the OpenStack community at `http://www.openstack.org/community/`

Index

Thank you for buying
OpenStack Cloud Computing Cookbook

About Packt Publishing

Packt, pronounced 'packed', published its first book "*Mastering phpMyAdmin for Effective MySQL Management*" in April 2004 and subsequently continued to specialize in publishing highly focused books on specific technologies and solutions.

Our books and publications share the experiences of your fellow IT professionals in adapting and customizing today's systems, applications, and frameworks. Our solution based books give you the knowledge and power to customize the software and technologies you're using to get the job done. Packt books are more specific and less general than the IT books you have seen in the past. Our unique business model allows us to bring you more focused information, giving you more of what you need to know, and less of what you don't.

Packt is a modern, yet unique publishing company, which focuses on producing quality, cutting-edge books for communities of developers, administrators, and newbies alike. For more information, please visit our website: www.packtpub.com.

About Packt Open Source

In 2010, Packt launched two new brands, Packt Open Source and Packt Enterprise, in order to continue its focus on specialization. This book is part of the Packt Open Source brand, home to books published on software built around Open Source licences, and offering information to anybody from advanced developers to budding web designers. The Open Source brand also runs Packt's Open Source Royalty Scheme, by which Packt gives a royalty to each Open Source project about whose software a book is sold.

Writing for Packt

We welcome all inquiries from people who are interested in authoring. Book proposals should be sent to author@packtpub.com. If your book idea is still at an early stage and you would like to discuss it first before writing a formal book proposal, contact us; one of our commissioning editors will get in touch with you.

We're not just looking for published authors; if you have strong technical skills but no writing experience, our experienced editors can help you develop a writing career, or simply get some additional reward for your expertise.

**Microsoft Windows Azure
Development Cookbook**

Over 80 advanced recipes for developing scalable services with the Windows Azure platform

Neil Mackenzie [PACKT] enterprise⊞

Microsoft Windows Azure Development Cookbook

ISBN: 978-1-849682-22-0   Paperback: 392 pages

Over 80 advanced recipes for developing scalable services with the Windows Azure platform

1. Packed with practical, hands-on cookbook recipes for building advanced, scalable cloud-based services on the Windows Azure platform explained in detail to maximize your learning

2. Extensive code samples showing how to use advanced features of Windows Azure blobs, tables and queues.

3. Understand remote management of Azure services using the Windows Azure Service Management REST API

4. Delve deep into Windows Azure Diagnostics

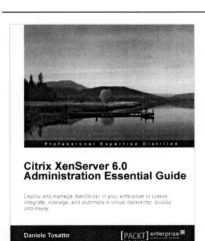

**Citrix XenServer 6.0
Administration Essential Guide**

Deploy and manage XenServer in your enterprise to create, integrate, manage, and automate a virtual datacenter quickly and easily

Daniele Tosatto [PACKT] enterprise⊞

Citrix XenServer 6.0 Administration Essential Guide

ISBN: 978-1-849686-16-7   Paperback: 364 pages

Deploy and manage XenServer in your enterprise to create, integrate, manage, and automate a virtual datacenter quickly and easily

1. This book and eBook will take you through deploying XenServer in your enterprise, and teach you how to create and maintain your datacenter.

2. Manage XenServer and virtual machines using Citrix management tools and the command line.

3. Organize secure access to your infrastructure using role-based access control.

Please check **www.PacktPub.com** for information on our titles